I FEEL LIKE GOING ON

LIFE, GAME, AND GLORY

RAY LEWIS

with Daniel Paisner

TOUCHSTONE

New York   London   Toronto   Sydney   New Delhi

T

Touchstone
An Imprint of Simon & Schuster, Inc.
1230 Avenue of the Americas
New York, NY 10020

First Touchstone paperback edition October 2016

TOUCHSTONE and colophon are registered trademarks of Simon & Schuster, Inc.

For information about special discounts for bulk purchases, please contact Simon & Schuster Special Sales at 1-866-506-1949 or business@simonandschuster.com.

The Simon & Schuster Speakers Bureau can bring authors to your live event. For more information or to book an event, contact the Simon & Schuster Speakers Bureau at 866-248-3049 or visit our website at www.simonspeakers.com.

Interior design by Kyle Kabel

Manufactured in the United States of America

10 9 8 7 6 5 4 3

The Library of Congress has cataloged the hardcover edition as follows:

Lewis, Ray, 1975–
    I feel like going on : life, game and glory / by Ray Lewis with Daniel Paisner.—First Touchstone hardcover edition.
        pages cm
    "A Touchstone Book."
    1. Lewis, Ray, 1975– 2. Football players—United States—Biography. 3. Baltimore Ravens (Football team)—History. I. Paisner, Daniel. II. Title.
    GV939.L49A3 2015
    796.332092—dc23
    [B]
                                                                2015025645

ISBN 978-1-5011-1235-5
ISBN 978-1-5011-1237-9 (pbk)
ISBN 978-1-5011-1238-6 (ebook)

This book, like everything I do,
is for my mother—my dear mama.
Like the great Tupac song says,
"Ain't a woman alive that could take my mama's place."
No, sir.

Though the storm may be raging,
and the billows are tossing high,
I feel like going on . . .

—Rance Allen and Thomas Allen,
"I Feel Like Going On"

CONTENTS

OCTOBER 14, 2012

When You Know What You Know, Do What You Do

Game six of the 2012 NFL season—a season that's meant to be mine, ours. We're meant to win the Super Bowl. Other folks, they don't know this yet, but I know it. My teammates, they might not even know it, but I know it. How do I know? Because I know. I can feel it in my bones. I can taste it. I can close my eyes and picture it. And I'm not shy about saying so.

Already, I'm on record—told a sideline reporter at the last Pro Bowl that it was my final trip to Honolulu.

She said, "Ray, this is your thirteenth Pro Bowl. Do you like coming to Hawaii year after year?"

I said, "Tell you the truth, this is it for me. No more Pro Bowls. I'm done with Pro Bowls."

Something to think about: this was right after we lost the AFC Championship Game to the New England Patriots. It stung, the way we lost that game. It hurts to remember that game. We gave up the lead on a fourth-quarter drive after a goal-line stand. I'd stopped BenJarvus Green-Ellis, cold, third and goal from our 1-yard line, but then Tom Brady came back and stole that touchdown from us on fourth down—a sneak up the middle. We had our chances after that—drove inside the New England twenty with less than a minute to go, but Lee Evans had the ball stripped from his hands after catching a Joe Flacco pass in the end zone on a controversial call, and then we ended up missing a thirty-two-yard field goal that would have tied the game with no time on the clock. So, yeah, it stung.

Told my teammates right after that game we'd be back next year—said, "This ain't over. I promise."

This was no end-of-season pep talk. This wasn't me sugarcoating our loss. I knew we had team enough to do it, drive enough to do it. I made it my goal. Nothing would get in the way of that. And I wanted the entire Baltimore Ravens organization to make it a goal, too. I wanted everyone to want it, same way I wanted it. Nothing else mattered. We'd worked too hard, come too close. No way we could let it lie.

Honolulu? The Pro Bowl? I was grateful for the honor each time out, and Hawaii was nice enough, but let's face it—the only folks playing the week before the Super Bowl are the also-rans. Lately, that's how they have the game scheduled. You can be an all-star or you can be a champion. You can't be both. We might dominate at our positions, we might get it done as individuals, but we're not winners. Not this year. This is how I took it in, all those trips to Hawaii, that bye week just after the AFC and NFC Championship Games. If we were champions, we'd be dug in, getting ready for the Super Bowl. The rest of us, we're just on vacation.

So that's the part on record. Off the record, I'd decided that 2012 would be my last season. It was time. All along, I knew that when my kids reached a certain age, when I'd accomplished everything there was to accomplish in the game, I would set it aside. My son Junior was going into his senior year in high school. I wanted to share that time with him, help him make the transition to college ball. My other kids, I wanted to be with them, too. Wasn't about football. Physically, I felt strong. Physically, I could have played another four or five years at this same high level, I could continue to dominate, but it wasn't about that. It was about family. About a life off the field. That's the thing people don't realize about this game—it takes the life out of you. I don't mean it saps your strength or beats you down, although it does that, too. I mean it takes you away from the life you're meant to be living. That's the trade-off. All that time in the gym, all that time in practice, all that time on the road—it pulls you from the people you love. You trade the game for family time, and I got to where I didn't want to make that trade. That's all.

First person I told was Junior. Told him right before that Pro Bowl game, when I was still lit by the fire of that loss to the Patriots. I took him aside and said, "Son, this is it for me. I'm gonna fix it so I can come to all your games next year."

He knew what I meant right away—said, "For real?"

I said, "For real."

Then he said, "But, Pops, you always said that when you start something you've got to finish it. You need to get back to the Super Bowl."

I said, "Junior, we're going to the Super Bowl. You can write that down."

I told my daughter Diaymon, too—but no one else. Wasn't any reason for anybody else to know, not yet. I didn't want to go out on some farewell tour. I didn't want all those distractions. I just wanted to play football, get us back to that AFC Championship Game, get us back to the Super Bowl, finish on top. The Baltimore front office, the coaching staff, my Ravens teammates—all those folks could wait for my news and join me on my journey instead. I didn't need them on my roller coaster. It would've gotten in the way of what we were trying to do—what we needed to do.

So this is my mind-set, going into this game against Dallas. The season is young, but we're off to a 4–1 start. We're playing pretty well, both sides of the ball, finding our way. There's a long way to go, but our championship run is taking shape. The pieces are in place. I've got my whole family with me at the stadium, up from Florida. Even my father is in the box, cheering me on. The whole time, leading up to the kickoff, I'm thinking this could be the last time my family is gathered like this for a regular season game—and just this one thought lights some new fire in me.

The game starts out close. We're on the board first with a field goal. The Cowboys answer with a touchdown, then a field goal. We tie it up at 10–10, then take the lead just before the half on a nineteen-yard touchdown pass from Joe Flacco to Torrey Smith.

We head into the locker room on a momentum run, and the whole time I'm thinking of my family in the box above the field, everybody gathered to watch me go through these motions one final time, nobody but my son and daughter knowing this is some kind of a last dance. It started out as this great secret, but it can't help but leak out. Already, there's talk around the league that I might be retiring. This is where I am in the cycle of my career. I'm one of the grand old men of the National Football League, I guess. After every game, there's a press conference, people sticking microphones in my face, journalists asking me if I'm getting ready to hang it up. I've gotten pretty good at dodging the question, but that's mostly because I've been asked the same question so many times.

Still, I can hear the talk, mostly in whispers. Folks in and around the game, speculating on what I might do next, nobody knowing the first thing about me, about what drives me. But I tune it all out. I have a job to do, a goal in mind. All that other stuff, it gets in the way.

Here's a little background to help tell this next part: Sometime during the week leading up to this game against the Cowboys, one of my fellow linebackers—Dannell Ellerbe, a good young player out of Georgia—asked me to join him in the weight room for a session. He said he wanted to stay strong, second half of the season, and I wanted to encourage him, push him, so I joined him, and the whole time we were lifting I felt a little off. At one point I said to him, "Bro, my triceps, my arms, they're feeling tight."

It was something to notice more than it was something to worry about. It wasn't even enough to get me to change up my routine or cut my workout short. I just put on some compression sleeves to help me get through the lifts, and everything was fine.

Now here's the next part. Fourth quarter, the Cowboys are driving.

Tony Romo hits Jason Witten for a big first down on an out route. The crowd is into it—it's a one-possession game, Dallas down 31–23.

I'm dug in, dialed in, leaning in. All of that.

Next, Romo drops back. I follow his eyes, see where he's looking to throw, so I drop back to meet the ball where it's headed, maybe knock it away. For a couple beats in there, I'm thinking about putting my hands up, thinking about it, thinking about it—and when I finally do, after just the slightest hesitation, I time my jump and reach for the ball in a funny way, come down in a funny way, land hard against the helmet and shoulder pad of one of the Dallas linemen.

As soon as I hit, I feel my triceps pop. It's more like a snap than a pop—same spot where I'd felt that tightness in the weight room earlier in the week. Here was that "something to notice" come back to bite me, shift into something to worry about.

Immediately, I know something's wrong, but I shake it off. I'm in full battle mode. My thing is, you don't leave the battlefield unless you die. You don't walk off a battlefield—you're carried off, on a stretcher. So I take that pain in my triceps and push it away, tell myself I can't show that I'm hurt. Tell myself, whatever it is, whatever I've just done to my triceps, it doesn't matter. And it doesn't. Only thing that matters is getting through this game with a win. Only thing that matters is making plays. I'll play with one hand if I have to, long as we come out the other side.

Turns out that's just what I do—try to, anyway. I get back to the huddle, my arm is just kind of hanging there, dangling, but nobody notices. My teammates, they're in full game mode, too. They're into their own heads, focused. They don't have time to think I might be hurt, and I'm not about to tell them. So I keep on keeping on. The fans don't see that I'm hurting. The coaches, the trainers—they don't see that I'm hurting. (Or, if they do, they don't move to stop me, because they're in it, too. They're not about to take one of their warriors off the field unless they're forced to.) Up in the stands, in the box, my family doesn't even notice.

The Cowboys, they absolutely don't see that I'm hurting—and I

XVI | RAY LEWIS |

take the time to think that this right here will be the killing piece, if my opponents see me vulnerable.

I fight it, keep playing, make a couple tackles. The crowd is pulling for us, but Romo keeps moving the ball. We're in our two-minute defense, short yardage, giving them a little room, middle of the field, protecting deep. We're counting on the clock to help us defend—counting on Romo to run out of steam, maybe make a mistake.

Finally, a bunch of plays in to my one-arm, tough-it-up, shake-it-off approach, this kid running back, Tanner, busts through the left side, barrels my way. I get it in my head that if I don't make this play, this kid scores. He's found a hole. We're out near our own 40, but it feels to me like I'm the last line of defense, so I hurl myself in front of him, grab him, turn him to the side, yank him down with my one good arm.

I make the play, the crowd feels it, but I realize it's costing us, me being out here. I can't fire, pounce the way I need to off the snap. I'm hurt, no doubt about it. I'm not worried about the pain. I don't care about the pain, don't even feel it. I'm not even worried about hurting myself any more than I already have—no, I'm worried about hurting the team. This is the equation I run in my head: If I can't fire, I can't make plays. If I can't make plays, we might not hold this lead. If we don't hold this lead, we might lose an important game in the standings. There's this whole ripple effect that gets set in motion if I can't do my job.

Deep down, heart of hearts, I know my triceps is in bad shape. I know I tore something. But it doesn't matter. What matters is shutting down this Cowboy drive. What matters is getting the ball back so Flacco can run off some clock, put another bunch of points on the board.

I head for the sidelines, and as I leave the field I let myself feel whatever it is I'm feeling. Finally. For the first time, I consider the pain in my triceps and think what it might mean. I have some idea. I know what a burn feels like. I know what a strain feels like. I know this is something else. A tear, most likely. I know it's not good.

Before I can call for help, I'm met by our team doctor, Leigh Ann

Curl. She's been with us my whole career, travels with the team, knows how I like to fight through all these aches and pains. She knows the game, knows her players. She saw me signal to leave the game in a key spot, saw me favoring my arm as I made for the sidelines, saw me wincing, so she crosses to meet me. She takes my arm at the elbow, pushes gently at the back of it, tells me my triceps is gone. She doesn't need an MRI to tell me what she can see with her naked eye, a gentle touch.

I say, "What?"

She shows me a dent, almost like a divot, on my upper arm. She says, "This tells us your triceps popped. It's just gone, Ray."

She presses on that dent and a pain shoots through me like nothing I'd ever felt before.

I say, "No big thing." And really, at just this moment, it isn't—not to me.

She starts crying.

I say, "Why are you crying? I'm the one busted up his triceps."

She says, "Because this is no way for your career to end."

It's like I don't even hear her—like I won't let myself hear her. I say, "My career's not ending, Doc." Certain, matter-of-fact.

She says, "Ray, nobody's ever come back from an injury like this. It's never been done. It can't be done."

I look at her and smile. It throws her that I'm smiling, confuses her. She knows what this pain must be like. She knows what her diagnosis means, the weight of her words. She's always been straight with me, same way she is with all her players, and here she thinks maybe she hasn't made herself clear. But she has—better believe it she has. It's just that those four words—*It can't be done*—are like lighter fluid to me. I hear those words, and it's like pouring a gallon of the stuff on an open flame. It lights me up and sets me off, leaves me thinking there's nothing I can't do.

She says, "Why are you smiling, Ray? This isn't good. Your triceps is torn."

I say, "I'm smiling because we're gonna win the Super Bowl. I'm smiling because this injury is nothing."

She says, "You're not hearing me, Ray."

I say, "Oh, I hear you, Doc. But you're not hearing me. I'm gonna be okay."

We must make an odd picture, the two of us. The doc, crying, trying to comfort me, trying to give it to me straight—and me, smiling, trying to tell her she's wrong about me, off in her diagnosis. We're both right, of course. In our own minds, in our own experience, we're each reacting to the same set of circumstances in our own way, each of us dead solid certain that the way we see it is the way it will go.

She asks me again why I don't seem more upset—because, hey, she just told me my career is over. My arm is hanging like a sack of flour.

So I'm straight with her, same way she's always straight with me. I say, "Man deals with the possible, Doc. God deals with the impossible."

Then I turn to face the field, knowing I'm in good hands.

I FEEL LIKE
GOING ON

ONE

Say My Name

Some folks have it hard.

Some folks have it harder still.

For me, the hard part was mostly in what I *didn't* have. I didn't have a father. I do now, but I didn't then. The man I now know as my father, Elbert Ray Jackson, is a father in DNA only. He claims the title, but he didn't earn it. He looks like me, moves like me, but he never took the time to know me, never played the part. He left the day I was born. He came back a couple years later—stayed long enough to father my twin sisters, Laquesha and Lakeisha, but not long enough to pick me up or change my diaper. Far as I ever knew, he was gone the next day, the same deal all over again, and as I write this I think of the cycle of abandonment that's colored my family. Every twenty years, there's been another link broken, another hard road laid, going back four generations. My son Ray Lewis III is nineteen years old; I am thirty-nine; my father is fifty-nine; *his* father, my grandfather, is seventy-nine; and my great-grandfather is ninety-nine. And the only one who's grown up with a father is my son.

And then on the other side of all that was my mother, Sunseria Smith. Oh my God, my mother had it *hard*, and it only got harder once she started having kids, but it was because of her strength that my younger brother and sisters were able to get by. It was because of her resilience that we had a chance. That *I* had a chance. Really, everything I do, everything I *am*—it's because of this good, sweet, proud woman.

My mother was fifteen when I was born, on May 15, 1975. She was a runaway—only, she ran no further than my great-grandmother's house in Mulberry, Florida, about a half hour south of Lakeland, where she'd been living at the time. She ran because she was pregnant and her mother didn't want her to have the baby—to have *me*. This right here was one of the great ironies of my life. My grandmother was a God-fearing woman, and she raised her family in a churchgoing household, but she chased after my mother with a coat hanger and tried to pin her down. She believed in the sanctity of life, my grandmother, but she was a full-blooded Indian woman who also believed that her fifteen-year-old daughter was too young to have a child. Guess you could say it was a conflict of blood and faith. My grandmother was a firecracker, with her own principles, and her daughter was not about to have a baby on her watch. No, sir. She did not *play*, that woman—in fact, this same scene took place a bunch of times, with other members of my family, aunts and nieces and cousins, but my mother was the one who lit out on her own and followed her heart.

My mother knows her mind. I'll say that. To this day, she expects things done a certain way, likes things *just so*. As a boy, this was made clear to me. I could not leave a dish in the sink. Everything had to be in the right place—from the rugs to the furniture to the picture frames. I could not go outside to play after supper. I could not have friends over, or leave the house in the morning without tidying my room. As I got older, as my baby sister Kadaja joined the family, and my baby brother Keon soon after that, I helped out around the house more and more. My mother worked three jobs, so a lot of the babysitting, cooking, cleaning was on me. I didn't complain then and I am not complaining now, because it was a blessing to be able to do for my family in this way. It's just how it was. Most days, my mother would come home from working the night shift at the hospital at two or three o'clock in the morning, dog tired, hoping to grab a couple hours sleep before heading back out the door. Her feet would be swollen, and it was my job to comfort her, even in some small, little-kid way. We used to keep a beige bucket by the side of her bed, and I would fill it with warm water and pour in some Epsom salts and rub her feet while she went to sleep. Then I'd go back to my own bed and lie down for another while, until it was time to wake my mother so she could get to her next job. I'd have to get my brother and sisters up and ready for school, then get my own behind to the bus stop. I was eight, nine, ten years old. This went on and on, for years and years. End of each day, it was the same deal, in reverse. I'd hurry home before the others, pick them up from school, the nursery, and get everybody started on their homework, on dinner. In between shifts, whenever she could find the time, my mother would prepare meals for us—meals that I could reheat, rework as the week went on. Pork and beans, wings, mashed potatoes, anything that could last us two or three days, until she could get back to it. When I was old enough to work the stove, she had me boiling weenies, making eggs.

I never questioned how things were. They just *were*, you know? This was how we lived, how we managed. The only piece I ever questioned was my name. My family tree, it was messed up, made no sense to me. There was no way to recognize the different branches, put them in the right spot, find a little piece of shade beneath one of those branches that I could call my own. My twin sisters had my mother's name—anyway, they had the name Jenkins, which was the name of my blood grandfather on my mother's side. My mother went by McKinney, which was the name of her stepfather, Gillis McKinney, a man

I grew up knowing as my maternal grandfather. My baby sister had another name—my brother, too. We were a mismatched set, and I wanted to know who was who, what was what, who had the same name as *me*.

One day, my mom took the time to explain it all to me—*some* of it, at least, and here it helps to know that we never talked about my father. He wasn't a part of our lives, wasn't even a part of our thinking, but there was no way to have *this* conversation without bringing him up. Come to think of it, this was the first conversation I can remember where we talked about him at all. My mother said, "Baby Ray, I will never say one bad thing about your father. Ever. Never. He's your daddy, after all."

I said, "Okay, but whose name do I have? We don't know no Lewises?"

She said, "I'm 'bout to tell you, if you let me finish."

I didn't know much, but I knew to stay out of my mother's way when she got going on a story.

She continued, plain talk: "Your father, he's chosen not to be in your life, so you're gonna have to figure that out. There is no one to teach you how to be a man. I can't teach you to be a man. That one's on you. But when it comes to your name, that's a whole other story."

That *whole other story* went like this: My mother was a good-looking young woman, stunning—hazel eyes, hair down to her freakin' butt, a smile to light up the night sky—just crazy beautiful. I look at pictures from when she was thirteen, fourteen years old, and I'm knocked out. My father was, too. That's why he'd come around in the first place. He was just a couple years older, but he used to babysit my mom when she was little; he knew our family; he took notice as she grew up—kept comin' round, long past the time she needed minding. Let me tell you, it was hard *not* to notice my mother. Those pictures don't lie. She turned heads. Folks around town, they knew who she was just by the way she looked. Folks the next town over, they knew who she was, too. The boys, they lined up just to talk to her, to be near to her. So when she finally got around to telling my father about me on the day I was born, the day he turned tail, there was this other young man next in line, and he stepped up and helped my mother with her hospital bills. Wasn't like he was fixing to hang around, wasn't like there was any kind of relationship between them, but the young man had taken a shine to my mother, said it was his privilege to help in this small way. And it was. To him, it was a small kindness; to my mother, it was big beyond big. He was a military man, and here he'd done my mother this great good turn, so she reached out to him a second time. She asked him to sign the hospital paperwork, where it asks for the name of the baby's father—and happily, mercifully, he agreed.

That young man's name was Ray Lewis, so my name became Ray Lewis. Just like that. My mother hardly knew this man, but it was a way to honor him.

I was a way to honor him.

I didn't meet him until many years later, when my own name was becoming well known. I'd been having some success on the football field and on the wrestling mat in high school. And this man, Ray Lewis, found a way to reach out to me, tell me who he was. He'd had no contact with my mother since he'd helped her out just after I was born, but he introduced himself—said, "My name is Ray Lewis, son. I used to know your mama."

I made the connection right away—said, "Thank you for giving me your name, sir. I will make it great."

Wasn't just Ray Lewis whose name shined down on our household. Wasn't just Ray Lewis whose name I vowed to uphold.

It was His name, too.

We were a churchgoing family. My mother introduced me to God early on. He was in the air and all around. By the time I was eight or nine, I was a junior deacon at the Greater Faith Missionary Baptist Church. I took my role seriously, felt it in my soul, in my bones. Other folks, they could feel it too—in *me*. Once, the pastor had me lead devotion, and I'll never forget, I prayed and prayed so hard that when I got up I could see my great-grandmother in one of the front pews, crying. She came up to me after and said, "God got a calling on your life, Baby Ray."

God got a calling on your life . . .

I didn't know what those words meant at the time. I only knew that my great-grandmother believed them, deeply. I only knew that I was moved when I spoke the Word of God. Underneath all of that, I only knew what I was tired of, what I would not let stand—and underneath all of *that*, I knew He would give me the strength to power through. Whatever it was holding me down, He would lift me up.

Wasn't just in church that I went looking for God. Wasn't just in church that He found me. I took to praying early on. My mother encouraged me, big-time. She taught me to read the Bible. She taught me the hymns. I learned to pray by watching her. She would drop to her knees and have at it, and when she saw I was a little tentative, a little shy about it, she'd push me toward Him, gently. She'd say, "Talk to Him, Baby Ray. He'll talk back. Just talk to Him."

So I did, and as I did I came to understand that there is something else outside of what man says is true. I learned that man is not the only ticket, not the only answer. I learned there is a spirit, a power greater than all of us put together. And He did talk back—He did, and His words were a comfort to me, a shield. In God's words, I felt this great sense of protection, left me believing that as long as I had my relationship with God, I was good. Didn't matter what was going on in the rest of my life. Didn't matter what was *missing* from the rest of my life, long as I was good with God.

My mother used to always say, "God don't make no mistakes." It was her answer to everything. Whenever I was angry or frustrated, she had me think things through—to look at things from God's perspective, get me to realize there was a plan, a reason.

God don't make no mistakes—that's a powerful message for a young boy to take in, but I did just that, in what ways I could.

And so I split my time trying to live up to the good name of Ray Lewis, to the name of God, while at the same time trying to live *down* the legacy of my father and the troublesome string of men that came in and out of my mother's life. Sad to say, she didn't always make the best choices when it came to men. Oh, they had money, some of them. They were good to us, some of them—two of them she even married. They put a roof over our heads, food on the table, maybe even a little stability in our lives. Outwardly, they were generous. One of them gave us my baby brother and my baby sister—another blessing. But none of these men lasted, not a one. It was the five of us who lasted—my brother, my three sisters, me. *We* were my mother's family. These men, they were just a means to an end, a necessary evil—and trust me, I don't choose that word lightly. *Evil.* Some of these men, they drank, and when they drank, they got physical. They beat my mom. They beat me. My brother and sisters, they were mostly spared; I took their hits, and this too was another blessing, that I was able to carry some of that burden, protect them in this way.

This one guy, he lasted longer than the others, but that just meant he stuck around long enough to cause us the most trouble, inflict the most pain. He used to drink, hard, but only on the weekends. All week long, he'd punch the clock at work, go about his business, sit down to table with us for family dinner. To look on at our put-together family, you'd have thought all was right in our little world. There were times he was actually nice to me. If he felt the need to call me on anything during the week, he'd ride me with his words, never his hands. He'd be on me about this or that, on my mother about this or that. He would raise his voice, but not his hands. Come Friday, he was a totally different person. Every week, it was the same damn deal. He'd cash his paycheck, buy a couple bottles, and get into it, and for the longest time I struggled to figure him out. My sisters, he would never touch. My baby brother, he would never touch. But me and my mother, we were like punching bags to this man. We were there to receive his anger. It's like it was building up inside him all week long and it came pouring out. On *us*.

I used to sit in my room and think, *Why does this man hate me so?* I couldn't understand why God put us on the receiving end of his blows. Wasn't until years later that I realized this guy's hatred wasn't for me. No, his hatred was for my father—something I couldn't see when I was but a child.

The way it worked, in our little town, my father's name went a long way. Lakeland, Florida, wasn't much—but to me, to my family, it was everything. We lived in a poor part of town, in what was known as the projects, only to call it the projects to someone from the big city, they'd have a different picture in mind. My Lakeland—*our* Lakeland—wasn't a place of high-rises and blacktops. It was country. It was simple. A lot of folks on welfare, struggling to get by. Everybody knew everybody's business. We were rich in tradition in Lakeland. Family histories, they ran deep. It was the kind of place that showed you what life could be, the good and the bad.

Lakeland was small enough that there were lots of folks

around who knew my father and would tell me about him. His deceptive charms, his athleticism, his competitive fire. But Lakeland was also plenty big enough that I never accidentally ran into him. He was one of the best athletes that part of Florida had ever seen. He was handsome, smooth, a sharp dresser. He used to have his nails manicured, back when he was chasing after my mother. And he could sing! Oh my goodness, the man had it going on—only, he was nowhere to be found once I came along, once my twin sisters came along. He steered clear, but he didn't go far. He was around. He ran with this crew of guys who ended up married to some of my aunts, some of my relatives, so our lives were all intertwined. This dude who used to beat my mom? He was a part of all that, and I think he felt like he was living in my father's shadow. My father never set foot in our house—and, still, his shadow got us beat.

And yet I could not hate this guy—this one man on a long string of many. I wanted to, but I couldn't. He was an obstacle to get past. That's all. He was bigger than me, of course. At ten years old, I wasn't much to look at. I wasn't big, wasn't cut, wasn't strong. I couldn't fight back for trying, but I could endure the blows. The physical pain, I could deal with that. I got used to it, what it came down to. I found a way to set it aside, wait for it to pass. But seeing my mom hurt—I never got used to *that*. I'll never forget this one time, we went to a family barbecue at my grandmother's house, and this guy had beat her so bad she had to wear these big black sunglasses to cover the bruises around her eyes. Her disguise didn't fool anyone, but she kept those glasses on all afternoon—inside the house, even. I wanted to help her, but I didn't know how. I was just a boy.

We talked about it, in ways that made sense to a ten-year-old child. We were tight, me and my mom. We were in this muck together—because, hey, ain't nothing like the love between a boy and his mama beaten by the same man. We were bound together by the force of this guy's ugliness.

She used to say, "We're gonna ride this out, Baby Ray. You with me?"

And I would nod and say, "I'm with you." I could not think what this meant, but I was with her, absolutely. I said, "Just tell me what to do."

There was nothing to tell me, of course. There was nothing to do. I'd see my mother with the bruises around her eyes, and I would cry for her. She'd see me crying and say, "It's me and you, Baby Ray. Just me and you. Ain't nobody's business but our own."

Meaning, I wasn't supposed to talk about this.

There was the pain of a beatdown, and there was the pain of humiliation. It was one thing to get beat; it was another thing to be shamed; and this man, he gave it both ways. Looking back, I believe the shaming was harder to take. To this day, I can close my eyes and picture one night in particular. It was raining. I was sitting by the window, wishing myself away, away, away. This guy was cursing, ranting, going off. His voice was wild, menacing, the way it got whenever he was into the bottle. For the longest time, I just sat there, staring, lost in the slap of the rain against the window. At some point—must've been drifting in my own thoughts for a good long while—this man stepped outside, grabbed hold of a garden snake, and returned with it inside. Tossed it right at me—just to mess with me, amuse himself. I couldn't figure what it was at first, couldn't make out what was going on, why, but that all came clear. I can't be sure, but I think I shrieked when I noticed this hissing, slithering snake in my lap. I called to my mother—tried to, anyway. I said, "M-m-m-m-m," struggling to call out "Mama!" But I was overcome by this sudden stutter—a stutter that stayed with me all the way to college. It would come on when I was stressed or worried, and it all started with this mean-spirited man standing by the doorway, wet from the rain, laughing at me, mimicking me, humiliating me, saying, "M-m-m-m-m . . ."

It stung, got to admit—damn near killed me, to be reduced in this way in the eyes of this guy. But there it was, and there was no shrinking from it.

Soon as I was old enough, big enough, I vowed to keep my mother safe—to take care of her, the way she'd always taken care of us. Being hurt by this guy, that was one thing. Seeing my mother hurt, that's a different hurt.

One night, without even thinking about it, I reached for a deck of cards I used to keep by the side of my bed. It was just something to do, a way to kill the time. I turned over the first card—five of clubs. I did five push-ups. I turned over another card—nine of diamonds. I did nine push-ups. I worked my way through the whole damn deck. Picture cards were ten push-ups. Aces were twenty-five. The two jokers, fifty each. There was no plan to it, no method. Like I said, just something to do. And when I flipped the last card in the deck, I shuffled the cards and started right back in again, told myself I would get strong. I would build myself up. I set my mind to it. I would not let this guy beat us down in this way.

Now, it takes a whole lot more than a deck of cards and a mess of push-ups for a little kid to stand up to a grown man, and I knew deep down that I would be on the losing end of these battles for a long, long time. But I wasn't about to let him have an easy win. He'd still win, but it wouldn't be an easy win. It would take something out of him—more and more, as I got stronger and stronger. And I did get stronger. Flipping cards like that, doing push-ups—it went from *something to do* to *something I needed to do*. Right away, I started adding sit-ups to my routine. I'd go through the deck doing push-ups, then

I'd switch. Then I'd go back to push-ups, then switch. Back and forth, up half the night.

I already understood pain. I try to explain this to people, but there's something lost in the telling. There's no way to communicate the doggedness of a small boy beaten down one time too many. I was so tired, so *worn out* by this guy's abuse, I could only will myself past it. Over it. Through it. The pain of all these push-ups, all these sit-ups. Hundreds and hundreds of push-ups. Hundreds and hundreds of sit-ups. They were *nothing* next to the pain this guy put us through.

In some ways, the pain I put myself through was like my comfort zone. It was my way out. With every push-up, I saw the light. With every sit-up, I saw the light. Every time I flipped the last card and shuffled up that deck to start in again, it was like my world was brand new. Anything was possible. And everything else fell away. All the bad stuff, it was gone—just, *gone.* All there was in front of me was the deck of cards, and in those cards, however they fell, however they turned, there was my escape. *Our* escape. It got to where I'd get a cramp in my stomach and I could only suck it up and tell myself the pain I was feeling was nothing like the pain waiting for me on the other side of that door, so I kept going. Why stop? All night long, I flipped those cards, did my thing. Some nights I couldn't sleep but for a couple hours at a stretch, and in between those stretches I was back at it. Push-ups. Sit-ups. Just *wishing* for an ace, a joker, so I could taste a little extra pain. Told myself that the more I worked, the more I would get back in return.

Every night, I'd work my way through that same deck of cards. Over and over. I was relentless. Seven of spades. Jack of clubs. King. Ace. Joker. I wore those cards out, man. And when that happened, I'd start in on another deck. Over and over. Some of those decks I took away with me to college, when I started playing at the University of Miami. Some I took to Baltimore. Some I carry with me to this day.

Turned out the last battle with this man had nothing to do with me or my cards. I was about three years into my routine. I was good and ready. But on this one night he came after my mother. My mom was in the kitchen, fixing us dinner. It was a Friday afternoon, and he was already into it. He walked over to where my mother was standing and slapped her, just for nothing. And my mom, she snapped. This was her *one time too many*. She got her back up, in a way I'd never seen, flashed him a cold, hard look that said she'd had enough. It was a look of strength, resolve—I'll never forget it. And this man, he shrank from it, backed off.

He left soon after that. Maybe he saw I was getting bigger, tougher, stronger. Maybe he didn't like that there were no more easy wins with me. Maybe he was just a coward, wanted to pick himself an easier battle. Whatever. The guy was gone.

One more thing, about my name: the story behind it tells what it meant to grow up without a father, to represent the fourth generation of men in my family to grow up without a father, to grow up in a house with three sisters and a brother, everyone with a different name. My mother, with a different name. All these other men—two of them my stepfathers, even—all of *them* with names of their own. And me with the name of a kind stranger who just happened to be there on the day I was born.

That kind of thing, it leaves you wondering who you are, who you're meant to be, how you fit. Anyway, it left me wondering. And like I said, my father left some pretty big footprints in and around Lakeland. Even though he didn't come to see us, he was still in touch with the friends he left behind. When I started playing football in high school, he knew. When I started wrestling, he knew. Word kept coming back to him, the kind of noise I was making on the field, in the gym, and after a while he must've started thinking some of that noise was meant for him. I was his son, after all.

So the man went out and changed my name—to *his*. Without even telling me, without reaching out, he hired a lawyer and changed my name to Elbert Ray Jackson Jr. The papers came in the mail one day, telling me what he'd done. No phone call. No heads-up. Nothing. He just sent them over, thinking we would accept this change like we'd seen it coming. My mother showed the papers to me, and I went off. Really, I was furious. I marched those documents out of the house, like the papers themselves could pollute the air, infect our lives with the stink of this man who'd left us for nothing.

My mother, she'd never seen me so upset. Even with all those beatings, at the hands of that other guy, I never let my anger show the way I let it show here. I'd grabbed a book of matches from the kitchen and set all those official papers down on the driveway, flattened them to the asphalt with a stomp of my foot.

I can't be sure, but I think I was crying—tears of rage, mostly. Tears of fury.

My mother walked over to where I stood on the driveway, saw I was fixing to light a match—said, "Baby Ray, what you doin'?"

I said, "I'm gonna burn these papers, Mama. I will never live a day in that man's name."

And my mom, she just kind of sidled up next to me on that driveway as I set a match to those papers. There was nothing to say, really. She put her hand on my back, and we stood there watching those papers burn—didn't take but a long moment for the fire to burn all the way through, and in that long moment I could see the whole of my life in the thick black smoke that curled to the sky. I can still see that plume of smoke. I close my eyes and there it is, and as it reaches up and up and disappears I can see myself shaking the hand of the man whose name I *do* carry, the man whose name I've chosen to celebrate.

I can see me talking to him. I can hear my voice.

Thank you for giving me your name, sir. I will make it great.

TWO

Pick 'Em Up, Bust 'Em

Things were better for a while.

Soon, there was another man to take this guy's place. He wasn't so bad. Then there was another man, and he wasn't so bad, either. The violence, the not knowing if you'd get whooped or menaced or called out. All of that fell away, a bad dream none of us wanted to remember. We still had a roof over our heads—that was the main thing. Everything else, we'd find a way to deal.

Somewhere in there I started playing football. First team I played for was the Lakeland Lumberjacks. I was ten years old, in the sixth grade. I wore a tore-up jersey with the number 85 clinging to the back in bits and pieces. It was the last jersey they had, because I was late to sign up.

Football—*real* football, *organized* football—couldn't have found me at a better time, because I needed to get out and do my own thing, find some way to channel all those emotions building up inside of me. I mean, when you grow up on the wrong end of a beatdown, you look for ways to put some of that rage and frustration back into the world, and football became my release.

I might not have signed up at all if it weren't for the coach—a good, good guy named Biscuit. He noticed me one day while I was running around in the park playing in a pickup game. I wasn't the fastest kid in the neighborhood, wasn't the quickest, wasn't the strongest, but when we got a game going I could figure it out. It was easy for me—reading the other players, getting to where the ball was headed. Don't know why, don't know how, but the game unfolded for me in this crystal-clear way, and what I couldn't figure out right away I learned soon enough. Mostly, I learned by watching, seeing the whole field—and not just the field I was playing on at the time. The park was just across the way from where the high school team played. Our little field was the same little field they used for some of their practices, so when I wasn't running around with my own friends I was studying these older kids, watching how they lined up, how they moved, how they made things happen.

I was a quick study, shot through with a confidence I'd yet to justify. Got to where I thought I knew a couple things. And I guess I did, because here was this coach, Biscuit, seeing something to like in my game.

He came over to me—said, "Son, why you ain't playing football?"

I said, "Football? Thought that's what we were playing." I pointed to the football that had come to rest at our feet, just to show him I wasn't being smart. (Okay, so maybe I was being smart—maybe it was some of that confidence shining through.)

He said, "No, I mean Little League. On a team. Uniforms and everything."

Little League football, that's what we called it. Other parts of the country—other parts of Florida, even—it was Pop Warner football, Pee Wee football, youth league football, but this was the first I was hearing of it, and Biscuit called it Little League. Anyway, it sounded good to me, and I said as much, but I also said I didn't think my mother would allow it. I was wide-eyed, excited to play organized football, but I was also realistic.

He said, "Let me talk to her."

I tried not to laugh, didn't want to be disrespectful—said, "You? Talk to *my* mama? That's the last thing you want to do is talk to my mama 'bout me playing football."

He couldn't know this, of course, but I would have had an easier time getting my mother to sign me up for astronaut school. But Biscuit was determined, so I brought him round to see what we could see. In a million years, I didn't think my mother would go for something like this—for one thing, we didn't have the fifteen dollars it cost to register—but what did I care if this dude wanted to talk to her about it? If anything, it would be fun to watch him dance.

Sure enough, my mother wasn't having any of it. She put her hand up before Biscuit could get through his pitch—said, "I don't want to hear it. You tellin' me this boy should take the time to play a *game*? He's got too much to do around the house. There's nobody else to watch these kids."

Oh man, she *shut him down.* Then she ran through a whole list of reasons why I couldn't play, said she couldn't get me to games or practices, couldn't pick me up from games or practices, couldn't pay my registration fee, and on and on.

When she finished her list, Biscuit put up his own hand—said, "I'll take care of all that."

Now, there's one thing you need to know about my sweet, proud mama—she wasn't about to be told *what for* or *shhhed* by this strange, biscuit-shaped man who'd come into her kitchen to talk football. She had a lot of questions, concerns, and she would run through all of them, in her own time. Probably, she wanted to know Biscuit's background, what he did for a living, whether he had children of his own, but this part of the conversation wasn't meant for my ears. That was the beauty of *back then*. Back then, grown-up business was grown-up business. Kid business was kid business. Nowadays, everybody's business is everybody's business, but I remember my mother flashing me a look, telling me I should disappear into another room for this part of the conversation.

She was on it, my mother. No, she didn't always make the best choices when it came to the men in her life, but she figured it out, best she could. Through it all, she had us kids covered. She had our backs. End of the day, *every* day, she was my hero, and I can't remember a time when I wasn't looking for ways to let her know how I felt about her. The best way was to tell it to her straight, with a little help from Tupac. To this day, every Mother's Day, I call her up and sing her a couple lines from "Dear Mama."

Now ain't nobody tell us it was fair
No love from my daddy, 'cause the coward wasn't there . . .

I put my heart all the way into it—same way my mother put her heart all the way into me, into each of us kids. And here she was, spread crazy thin by work and life, stressed, with hardly enough time to even *breathe*, and still she made time to think about something that might have been important to me that seemed foolish to her. Bottom line: she fought for us, even if it wasn't always clear to her what she was fighting for, and here she had no way to know how important this was to me—how important it *could* be, anyway.

Don't remember how long they talked, Biscuit and Mama, but it seemed like forever. It felt to me in my little-kid head like my future hung in the balance. For the first time in my life, I wanted something that had nothing to do with the care and feeding of my family. Something for me—just me. I hadn't even realized I wanted it so bad, until Biscuit came through the door and started making his pitch. Still, my mother wasn't ready to sign me up. She had to think about it, and think about it. Every day, I begged her to let me play. But she put me off until the last day of sign-ups, when she finally gave in. That's why I got the last jersey in the pile, the number practically falling off. It was such a sorry-looking thing, but I didn't care. To me, it was like an official NFL jersey. To me, it was like a rite of passage just to be able to put on a uniform—*any* uniform.

Anyway, it was 1985, and my number was 85, and I thought that was some kind of sign, the numbers matching up like that. My mom keeps a picture of me in that jersey, and every time I see it I get this big old smile on my face. It takes me back—my first taste of the game, dressed out in a shabby, worn uniform with the jersey number tore off and half gone.

My mother came to the first organized game. It was the only time she ever made it to one of my games, all the way through high school. Wasn't that she didn't support her kids—she couldn't. There just wasn't time. In her heart, she supported us, but her heart had to punch the clock at three jobs, be in all these different places at the same time. She was always working, always chasing after my sisters and brother, so she didn't have time to come out and watch me play football—or, later on, to watch me wrestle. That's just how things were, and I understood it, but she did make it to that first one. She made a special point of it. She came as much to check me out, to see what I was up to, as she did to cheer me on.

We used to play our games at Bryant Stadium, a run-down place right across the street from the projects where we lived. Wasn't much of a field, the grass had been run down to a ribbon of dirt reaching from end zone to end zone, but to me it was like playing in the Orange Bowl. So there I was with my ragged Lakeland Lumberjacks jersey, number 85, and my mom was at the field to see me get the first reverse on a kickoff and run the ball back seventy-five yards for a touchdown. As moments go, it was pretty damn great, but I don't think I'd remember it thirty years later if my mother hadn't been there to see it. It's through her eyes that this one play has lived on in my memory. Here's what she saw, behind the gate in the end zone: me, crossing the goal line and still running, running, running to her. Here's what I remember: me, crossing the goal line and thinking I wanted to collect my mother in my arms and twirl her around like we'd just won the Super Bowl or something. That's how happy I was to be able to run toward her like that, in that moment.

I gave her the ball. It wasn't hers to keep, mind you—don't think we had but one. It wasn't mine to give. But I gave it to her like a big grand gesture, like I was thanking her for letting me play, for filling up all those spaces where my father might have been. For being a hero to a boy who needed one.

Coach Biscuit felt bad about handing me that torn-up jersey, but he was an old-school coach. He was tough, but fair. He was a product of his time, which meant he was willing to do a lot of things a father would have done for a bunch of kids who didn't have one at home. Just in terms of getting my life organized, finding a way to fit football into what I had to do at home, what I had to do at school—he was all over it. He was good to his word, picked me up to take me to practices, made sure I got home after, covered my registration fee. But it went beyond that, of course. It went all the way to teaching us what it was like to be a part of a team, a part of something bigger than just ourselves. Wasn't just me taking this in—no, we were a team full of lost, misfit kids. Most of us came from single-parent homes in the projects. Most of us couldn't afford to be out there every day during football season. We had someplace else we needed to be, chores we had to do at home, whatever. But Coach Biscuit knew we *needed* to be out there on that field, with him. He knew it ran deeper than just football.

It put me in mind of the words I took in from my mother,

trying to explain how things were with my father: *I can't teach you to be a man.* No, she couldn't. But Biscuit, he could teach me some of that. Not all of it, but some.

Survival—that was the big message that came through in practice. We'd go at it, hard. One-on-one. And the boy who survived these battles was the boy who could get it done. Football, the game itself, was almost beside the point. It didn't much matter. The scoreboard, it didn't much matter. What mattered was what the game could teach you. What mattered was a sense of discipline, the structure the season could give to our days. Also, the Lumberjacks gave me a sense of community, a place to belong. In addition to Biscuit, there were three or four assistant coaches, and they took an interest in us, mentored us, checked in with us to see how we were doing off the field.

For me, the game became my sanctuary. It took me out of my own head and whatever ugliness was around me and just set me loose. And the game itself, the way Biscuit had us playing it, was a revelation. Before I started playing with the Lakeland Lumberjacks, it was every man for himself. Our street version of football was a game we called "Pick 'em Up, Bust 'em," which was pretty much like what it sounds. Everybody chased after the guy with the ball. No pads. No boundaries. That was the game. When I had the ball, I just had to *deal with it*, you know? And when I was chasing after the guy with the ball—well, then he would have to *deal with me*.

Little League football was different—way different. There were rules. There were set plays. Full pads. Refs. But my "Pick 'em Up, Bust 'em" training? It gave me a great foundation. It set the course.

One of Biscuit's drills was to have us lie on our backs, middle of the field, head-to-head with one of our teammates. Coach would blow the whistle and we'd have to spring up off the ground and do battle. One dude would have the ball, one dude would be the defender—he'd keep switching it up. We'd lie there, ready to spring to our feet at the sound of that whistle, and the kid on D would have to get the other dude back to the ground or force him out of the circle. It was a grudge match, man. It was *on*. And a couple times through I started to realize that this was the essence of the game—all there was to it. Football, it was just one-on-one. All I had to do was beat this one other person across the ball from me. That's it. One and done. Soon as I figured that out, I waited for the rest of it. *Me, beating another person?* That was easy. That was nothing. Had to be more to it than that, right? But there was never any more to it. This was football, at its most basic. This was football, all the way up to my time in the NFL. Beat the guy on the other side of the ball—all the time if you can, more times than not if that's the best you can do.

Biscuit, he had us running into each other, hurting each other. Kids today, you can't coach them in this way, but this was how we went at it back then. We went at it *hard*. First to break, first to complain, first to cry—well, then we knew what *he* was made of. First to *cause* another kid to break, first to *cause* another kid to complain, to cry—well, we knew what that dude was made of, too.

Game day was Saturday, and that was a whole other deal, but practices were every day after school. I'd race home, help out with my sisters and brother, take care of the house, get started on my homework. Maybe I'd have to braid my sister's hair, sew a patch on a torn pair of jeans, do the dishes so we had clean plates for dinner, whatever it took. Then, a little before five o'clock, Biscuit would be outside with a car full of Lakeville Lumberjacks to ferry us to the field. Practice ran from five to seven. A lot of times, I'd have to make my way home with a couple other kids who lived in the same projects—we'd race each other back, before the street lights came on.

The deal at home was if I kept my grades up I could keep playing, so I kept my grades up. I wasn't about to let anyone take this away from me—no, sir.

I'd get so excited after practice, I'd burst into the house and start running my mouth. I'd say, "Mom, I'm busting these boys up."

She'd look at me like she had no idea.

"Mom, I *ran over* this dude. Just destroyed him."

She might not have known what I was talking about, but she could see I was pumped. She could see I was filled with a sense of pride and purpose, a sense of possibility—good things, all.

A lot of the kids on my team lived in Washington Park, but some of the kids in the projects played on other rival Pop Warner teams in town—the Patriots, the Gators, the Volunteers. I didn't pay much attention to rivalries or anything like that—wasn't about that for me. No, the kid on the other side of the ball—*he* was my rival. Didn't matter if it was my own teammate or some dude in another uniform—if you went up against me, you were going down. And after a while, it wasn't enough for me to just beat you, knock you down. I had to put a hurt on you, too. That was my mind-set, and out of that mind-set I began to make a name for myself in town. How you played, that's how you were known. If you wanted to be the best in Lakeland, you had to outrun somebody, beat 'em in a fight, beat 'em in wrestling, beat 'em to the ball. That's the path we were on. All of us. That's the path my father had been on, back when he was in high school—only, his path didn't exactly take him up and out, more like around and around. But I was determined to have a different future than my dad, and I started to see that sports might just be the way to get there. I didn't have any plan at this point. Just a vague notion.

Football taught me that I hated to lose. Lakeland taught me that I needed to win—because, hey, in my neighborhood, you were known by the things you won. I wouldn't trade growing up there for anyplace else. Wasn't a place to stay, though. It was a place to leave, but it gave it to you straight. It showed you what life sometimes hides. Our days were filled with hundreds of tiny battles. You'd get in the dirt and go at it. Some of those battles you'd win. Some of them you'd lose. But you kept score, man. Everybody kept score. And after a while of this, day after day of going at it, you'd see where you stood. You'd look around and start to see what was possible, just by how you measured up to the folks who were doing it before you, with you, against you.

On some level, I must've known these things going in, but it took all those drills for me to recognize how I was wired. It took being around the game, playing on a good team with good coaches, for all of this to register. Sprints—that was the be-all and end-all for me. Like I said, I wasn't the fastest, but I would not let myself be beat. Coach would end his practices with sprints, and for him it was all about fitness, stamina. He was building us up so we could run our opponents into the ground. That's all. But for me it was a race, plain and simple, and if I lost one time I would race you ten times more—just, you know, to run *you* into the ground. Sooner or later. Didn't matter that you were my teammate. Didn't matter that we were friends. It only mattered that you were lined up against me.

One of my closest friends early on was a dude named Willie Buford—Skeet, to everyone in town. He was way older than me, but he took a shine to me. And I looked up to him, carried myself like him, followed his lead. Skeet was one of the best athletes I've ever seen—nobody could deal with him on the field. He played high school ball for the Lakeland Dreadnaughts, and I used to watch all their games, all their practices. That team ended up winning the state championship—and to a little kid like me, where I grew up, *how* I grew up, that became the goal.

We had our role models out there on that field. Those high school players, Skeet and them, they were our ideal. They were like rock stars to us little kids. The Dreadnaughts had this one dude playing for them, Earl Motherseal—I just fell in love with his game. He wore number 42, and he moved just like Eric Dickerson. He had Dickerson *down*, all the way to the Jheri curls and the goggles. He was slick, slippery, smooth. I wanted to be just like him, too.

Friday night was game night at Bryant Stadium, and the whole town came out to watch the high school team play. Talk about *Friday Night Lights*—this was what mattered, where I grew up. It's like the rest of the world was silenced on Friday nights. In Lakeland, you lived and died with your team, so we weren't about to miss those games. Trouble was, we couldn't pay our way in, so we jumped the gate after our Friday night practice and slinked in by the side bleachers and hoped no one would notice us and throw us out. I couldn't stay for the whole game, though. My mother was expecting me home after practice, so I'd watch the first quarter, maybe the first half if I was feeling it. In those moments I was transported, lifted by those high school players. I began to see what was possible. And it's not like I watched those dudes and started thinking I could maybe play ball at their level, maybe even at college. Wasn't about college, just then. No, the game was a way to prove myself. That's all. A way to test myself.

Eventually, it became a way up and out for me, but at the same time I could see how it didn't always work out for everyone. That was a hard lesson, man. Earl Motherseal, Skeet, and plenty others had the talent, but it didn't shake out to the good for them. They caught some bad breaks, got knocked to the ground by life. But that didn't stop us from rooting for them, seeing ourselves in them, growing our games to look like theirs.

Probably my biggest role model back then was my older cousin, Tony Stancil—T-Boy. He was much older than me, but he had my back, too. I didn't want to be like anybody else but my cousin Tony. We lived in the same house for a while, so we were super close. I stayed for a couple years during middle school at his house in Mulberry, and he took care of me.

How I got to Mulberry was simple. My mother couldn't afford to feed all of us kids. Once that first guy left, we were up against it. Money was tight—we hit a bunch of rough spots. And me, I had a big old appetite. The way I used to eat, folks really meant it when they used to say, "That Baby Ray, he'll eat you out of house and home." So when I got old enough, seventh grade, when my appetite got big enough, when my twin sisters were able to pitch in a little bit more with the younger two, my mama got it in her head to send me to live with her family. It was a way to keep ahead of our bills. That's all—and it wasn't meant to be permanent. It was just for a while.

Mulberry was where my mother's people were. It was in a whole other part of the state, a long way from home, so I had to make a new name for myself, start fresh. That could have been tough, but Tony never let anybody mess with me, never really let me talk to girls, kept me out of trouble. Those days, when you were a new kid in a new city, you needed someone to stand up for you, and Tony did that for me. Lakeland and Mulberry, they were like different worlds. You came from one, you could never be a part of the other, so it was a good thing, him looking after me like that.

Nobody messed with T-Boy, and I got to ride his coattails. His reputation became mine. He was the cornerback for his high school team, so he could *play*, and because he could play, folks just assumed that I could play, too. But in my mind, Tony was playing at a whole other level—an *impossible* level. There was one particular game, Mulberry facing off against the Bartow Yellow Jackets, their archrivals. It was a big, big game, the season on the line, and my cousin showed me what it meant to show up, to put in a full effort. This one play, it was like a life changer for me—a game changer, anyway. What happened was this dude on the Yellow Jackets broke out, had the field to himself. Really, he was *gone*, but T-Boy, he saw this kid break and he took off after him. Like a lot of high school football players, Tony played both sides of the ball, so here he was on D, trying to keep his team in the game. This Bartow dude must've been on his own 40-yard line, and my cousin was back around the Bartow 20, but he gave chase, never thinking for a minute he wouldn't catch up to him. Didn't have a whole lot of field to work with, had to close those twenty yards before his opponent ran sixty, but he tore after him just the same.

I've always been a fan of a good footrace, and this was crazy. Tony had no shot, but he kept closing the gap and closing it, until he ran out of field. Really, it was one of the greatest efforts I've ever seen. Another ten yards, he would've had him, easy, but the takeaway for me was to never give up. All my years in the game, at the highest levels of the game, I never saw anybody hustle like that. Never. My cousin was just relentless, determined, and out of that one play, I found my game. I told myself, no matter what, if the guy on the other side of the ball breaks out like that, no matter where he is on the field, no matter where I am on the field, I will take off after him. Hard. Relentless. Determined. I will chase him down. I will run through my own end zone if I have to. Just like my cousin Tony. And I won't stop until I touch him, and when I touch him, if the ball's still in play, I will punish him. I will make him remember me.

Tony lit a fire in me that night, under the lights in Mulberry, in front of the whole town. Taught me what it was to play the game all out, all the time—no matter what. And it spilled over into how I played. Right away. Left me thinking, *Can't nobody beat me to the ball.* Left me thinking, *Ain't nothing I can't do.* And it wasn't enough just to edge the other guy out. No, I had to run him into the ground, punish him. At ten, eleven, twelve years old, this was how I learned to play the game.

Out of all that, there was this hard truth: there is only one way to win, one way to play. All out, all the time. And I *owned* that hard truth, man. I did. My thing was to hit the other guy so hard, I'd make him think about quitting. He'd have no choice in the matter. That's one of the things about today's game that frustrates me, the way they've changed the rules to take the edge from the defender. Telling a defender he can't hit, or he can't hit a certain way—it's like telling a quarterback he can't throw the ball deep. It takes away a key weapon, and for me that key weapon was putting a hurt on my opponent, making him think twice about coming across my field.

In football, the only way you're remembered is by what you did to somebody. I took that in, early on. It's not how many yards you gain. It's not how many passes you complete. It's how you hit, how you hurt. In my town, that's the way you earned respect. It got to where I'd look for my moments. In a game, there'd be just a couple opportunities. Two or three hits—that's all you needed to change the game, make your mark. Let them know you're there.

End of the day, it was just like those "Pick 'em Up, Bust 'em" games we used to play as kids. No rules. No boundaries. No set plays.

End of the day, you had to deal with *me*.

THREE

Respect Me Like You Sweat Me

Growing up, the only real connection I had with my father was through my grandmother, Minnie. She was my heart, my everything. Oh my goodness, she was one of the greatest angels to ever walk this earth. She never raised her voice, never swore, never judged. Her two boys, my father and his brother, Curtis, they struggled, gave their mama a lot of heartache. But she had a way of taking their troubles and setting them aside, moving on.

As I got older, on into high school, I used to go over to Grandma Minnie's house more and more. She got along real well with my mother, so that was never an issue. And she was used to folks being disappointed by her son, so that wasn't an issue, either. Anyway, I was Minnie's first grandchild, so she always said she had a special place in her heart for me, and one of the reasons I was drawn to her was to help me understand who I was, where I'd come from. She had pictures all over the place—pictures of me, my sisters, my father, my uncle. That was her big thing, all these pictures. Those pictures of my father, they could get her going. She'd pick up a frame and stare into it and start to talking. Every picture came with a story.

My daddy had been such a good-looking young man, with his big old Afro, his big old swagger—it killed my grandmother what his life had become. Tore her up inside. I think she was ashamed by his behavior, the choices he made. She never said as much, but I could see how it weighed on her. And the thing of it is, a small place like Lakeland, his bad choices were *right there*, on display. Everybody knew everybody's business. Everybody knew my father was caught in the swirl. He made some bad choices, every which way. He was what we used to call "a good for nothing," but this was where Grandma Minnie drew the line. It was okay for her to speak the truth about my father's behavior, but she didn't like it when other people talked. She might have used the phrase herself, but coming from someone else she would have argued that "good for nothing" tag into the ground. There was goodness there, she kept telling me. There was hope. Somewhere, down deep, my father was a decent man.

She used to say, "You'll see, Baby Ray. One day, he'll come round, you'll come to know him."

I'd say, "When, Grandma? When will that day come?"

And she'd say, "Your daddy, he's off doing his thing. He ain't ready to deal with you, not just yet."

Somewhere in there, I got word that my father was back in town. I was thirteen, maybe fourteen. I was back living in Lakeland, after spending two years in Mulberry. By this time, my mother had moved in with another man, who had a little more money, and we were living in a little bit nicer part of town, in a development called the Pines. It was a proper house—only, there weren't enough bedrooms to go around, so I had to sleep in the garage. Wasn't as bad as it sounds in the retelling. We fixed it up nice, private, but I was off by myself a lot, had a lot of time alone with my thoughts. So that's where I was living, *how* I was living when I heard my father was in Lakeland. It was around Christmas time, and he sent for me—anyway, he sent word. My mother told me he'd be by to collect me, take me for a visit, so I packed a couple things and went outside to wait for him by the curb. I took a toothbrush, a clean shirt, a pair of socks, bunched it all up in a brown paper bag and sat myself down. I remember that it was cold that night—winter, coming full on.

I was *excited*. Didn't have the first idea what I would say to this man. Didn't know if I was pissed, or ready to make some kind of room for him in my life. I was of two minds, guess you could say. But I did want to see him and I did want to know him. I kept hearing Grandma Minnie talking about the good he had to offer. There was plenty of good in my life, but there was always room for more. I wanted some of that from him. And, so, I waited. The whole damn night, I waited. Past dinner. Past bedtime. Past when the cold didn't bother me. Finally, my mother came out and tapped me on the shoulder—said, "Don't think he's coming, Baby Ray. Not tonight."

I went back into the house and cried. At thirteen, fourteen, however old I was, I just cried and cried, like a big old baby. Don't know why I was so tore up over him not showing, because I was used to him not being around, I was schooled in being disappointed by this man, but there it was, and when I got through crying I jumped back on my push-ups, my sit-ups—started flipping through that deck of cards like crazy.

I got tired of waiting for my father to come round. Got tired of hearing people make excuses for him. Got tired of people telling me I looked like him, walked like him, played ball like him. Got tired of hearing his name.

Things went back to how they were after that long night waiting by the curb, but now I was angry—not just a simmering kind of anger that attaches to you over time, but more of a boiling anger. A fury. His pictures, his name, his legacy. It got to where I wanted no part of my father. And it worked out that this fury was coming on right about the time I started high school. I'd been away for a while, but now I was back, living in the garage, doing my push-ups and sit-ups, trying to make myself strong, to make my own way.

Playing ball, that was my release. I'd play whatever was in season, but I didn't last too long on the basketball court, which is how I eventually ended up wrestling. In ninth grade, I was playing on the freshman basketball team, and at one practice I was up against one of my teammates. We were running full court, and he was driving for a layup. He had me beat. Only way to stop him was to foul him. I didn't have position to go up and try to block the ball, couldn't make a clean play, so I defended the only way I could. The only way I knew. Hard. It wasn't a dirty play, but it was aggressive, I'll admit. On a football field, it wouldn't have even drawn a flag, raised an eyebrow. On a football field, this kind of play was second nature to me. But here in the gym, a stupid little scrimmage, the kid went into a little tantrum. The coach seemed to take his side. Words were exchanged. For ten minutes, we were all standing in the middle of the court, yelling, giving each other *what for*. Finally, I just threw up my hands and stormed off—said, "This game is too soft for me, man."

I quit. Right then and there. Wasn't a temper tantrum kind of quit—no, it was more of an *I don't have time for this* kind of quit. And as soon as I walked out of that gym, I ran into a man who would go on to have a huge influence on me. His name was Steven Poole, and he was the wrestling coach. He saw me storm through those gymnasium doors, saw that I was a little riled up, and took the time to find out what was troubling me. He was one of those coaches who really took the time to connect with us kids—an educator, more than anything else. He heard me out, let me vent and moan about how basketball players were soft, whatever it was that had gotten me going.

When I was through, he said, "Got something I want to show you."

He took me to see the wrestling team, which used to practice in the cafeteria. They didn't even have gym space for these guys—that's how far down the ladder they were in terms of being a popular sport in our junior high school. They'd moved all the tables to the side, set down this giant mat on the floor. It was the strangest thing, because this was where we took our lunch, every day, and here the place was completely different. First thing I noticed was the smell—it smelled like a locker room, all sweaty and grimy. All that time eating lunch in that same big room—a lot of times, the only decent meal I'd have all day—I'd never had a whiff of what went on in there during wrestling season. And it was super hot, like someone had cranked the heat all the way up, and there on this mat were all these sweaty kids, just going at each other, working on drills, grips, moves—all of it.

I didn't want any part of it then, but it must have made an impression, because I came back to wrestling a year later, when I was up at the high school. What happened was I met a man who used to coach my father, who'd been a big-time high school wrestler. This man was now a referee, and he sought me out one day in the gym and handed me a small booklet, almost like a magazine. How he came to find me, I never knew. I had no idea who this guy was, or what he was handing me, so he went to explain. He said, "Boy, you open that book, you might see something."

So I did. Turned out this man had given me the Kathleen High School wrestling yearbook from 1975. The year I was born. The year my father set a whole bunch of records. There it was, on the very first page. Elbert Jackson, Elbert Jackson, Elbert Jackson . . . and as I tore through that yearbook I saw the man didn't just set a bunch of records—he'd set them all. There was his picture—a face that could have been mine. And there was his legacy—a legacy I could not let stand.

His name was all over that book. Most wins. Most pins. Fastest pin. Everything you could possibly win or accomplish, he'd done it. And as I kept looking at his name, over and over, up and down the page, it set me off. Got me thinking his name didn't deserve to live on like that, not with the way he'd stepped out on me and my mother, me and my sisters.

I took that book home and showed it to my mother.

She said, "Where'd you get that?"

I said, "This man gave it to me. A referee. Said he used to be Daddy's wrestling coach."

My mother looked at the book for another few moments, looked at my father's picture, then handed it back to me—said, "Well, what do you know?" There was nothing else to say.

I took that book to my room in the garage and studied it. Then I hung it over my bed, opened to the page with my father's records. Every night, I'd look at that book and get mad. That fury I'd started to feel? It grew in ways I couldn't even recognize. Seeing my father's name like that, seeing him *celebrated*. It set me off. I'd drop to the floor and start flipping through my deck of cards, doing my push-ups, doing my sit-ups. Just then, those push-ups and sit-ups came from a place of pure anger. And as I worked, as I raged, I said to myself, "His name will never be remembered."

I actually spoke these words out loud, to the empty room.

I said, "I will erase that man's name."

I said, "It will be like he was never here."

So I wrestled.

Sophomore year, I moved up to Kathleen High School. A lot of athletes at the school played multiple sports, so it wasn't a big deal for me to be doing football in the fall and wrestling over the winter.

Coach Poole was still over at the junior high school my tenth-grade year. For now, the wrestling coach was a science teacher who didn't know the first thing about wrestling. I won't give his name here, because there's no need to embarrass this man, but he would just kind of stand around in these big dorky glasses with his clipboard, his arms folded, and tell us to keep practicing, hard. That was all he could say to us—"Keep practicing hard, boys."

He had one or two assistants who knew the sport well enough to teach us a couple moves, teach us some strategy, but for the most part we were on our own. We wrestled by instinct, by watching our teammates, our opponents.

First thing we had to figure out was my weight. Me and a couple dudes were in the same weight class—165 pounds. But we didn't have anybody to wrestle at 189. I must've weighed about 167, maybe 170, so I raised my hand, said I'd take on the bigger guys—said, "It don't matter." And, really, it didn't. I was cock-strong, country strong. Anybody under 200 pounds, I could kind of deal with them, even with my lack of experience. I could give away ten pounds, twenty, thirty. I figured out straightaway that wrestling wasn't all that different than football. It was one-on-one. That's all. Even with my lack of experience, my lack of coaching. Long as I could outthink you, outhustle you, outdrive you, I could deal with you.

I had my way, my style. My thing was to bait my opponent, keep after him, make him go after me. I was aggressive, but I had this switch in me, needed to be flipped. I needed to be *confronted*. If it was just strategy, just tactics, you could maybe outwrestle me, but if you got me *riled*—well, then it was on. My go-to move was to get my opponent in a big old bear hug, turn it into a hip toss, pin him to the ground. Ninety percent of my matches, that's how it would go. Once I got my hands on you, that was it. Nobody was picking me up off that floor, throwing me down. Kids weren't into lifting the way some of them are today. And you can bet I was the only high school wrestler with my crazy regimen of push-ups and sit-ups, so nobody could match my strength. Even if you were two hundred pounds, you couldn't match my strength.

I made it all the way to states that first year. Nobody from my school had ever won a state title—not even my father, with all his wrestling records. But here my lack of experience finally caught up to me. I sailed through the first couple rounds. Outflanked this one dude—boom! Pinned this other dude—boom! Next thing you know, I came up against this kid from Miami in the semifinals. He was wearing an orange singlet. I never knew his name. I didn't want to know. Names, they make it personal, get in the way. Even on the football field. I had your number. That's all.

But this dude from Miami, I can still see his face. I can still see that stupid orange singlet. He was well coached, I'll say that. He had a plan. Me, I had no such thing. He knew my strength. He was prepared for it. I could only try to dominate—and I did, first two periods. I was up in the match, in control, but then I made a fool move. We were grappling, each of us looking for an opening, and finally I underhooked him, clamped my hands around his chest. Usually, when I clamped my hands, it was all over. If I got up under you, that was a bad day for you, because there's no easy way for you to come back from that hold. But this guy was cock-strong, same as me. He was country strong, too—probably one of the strongest guys I ever touched. The fool move came as I was getting ready to twist him, toss him. He hit me at the exact same time. He'd seen what was coming from me and he reacted to it, like he must've been coached. It was a smart move—the *only* move he could have made, really.

See, when someone's fixing to twist you like that, the response move is to hook your opponent's arm and roll with him, so that's what this orange kid from Miami did to me, and he was so swift, so sharp, so strong I didn't notice what he was doing until it was too late. I caught myself as I went to the ground—thinking, *No, don't let your left shoulder go down.* But sure enough, he drove that left shoulder down and pinned me, and the moment the referee whistled the match it's like all the air was let out of me.

I was devastated—although, truth was, I had no business being devastated. I just didn't know how to wrestle, was all. I could battle the heck out of people, I could deal with them, grapple with them, drive them to the ground, but I was just throwing my strength around. I didn't have a plan, didn't have a clue.

So this was where Steve Poole checked back into the picture. Our principal from Kathleen Middle School came up to take the job at the high school, and he brought a bunch of faculty with him, including Coach Poole, so when I went out for the wrestling team the next year he was waiting for me. He knew about my run to states the year before, of course. He actually sought me out in the hallway one day during football season, before wrestling even started. He said, "I finally got you to wrestle, huh?"

I said, "It's good to see you again, Mr. Poole. I could have used your help last year."

He laughed, shook my hand—said, "It's a new year, Mr. Lewis."

Coach Poole knew wrestling. He was known around our little town as "The Magician on the Mat." Folks actually called him that, if you can believe it—but the name fit. Coach Poole had it down. He was short, didn't look like much of an athlete, but he knew wrestling. He was powerful, knew how to harness that power. As much as anyone else in my life to that point, he prepared me for battle. All that mixed martial arts stuff you see today, he had me working on those types of moves back then. I had moves, countermoves, moves to counter *your* countermoves.

He asked me, "How good you want to be?"

I said, "The best ever."

He said, "How much time you willing to put into it?"

I said, "How much time you got?"

I was always one of the last to leave football practice, and I brought that same mind to wrestling. I'd be there until Coach Poole shut the lights off, and then he would drop me off at home in his blue pickup truck. His big thing was to keep moving out there on the mat, so my hands were always moving. He had me bouncing on the balls of my feet, ducking, juking, weaving. He had me doing a ten-play move, a twenty-play move. He had me firing like a machine—wasn't anybody in the state of Florida could keep up with me. I made quick work of my opponents. It was just too easy. Ten or twelve seconds, my matches were over. My whole junior year, working my way back to states, I don't think I had a match last longer than twelve seconds. I would come at you—hard, quick—and touch you and slam you into the ground and it was over.

Nobody could deal with me on that mat. Nobody. States? It's like it was a foregone conclusion, you could write it down. But then I messed up in the finals. I let myself be beat, gave away a point late in the match, didn't think all those steps ahead like Coach had trained me to do, and I was devastated all over again.

Coach Poole was just as disappointed as me—hard to believe, but it was so. He felt for me, man. He knew how hard I worked—how hard we *both* worked. He knew what it meant.

I said, "I'm coming back to finish this."

So we went back to work, but there was a whole other football season I had to get through before I could wrestle senior year. And do you know what? I took wrestling with me out onto that football field—because, back then, wrestling mattered most. Football was just a way to lift my wrestling—a way to fill the time *until* wrestling. Slipping blocks, getting up under people, staying low, engaging—this became my off-season workout. I'd always approached football as a one-on-one game, hand-to-hand combat. That's how I broke it down. But now that I knew what I was doing, now that I had all these moves, it's like I was cut a whole other way. This was my first football season as a *wrestler*—a real wrestler, working with all the benefit of Coach Poole's training. And I was a different cat out there. I was. I'd learned from all that time in the gym, all that time on the mat, that I could make you react or lean a certain way. Running backs used to always wonder how I could find the same hole as them, the same time as them, and it was because of wrestling. I was working through all these ten-play moves, twenty-play moves, got to where I was outthinking everybody on that field before the ball was even snapped. And that was all wrestling, man. That was all Coach Poole, teaching me to work with my hands, to bounce on my feet, to think ten steps ahead.

By the time wrestling came back around, senior year, I was good and ready. I was confident. I'd already snapped every one of my father's records. Most Wins. Most Technicals. Most Pins. Some of those, I snapped off sophomore year. The rest fell in my junior year. Each time, I'd come home, take that book off the wall, make a little *x* through my father's name in the record book, say a little prayer, hang it back up. I did that about a dozen times. The last record to fall was his Fastest Pin record—seven seconds. Snapped *that* one my junior year.

After that, there was just one record left—only, it wasn't a record; it was the state title. He'd never won one of those. No-body from Lakeland had ever won one of those, so this was my goal. Even with football heating up, lots of attention coming my way from college coaches, this was my one and only goal.

One thing I want to make clear: my father didn't *just* wrestle. No, he was the cornerback of the football team, too—and a stud cornerback at that. From what I could tell, he was probably the roughest athlete to ever come out of Lakeland, but I didn't care about what he did on the football field. I didn't have *that* record book tacked to the wall over my bed.

Erasing his wrestling records and making it like he'd never even been here—*that's* what drove me.

Coach Poole knew this was my motivation, and he fed into it. It was him, reminding me my daddy had never won a state title. It was him, telling me football was just a way to get ready for wrestling. It was him, egging me on. He was in my head, that whole off-season, after that loss in the state finals. He used to always ask me, "Ray, you're always so angry when you wrestle. Why you wrestle so mad?"

And I'd say, "Because I'm chasing demons, Coach."

All through high school—sophomore year, junior year, senior year—I didn't take a break. Not once. All through college and pro ball, too. I didn't know what taking a break felt like until all that confetti dropped in New Orleans after we won that last Super Bowl. I didn't know what *break* meant. I didn't know what it was to go to sleep with a sound mind, to rest easy. It wasn't my way. Even when I was hurt, when I had my surgeries, this burning inside of me would not let me be still. If it's just pain, then so be it. If it's just stitches, may or may not pop out, so be it. I never had time to lie down. There was always work to do, and it was in high school that I developed this mind-set. It was working with Coach Poole, trying to grab that state title, and it came from pure anger. It came from wanting to erase my father's name from that record book.

To lift myself up by beating him down.

• • •

Senior year, I had a plan.

I showed up to wrestle, first day of preseason, and put it to Coach Poole—said, "You ready?"

He looked at me like I was out of my head. The man lived and breathed wrestling. It was the first day of preseason. The newspapers were talking about me as one of the best wrestlers in the state. Of course he was ready. So he said, "Ready? Me? What you talking about, Ray?"

I said, "We're not wrestling one eighty-nine no more. I'm done with that. We're wrestling two twenty."

He wasn't expecting this. It went against the way the sport was played, to give away all that weight for no good reason. But that was just it—I had a *good* reason. Already, I'd gone up in weight my sophomore season, because we had too many guys my size and it didn't much matter, but that's not what I'd call a good reason. That was just necessity. That was just me taking the hit for my team. Now I was bigger, stronger—wrestling at 189, legit. But to give back twenty or thirty pounds? Just *because*? It made no sense to Coach Poole.

He said, "Ray, they outweigh you by thirty pounds. What are you thinking?"

I said, "That's just it, Coach. I beat these guys all season. Ain't nobody can deal with me at one eighty-nine."

He took my point—and that's how we played it.

All season long, there were just two dudes who pushed me—both of them from Auburndale, one of our rival high schools. Even though I never bothered to learn my opponents' names, I knew these two dudes. We went at each other so often at county tournaments, there was no avoiding each other. One of them, Victor Johnson, I ran into at the Polk County Invitational. Victor was about the same as me on the scales, but he had huge hands—just massive. And I knew him from football, too—he was a running back. But on the wrestling mat, those hands could be trouble. He'd grab me, and it was like he was trying to lift a sack of flour. He had a *vise* grip, man—like I said, trouble. He was an animal. If you let him ride you, you were done.

Coach Poole had me wrestle Johnson on his feet. "Make him stand up, Ray," he said. "He can't beat you on your feet."

Only thing was, I couldn't get Victor on his feet too early. The move was to wait him out, pick my spots, find some moment late in the match and make it my own.

It worked out that this one match went into overtime. I was hanging on. Victor Johnson was hanging on. Each of us was kind of waiting for the other one to make his move. Finally, I made mine. There came a point when I realized I could either try to roll him and ride him, or I could let him up—just like Coach Poole had said. So I let him up, got him on his feet—but he got a point out of it, and I could see he was surprised that I'd given him that point. In my head he was about to play *my* game. I was lining him up. And as the clock was winding down I saw my opening. I shot toward him, anchor-dove at his shins, hard. He started to twist, but by that time I was already on him. He was done.

After Victor Johnson, I had to wrestle Mark Smalls, his Auburndale teammate, and I found a way to beat him, too. At *my* game. After these two wins, I was feeling pretty pleased with myself—a little *too* pleased, maybe. It ratcheted up my swagger, conquering these two giants. I wore those victories on my sleeve as I headed into states.

I actually wore my victories around my neck. I had my idiot moments, back then. Absolutely. I guess we were all idiots—because, hey, we were just teenagers. I started wearing all my wrestling medals into the gym before my matches. Also, this

jacket I had printed up—a letterman jacket with a white butterfly collar, the zipper down in front so you could see all my
medals, like I was Mr. T or Stone Cold Steve Austin. I had it
going on. On the back of the jacket, I'd had my named stitched
in, and on the bottom, it had these words: RESPECT ME LIKE
YOU SWEAT ME.

This was my strut, my swagger—and in those days, Florida
schoolboy wrestling was all about the strut, all about the swagger. That's how I walked into the state tournament that year,
done up in all that swag and leather. But those medals, they
were like my badges, my stripes. They showed what I'd done,
proof of the battles I'd won.

Respect me like you sweat me.

Somebody should have smacked me around some, knocked
some sense into me, but this was my game, and I took that
swagger straight to the bleachers as the tournament was getting under way, headed right for this one dude from Orlando
I just knew I'd be facing in the finals. He was undefeated in
the season—33–0, some sick record like that. This kid was *all
that*, and he knew he was all that, and there I was, strutting, all
those medals dangling from my neck.

Crazy, right?

I walked over to the kid, introduced myself. He knew who
I was, same way I knew who he was, but I introduced myself
anyway—said, "Name's Ray Lewis. I hope to see you in the
finals." Then I held out my hand.

He shook my hand, and I was in his head. The tournament
hadn't even started yet, and I was in his head.

Those days, the state tournament was at the Lakeland Civic
Center, just up the road from where I lived. Still, my mother
wasn't able to make it to the finals. Nobody from my family

came. I was out to make history, the first wrestler from Lakeland to win state. I was out to erase my father's name, and I didn't have my family with me. It hurt, but I wasn't completely on my own. My best friend, Kwame King, was there to see me do my thing, along with his girlfriend, his sister, his big brother—might not have been *my* family there to cheer me on, but it was family just the same.

Coach Poole found me in the locker room before the match—crying, praying. He got down right there with me and cried and prayed, too. He was *feeling* it, man. Same as me. He said, "Nobody can keep you from this moment, Ray. Nobody."

I could close my eyes and picture it. The referee, holding up my hand, calling out my name. I could see this kid from Orlando, all tore up, the way I'd been tore up the year before. He wanted it, same as me. He was probably picturing it, same as me. But I told myself I would *die* before he beat me on this mat. And it would've come to that, because this dude was big. He was rough. He was agile.

I'd been wrestling for three years by this point, and I'd never come up against someone like this. This dude, he was like *a force of nature*—but, still, I would not allow him to compete with me.

So we went at it. First round, we were mostly feeling each other out, seeing what was what. Second round, Coach Poole hollered at me from his corner—said, "Go to work, Ray!"

And boy, I went to work. And what it means, when you go to work against a big-time wrestler like this dude, you shoot, he blocks, you make him sprawl. You work him like that, up and down, over and over. A time or two, maybe he can recover. But you make him sprawl five times, seven, ten and he's going to be sucking air. And that's how it played out here. This Orlando dude was a big boy, so when he lost his wind, third period, he was about to crumble. The score was still close, but he was weak. He'd gone from invincible to vulnerable, just on the back of all those sprawls.

Middle of the period I heard Coach Poole again in my corner, giving it to me. He said, "Finish him!"

And I did, and all this time later I catch myself wishing I had a tape of that match, because for the first time in my life I felt like I had mastered something. That's why I always loved those Bruce Lee movies, because the man was such a master. Nobody could touch him—and you could see it in his eyes that nobody could touch him. He *knew*. That's the way I felt as the clock clicked down—like nobody could touch me. I *knew*. I was on the absolute top of my game, everything was flowing, just right. It's like I was floating, those last couple minutes—working it, working it. Just like we'd done it in practice. Just like I'd pictured it. And then there was this thought, knocking on the door of my thinking: *I'm gonna be state champion!* It just hit me, and it grew, and it grew. The match was still going on, and here was this thought, growing inside my head, and underneath that thought I could hear Coach Poole, off to the side, telling me, "Thirty seconds!"

I heard that and went into beast mode. I rushed this dude, picked him up—boom! Let him up, picked him up again—boom! Then I got on top of him, hooked him, and let the clock run out.

It wasn't about pinning these dudes anymore. Once I'd snapped my father's record for the fastest pin, once I got so dominant, Coach Poole didn't want me pinning anybody—said it cheated me of all that time on the clock, time I could have used to work on my game. A wrestling match is supposed to be six minutes of hell, he always said. Made no sense to let my opponent off the hook, all those extra minutes. Made no sense to give back all those extra minutes. Got to where he started making me run extra if I pinned somebody. He was a technician, a craftsman. And here he'd turned me into a master—a state champ.

And this right here was my finest moment as an athlete. Hands down, no doubt. Those two Super Bowl victories? They were probably sweeter for the fans. Those Super Bowls will probably live on a little longer, a little louder, but for me there will be no greater high than that state title at the Lakeland Civic Center. No, sir. After all, it was just me. Ain't nobody dropping no pass. Ain't nobody throwing no ball. No, it was just me and this other young man, walking out on a mat and finding some way to deal with each other.

First thing I did was race into Coach Poole's arms, and as I pulled him in close I said, "His name is forever over."

Coach knew what I meant. He knew what this moment meant to me. Wasn't just about wrestling. Wasn't just about the beauty of hard work, and pain, and chasing demons. It was about setting my father aside, burying his name—and freeing me to live my life my own way, here on in. On my own terms.

FOUR

One Alligator

Alongside of wrestling, there was football.

I always tell folks that wrestling showed me how to truly channel my heart and mind, but it was football that woke up the sleeping giant inside of me. Little League, Pop Warner, that was one thing. Street football, that was a whole other battle. It went all the way back to those "Pick 'em Up, Bust 'em" games we used to play in the streets. And when I say *streets*, I do mean streets. We played on the grass when we could, but we mostly played on bumpy little dirt roads, little back alleys, driveways, wherever there was a stretch of mostly empty space and a way to mark it out, pole to pole. However many guys turned up to play, that's who played. Whatever we had to work with as markers—street signs, light poles, parked cars—those become our first-down lines, our end zones. We had our little rivalries, kids from other neighborhoods, other projects, but there were no set teams, no set rules. If you showed up, you played. If one side had too many kids, we'd swap out, try to make the teams even—but if it was a grudge match, we tried to keep those grudges going.

The only rule was if you were on the field and the ball was live, you could get hit. Didn't matter if you were on the grass, on the dirt, on the asphalt—you were going down. And we hit hard. No pads, no helmets. And none of that *touch football* nonsense. We played *tackle*, and we played it for real. There weren't always enough guys to put together a full front line, so we played that you could rush the passer on a certain count. Other parts of the country might have counted by *Mississippis* or *one thousands*, but in Florida, you counted by *alligators*. That's just how we did it—no reason, except it's how the big kids did it, our older brothers and cousins, so we could only follow.

When we were little—seven, eight years old—we might have to count to four or five *alligators*. You had to give the play a chance to develop, right? But by the time we got to junior high, we'd thrown a single blocker on the line and moved the count to one or two, and after that it was just a straight rush.

My thing was to play barefoot. Wasn't ideal—you'd get stepped on, tore up, but it was better than the alternative. None of us could afford decent running shoes, so we'd kick 'em off and run on the ground. We thought it made us faster, and I guess it did, but it's a wonder nobody got seriously hurt, running barefoot up and down those dirt roads, hitting the hell out of each other without any pads.

I never had my own football—come to think of it, I never knew *anybody* who had his own football. And yet, somehow, there was always a ball. Don't know how it got there, don't know who brought it home with him, but there it was. Always. Like magic.

And here's the thing: everything about our game was spontaneous, same way it was with the football just showing up like that. It all happened by word of mouth, like the games were some kind of force of nature. Nobody set them up. Nobody had to call nobody. You just came out and played. Nobody was in charge. The games just kind of sprang up on their own.

We had our field generals, kids who liked to call the plays, but it was always changing. A lot of times, a lot of neighborhoods, the best athletes would run everything, but that wasn't how it was with our group. We all had a shot. Me, I was a little louder than most, because I was *always* a little louder than most, and because football was my thing. My game did the talking. I saw it all a little differently than everyone else, even then. If we didn't have anyone on our side who could throw the football, I'd be the quarterback. If we didn't have anyone who could run with it, I'd take the ball. If we didn't have someone to match up with the fastest dude on the other team, the biggest dude on the other team, whatever it was, I'd get the assignment. And if you didn't pick me first when we were choosing up sides—well, then it was about to be a bad day for you.

I'm sorry, but that's just how it was.

I used to run my mouth on defense—I'd say, "Long as you don't put that ball in the air, you're good." This was me, trash-talking, but it wasn't really trash. It was the truth. If you tried to throw the ball on me, nine times out of ten I'd come down with it. Nine times out of ten I would make you pay.

At some point in there, I started watching football on television. In the 1983 NFL season, the Washington Redskins were trying to defend their championship, win their second Super Bowl in a row. That was my team. John Riggins, he was like a battering ram coming out of the backfield. He was *the man*. Nobody could stop that guy. Couple years later, the Chicago Bears won it all, and it was the same thing all over again, only this time it was *an entire team* of beasts, out to beat you down. The more I watched, the more I took back out on the field with me, back out on the street, next time we played. Even in the pros, even at the highest level, it was *still* just a game of one-on-one battles. It was man-on-man. So that remained my mind-set, but as I got older, as I played at all these higher levels, it took in a deeper way: *Oh, you busted my nose—that's okay, I'm good. Oh, you busted my lip—that's okay, I'm good.* You had to do a whole lot more than that to keep me from what I was trying to do, and what I was trying to do was hurt you.

In my head, I was climbing a ladder, a way up and out. And it ran through the game. This was back before I started to wrestle, so when that happened it kind of changed things up for me. But through it all, there was always football. The game might have had to fight for my attention a little bit in there, might have even taken a backseat for a while, but football never stopped mattering. Wrestling might have been a way for me to stand on my own and beat down the name of my father, but football was the path I was meant to follow. It's how I took my measure. If you beat me playing football, I would look at what I did wrong, what I could do better. If you outran me on the field, I didn't moan over losing a footrace—no, I figured out how much you beat me by, what I could do to cut that distance the next time we ran.

I was on a journey. Like I said, it was all about climbing that ladder. If I was playing on the Pop Warner D squad, I watched the kids on the C squad, tried to learn from them. On the C squad, same thing—I looked to the B squad for my next moves. I started to realize that football was a lot like life. If you want to get to a certain level, you have to study how folks are doing it ahead of you, model your game after theirs, kick it up a notch.

Making it to the Pop Warner A squad, that was my first real goal. That was the ultimate. It never quite worked out that way, because my time on the A squad would have come during those years I was sent to live with my cousin in Mulberry, seventh and eighth grade, but for a time it was all I ever wanted out of the game. Every chance I got, I watched these older players do their thing. There was this one kid, Charles Hilary. We all knew him as Mickey, and he used to play quarterback for the Lakeland Patriots. He wore number 11. The team colors were red, white, and blue, but Mickey was the only one who wore a red helmet—only he didn't need the red helmet to stand out. He was all about the extra effort, didn't have an ounce of quit. I was ten years old, watching this kid in a red helmet maybe two or three years older than me, realizing I didn't have to be the biggest, or the fastest, or the strongest—all I needed was to put in the best effort.

All I needed was to be relentless.

Ceon Carr was a dude I remembered from my time in Mulberry, living with my cousin Tony. Ceon wore number 3 for the Mulberry Buccaneers. Their team colors were orange and white, modeled after the Tampa Bay Buccaneers, and Ceon could tear it up out there. I could watch him do his thing, squint my eyes just a little bit, and imagine he was tearing it up for Tampa Bay—that's how dominant this kid was. And he had a teammate with him, a dude named Anwar Hardy, number 33. Together those two kids were unstoppable. To look at them, you'd think they could compete with the Tampa Bay Buccaneers for real. That's what the difference of a couple years can mean to a little kid. It can set it up in your head that these older kids were playing at a level just out of reach, like they were playing a man's game.

The more I watched, the more I started to see all these different levels of play.

I always tell people to go at it all out, all the time, because you never know who's watching. All the way to the NFL, last snap in the Super Bowl, I played like there was some little kid out there, eyeballing me through the rusted metal of a chain-link fence, modeling his game after mine.

My first high school coach was a man named Grady Maddox—and he was old school, all the way. Hard-nosed. Ram-tough. All of that. I only played for him my sophomore year, but the man gave me my first real shot—and for that, I'll always be grateful.

I came up just around the time our high school program started to struggle—and looking back I have to think those struggles started off the field. Coach Maddox, he had some glory days at Kathleen High School, some championship-type teams. He sent a lot of players off to college careers—even a few on to the NFL. For years, Lakeland had been a real proving ground for a lot of athletes, but the community was hit hard by drugs, alcohol, and gang violence. In this way, we were just like every other community where folks were struggling to get by, but I *knew* these folks, so it felt different to me. It felt like it was happening in Lakeland and no place else. A lot of our very best athletes got caught in a swirl of some very bad decisions—going back to my father, my uncle, and that whole generation, and continuing up to the kids I used to watch through the fence on those squads ahead of me. It was like a cancer.

One by one, these dudes started falling off that ladder. We still had a bunch of good athletes when I got to high school—some big, big dudes, some big-time players. Coach Maddox put me behind an upperclassman named William Campbell, at rover back. I didn't like it, but I couldn't argue—I was just a sophomore, and that's how it goes when you're just a sophomore. You have to wait your turn. I was busting my butt in preseason, working harder than anyone in practice, dictating the play, doing my thing, and Coach Maddox couldn't help but notice. I'll never forget, one afternoon I heard him chew someone out and say, "I need more players like Ray Lewis."

He just said it in this tossed-off way, and I just happened to be in earshot. But it lifted me, hearing a comment like that, even though it didn't earn me a starting job. That only happened when Campbell got into a fight and ended up breaking his jaw. The starting spot was mine, but only in this backdoor way, and this became a kind of recurring theme for me. Every chance I ever got on a *real* football field, it didn't come about because I'd earned it outright. It didn't come about because I was picked first to fill this or that spot. No, it came about because of an injury *and* because I was good and ready when the guy ahead of me went down. This first time that theme came into play happened before our first game of the season, against Clewiston. Coach Maddox called my name, and I stepped in at rover back. Back then, a lot of Florida high schools played with a rover back—kind of like a strong safety. If you were playing rover back, you were *the dog*, so it was a big deal. And in that first game I found a way to shine, man. I recorded twenty-two tackles. Twenty-two! That's the kind of number that's just off the charts, and this was back when they didn't keep such thorough statistics like that. But this was how *I* kept score, man. I was counting—better believe it, I was counting, and twenty-two was how far I got before the final whistle.

There was this one Clewiston dude, I hit him so hard, I knocked him to the team bench, got him all tangled up on the sidelines under the fence. I can still *feel* the impact of that one hit—a clean play, but it was *nasty*, sent a signal to anyone paying attention that I'd come to play. Put it out there that William Campbell could take his time healing, because he wasn't about to get his spot back.

I was the big dog now.

The rest of the guys on that team, they came to play, too, but we couldn't get it done. We ended up losing that first game to Clewiston, and almost every game after that. It was the story of our season. The games were close, but we couldn't close them out—got to where we started to think our team was cursed. We were 1–9 on the season, and this was coming off a big year, with a lot of returning players. We kept beating ourselves, was what it was. A lot of our seniors, they were checked out. They were superstars already, in their own minds, some of them headed off to college, on to do bigger things on a bigger field. Me, I was only thinking about the game in front of me, the player lined up in front of me. It was back to that one-on-one battle. By the fifth game of the season, all those losses were starting to weigh on us as a team, but I made my own peace with it—told myself, *Hey, we might not win another game, but I guarantee, nobody will beat me in tackles. Nobody will beat me to the ball.*

And I saw to it. I gave it my all. Wound up leading the team in tackles . . . *from the safety position.* And somewhere in there I caught myself thinking this was what I'd been dreaming about all along. This was me, climbing the ladder, playing with the big boys—same dudes I used to watch and model myself after when I was coming up.

The style of play, it was a little different than I was used to in our local pickup games. When it was just us, just a bunch of kids running around in the dirt, the game felt a lot like jazz. We improvised, a lot. We figured it out. There were busted plays every which way, and nobody really stuck to their assignments, because the thrill of the game was getting your hands on the ball, getting in on the tackle. Here at the high school level, though, you were playing in a system, so things were a little more regimented. Wasn't exactly rigid, what we had in place under Coach Maddox, but we all had our roles. We had to run our lanes, follow the set plays.

The refs mostly left us alone. They were old school, too—the game was still a man's game. There was no bailing out. If you got hit in the mouth, you took it. Didn't matter if the other guy got there early or you were hit late, you just had to deal with it. It was not a fixed fight, the way it is today—at the professional level, all the way down to Pee Wee. More and more these days, we've got these rules in place so that nobody can hit, and that's not how the game is meant to be played. Don't know that I would have stayed in the game, the hands-off way it's played today, but Coach Maddox let us play. The refs let us play. And even though we didn't win but one game, we started to find our way.

Unfortunately for Coach Maddox, he wasn't along for the rest of the ride. Wasn't his fault we'd put together such a miserable record, but I guess he took the fall for it, because when my junior year rolled around we had a new coach. His name was Ernest Joe, and he'd graduated from Kathleen High School the year I was born. Coach Joe brought a whole different vibe with him to the field. He knew Lakeland, knew all these distractions lining up away from the football field, looking to do us dirt. He was a new-school coach with an old-school mentality. He still had us playing hard and working our tails off, but he found a way to mix in a shot of pure joy. He had us dancing, man. He used to do this thing at our pep rallies before games. He'd write these crazy-funny raps, work in the names of all his players. He made football *fun*, and it carried over to the way we played. He changed the spirit of the whole school. He really did.

Winning was a part of that, but the change was in the air before our first game. And we had a lot of those good players from the year before still around so we came out strong. We started out 5–0 that year. We were a dominant team defensively. I played alongside a dude named Torrian Gray, who went on to play at Virginia Tech. The two of us together—man, *we were problems*—like, real problems. Torrian was smooth, fierce. I just loved playing with him—but our season took a turn before it even got started. Trouble was, we weren't ready as a team. We had a rough time on the other side of the ball, lost three out of our next five games, ended up missing the playoffs, but it was a step forward for us. It was a good season, a fun season, an important season.

I'll never forgot one of our toughest losses that season, against the Lakeland Dreadnaughts, our big crosstown rivals. That's the game that put us out of the playoffs—and for a guy who hated to lose, that was like losing *twice*. We played the game at Bryant Stadium, and we held the Dreadnaughts close most of the way. We ended up losing by a couple touchdowns, and the guy who killed us was this one dude, Steve Franklin. He wore number 32, and he kept making big plays. After the game he came over to me and did the most remarkable thing. I was sitting on our bench, my head hung low, waiting for my disappointment to pass, when Steve crossed to our side of the field to shake hands.

Now, I'm a sore loser. I am. I *hate* to lose. Been that way my entire life, so I knew back then to keep to myself when a game didn't go our way. But there was Steve, holding out his hand—saying, "Pick your head up, Ray."

I didn't want to talk to him just then, not at all. We were *rivals*. I respected him as an athlete. We lived in the same town, went to rival high schools, so we were always hearing about each other's accomplishments on the field. It was decent of him to come over like that, but I didn't want any part of it. I just wanted to be by myself.

Still, he kept his hand out, told me again to pick my head up—said, "Next year, it's gonna be different."

It took me back, a line like that. *Next year, it's gonna be different.* I couldn't think what he was getting at, so I looked up, finally, and Steve could see he had my attention.

I said, "What you mean by that?"

He said, "I'm coming to play with you next year. Me and Jason Mitchell. We're coming to Kathleen."

Jason Mitchell was another demon on that Dreadnaughts

team—six foot five, could throw the football eighty yards. *From his knees.*

I said, "Steve, I don't got time for this. Quit messing around."

He said, "No lie. Go ask Coach Joe. He knows all about it."

Sure enough, Steve was telling the truth. Those two families switched districts, and he and Jason came to play with us, and we were loaded with talent my senior year. At every position, both sides of the ball. It ended up Steve became one of my closest friends. I used to call him Black—and me and Black, side by side, we did a lot of damage. All the way back in preseason, we had our eyes on the state championship. That's how loaded we were, man—and Coach Joe, he had us playing with such joy, such exuberance. It felt to us like there wasn't anybody who could touch us.

It was our world and all these other teams, they were just lucky to be on the same field as us for a while. That was our attitude, going into the season, but unlike wrestling it didn't exactly play out this way.

Our first jamboree game, senior year, our star linebacker, Jason Bamberger, went down with an injury against the Lake Gibson Braves. A jamboree is like a preseason scrimmage, only you don't really keep score and you only play for two quarters. You weren't supposed to get hurt in a jamboree game, but Jason was out, and Coach Joe came over to me on the sideline—said, "Ray, would you do me a favor?"

I said, "What's that, Coach?" I'd only played for Coach Joe a short while, but already I trusted this man like a father. Already I knew I would run through a wall for him.

He said, "Would you fill in for Jason, play a little linebacker for me?"

I didn't even have to think about it. I said, "No problem, just tell me what you want me to do. I never played linebacker before."

He said, "Just go to the ball, Ray. All you gotta do."

So I went to the ball. And I went to the ball. And I went to the ball. I know we weren't supposed to keep score in a silly little jamboree game, but I did, in my own way. I kept score the way I always kept score—I counted my tackles. Every change of possession, I'd run over to the sideline with a big old smile on my face and say to Coach Joe, "This is too easy." It was like a revelation. From the linebacker spot, I could get to the ball a lot quicker than I could from the safety spot. I was making tackle after tackle—seventeen in all. *In just two quarters!*

So out of that one injury, my whole career took a turn. When my name was called, I was ready.

High school wasn't *just* about sports. No way. It was also about girls—and, got to say, the one kind of fed into the other. Somewhere in there, I started dating the captain of the cheerleading team—a beautiful girl named Stephanie Davis. And she wasn't just beautiful—she was super smart, with a 4.2 grade point average, could talk to you about anything. She ended up going to Florida State, but not before she broke my heart.

You see, this was around the time when this one song was getting a lot of play—"Let's Chill," by this R&B group called Guy.

Let's chill . . .

Let's settle down . . .

Every time I heard that song, it put me in mind of my girl, and one day they announced on the radio that it was coming up, so I sprinted the two miles or so to Stephanie's house, because I wanted to play it for her. Well, I pulled up in front of her house, and there behind the bushes I saw Stephanie kissing this other dude, and I was devastated, man. I was *struck down.* So I turned on my heels and sprinted over to my best friend Kwame King's house. And wouldn't you know it, as soon as I got to *his* place, that's when the song came on the radio, and I just lost it. I started cryin' like a great big baby.

Kwame sat me down and said, "Let me help you understand women, right now." And he walked me through how it was—how *he* saw it, anyway, all of fifteen, sixteen years old. Like *he* knew.

We'd been on Coach Joe to start letting us play on both sides of the ball. A lot of programs in the area, you'd see a lot of two-way players, and I was itching to carry the ball. Coach kept saying, "I'll think about it, Ray. I'll think about it." But other than a couple carries in practice, a couple kick returns, I never really got to do my thing.

That all changed when our star tailback, Carlos McCaplain, went down in a game against Lake Wales. We'd started the season on fire, 3–0. Nobody could deal with us. We had the two best linebackers in the county, in me and Black. We had Carlos and a big, fast sophomore named Ken Bridges in the backfield. We had Jason Mitchell at quarterback. We were a handful—we were *too much*. But then Carlos snapped his knee something awful. I could hear it from the sidelines. And Carlos, he screamed—a chilling sound. First time I ever heard somebody in that kind of pain. I felt for the dude, I really did, but before they could help him off the field my mind was already racing to the rest of our season. Carlos was a big part of our offense. Without him, we'd have to rely more and more on Kenny, and he was young, untested. Also, that boy played *soft*. I don't like to knock on one of my guys, but that's how it was. The dude could run. The dude was ripped. He had a body like Tarzan, but he took a hit like Jane—just sayin'. So we couldn't rely on him the rest of the way. He was a good option, but he couldn't carry us the way Carlos could have carried us.

That sense of joy we'd been playing with? It snapped, right along with Carlos's knee—it seemed to take all the air out of our team, just that one play.

Coach Joe responded by having our quarterback run the ball on our rushing plays—QB Sweep Left and QB Sweep Right. We tried this, first couple possessions, but Lake Wales had us figured out. It took away one of our weapons, lining Jason up in the backfield like that. It signaled the play. Instead of having all that firepower, we were down to just a little bit of juice.

So I went to Coach Joe and pushed him again on letting me run the ball. I said, "Don't put Jason back there, Coach. Run me instead. I know the plays."

Remember, I'd been on Coach Joe all season to let me run with the ball, so he must have thought this through a time or two, but it wasn't until I made this one last push that he gave in. He said, "Okay, get in there at tailback."

I ran out onto that field with a song in my heart, man. It about killed me to see Carlos go down like that, to look ahead to the rest of our season without him, but at the same time I was excited. I'd been looking forward to this kind of spot, long as I could remember.

Coach called my number straightaway.

Twenty-Eight, Toss. Twenty-Nine, Toss.

And I was off.

Oh man, I was flying—kept us in the game. I ran left. I ran right. I found a bunch of holes—and, once or twice, no hole to be found, I plowed my way through for a couple yards anyway. We ended up losing, but it felt to me like we'd found ourselves a running back. Felt that way to Coach Joe, too. He came up to me after the game and said, "Boy, you can really touch the ball."

I said, "Yes, sir. Just let me touch it any chance we get."

From there, he started putting me in on kick returns, at

running back, wide receiver. Whatever he thought we needed. And I kept flying, man. All on the back of that first series when Coach Joe called my number, we were playing with joy, energy, all of that. We put in this one package, a wishbone package, with me and Black on the wings and a 292-pound fullback named Tommy Lane in the middle. We had a little hand signal for it, called it the "Bone." And man, let me tell you something, when Coach called for that Bone, when he flashed that signal, folks sat up in their seats. It woke up the stadium, because that was the kind of football Lakeland hadn't seen in years—not out of a Kathleen High School team.

It was electric.

I can still remember the first time we went to the Bone in a key spot. We were down 13–0 to the Bartow Yellow Jackets, at home. Bartow always had a physical team. They came at you, hard, and here we couldn't get anything going. At halftime, our principal came to the locker room to speak to us. Mr. Wright— he'd come to us from Bartow, so the game was personal for him. He gave a really rousing talk, moved a lot of the guys to tears—Mr. Wright was crying a little bit himself. And when he was finished, I stood up and said, "Mr. Wright, I promise you, we won't lose this game."

That's when we went to the Bone.

First possession, second half, third down and long on our own forty-five. Tommy Lane went one way and sealed the line-man coming at him. Black went the other way and sealed his guy. And I shot through this little hole, just a sliver of daylight, but then I stumbled, about three yards from the first down. I started to fall—thinking, *Oh no*. But as I fell I managed to right myself, thrust myself forward another couple yards, and when I finally went down I fell backward, my arm stretched out over my head, the ball in my hand. Put that ball right on the first down marker, kept that drive alive.

Next play, I got the ball again—this time, boom, seven yards more.

We drove in for the score, and then I scored three times more. One of those was a punt return of about sixty yards. We won that game going away, 28–13.

We didn't lose a game the rest of the regular season, but we did lose a bunch of players—too many players, really. One injury after another. And the thing of it is, we only had so much depth to go around. Not to make excuses or anything, but we about ran out of bench. By the end of the year, half our guys were playing both ways, and we were *tired*. But it didn't matter. We kept playing, kept winning. It's like we'd caught a piece of magic. Our opponents, they couldn't run on me and Steve, and no team in the state had the passing game to make up for it.

We were playing with *swagger*. By the time we went up against Winter Haven, another big rival, my swagger was at an all-time high. One of the ways I would taunt my opponents was to cut their names into the fade of my hair. My uncle was a barber, and a good sport, and he hooked me up, and for the game against Winter Haven I had him cut in the name of Dmitri Denmark—one of their key guys.

Oh man, I was out of control. But I was feeling it. We were all feeling it—and this was a part of that.

That game against Winter Haven, it was a dogfight. Up and down. Back and forth. All game long, I kept my helmet on, picking my spot. Usually, I didn't take my helmet off unless I scored, and here I hadn't taken one in just yet, but I started thinking if I didn't score soon I'd have to take it off anyway. Didn't want to waste a perfectly good haircut. Second half, we were down two touchdowns, and I went back to receive the punt at about midfield. Broke two tackles, then broke another and high-stepped it into the end zone, and *that* was when I finally pulled off my helmet. Caused a big old commotion. I heard one of those Winter Haven dudes yell, "Dmitri, he got your name shaved onto his head! He ain't got no respect!"

And then it was *on*.

Fourth quarter, Winter Haven was driving. They had this little pop pass they used to run—kind of like a Peyton Manning play. They'd fake a run, roll, toss it to the tight end real quick. They'd just made a big play on us, they were closing in, and I knew they were coming back with that little pop pass, to the right. I just knew. So I was good and ready. Sure enough, they ran that play, and I took a half step toward the ball, made the pick, and ran it down the field another ten, fifteen yards, and it set up one of the most dramatic finishes of the season. Coach Joe wasn't liking our passing game that day, didn't want to throw the ball anymore. It was late in the fourth quarter, time was running out, and we needed to score. Mostly, he didn't want to throw because it was raining, and he didn't trust the ball to that slick field. Trouble was, we had about sixty yards to go to reach the end zone, and no way to mix things up without throwing the ball a time or two.

Coach called me to the sideline on the changeover—said, "I'm gonna lean on you, Hoss."

I said, "Yes, sir."

He said, "You're gonna touch it every play."

And I did. I touched that ball seven straight times, carried us across those sixty yards like nothing much at all.

After the game, I went up to Coach Joe to talk about the game. I said, "Coach, I know you like to run me in the fourth quarter, but a lot of times, in the fourth, I'm already run down, kind of tired."

He said, "What you have in mind?"

I said, "Run me early. Just one time, let me touch it early."

The very next week, we drew Haines City. They had a linebacker—six foot four, 240 pounds—named Derrick Gibson. He was the number-one linebacker in the county—*they* said. (In Lakeland, we said different.) First play of the game, Coach called my number on a 21 Trap, straight through the middle. He said, "You said to run you when you're fresh. This is as fresh as it gets, so let's see what you can do with it."

I ran that trap play all the way to the Haines City end zone, eighty yards down the field.

To this day, Coach Joe tells that story—me, asking him to get me the ball early. And every time he tells that story, he ends it the same way. He says, "From that day forward, every time Ray Lewis asked for the ball, I gave him the ball."

He's turned it into a kind of joke over the years, but the truth is he trusted me. We trusted each other.

We made a lot of noise that season. It was shaping up to be a special, special year. Truth was, in 1993, in and around Lakeland, Florida, if you were any kind of football fan, you *had* to come out to see me play. It was almost like you had no choice in the matter. The stands were filled to overflowing. Every week. People came out of the woodwork. And one of those people, I started to hear, was my father. I can't remember who told me he was fixin' to come to my last game of the season. Maybe it was one of my aunts or my cousins, but I got word he would be in the stands.

I didn't know how to feel about this, quite honestly. I was confused, excited, nervous, pissed. All these emotions were just kind of churning around inside me. I didn't even know if I wanted to see this man, but I can't deny that it meant something to me, him coming out to watch me play. It ate at me, a little, that he'd never come to see me play, never come to see me wrestle. I had no room for him in my life, no place for him in my heart, but it lit me up inside, him wanting to check me out after all this time. I had nothing to say to him, couldn't imagine what he had to say to me, but that didn't matter. Only thing that mattered was that he would be there, watching. Only thing that mattered was that he could see with his own eyes what I had become without any kind of push from him.

We hadn't beaten the Lakeland Dreadnaughts, the team that tossed us out of the playoffs the year before, in forever. There were a lot of emotions attached to that game. Wasn't just me, looking to the stands, not knowing if I would see my father. It was my buddy Black, going up against his old teammates. It was everyone in the stands, hoping to see us finish out the string.

There was so much going on in my head, it was hard for me to concentrate on the game. Wasn't hard for me to play, mind you, because by this point in the season I was on autopilot, but I was moving on pure instinct out there on the field. Muscle memory. Adrenaline. If I stopped to think about the game, what it would have been like to see my father after all this time, I might have just crumbled.

All game long, I caught myself checking out the crowd, looking for my father. I couldn't even tell you what the man looked like—but there I was, looking for him. I'd seen pictures, but not since he'd been a young man. I was told I resembled him, a little, but I didn't know what that could mean, seeing my face in his. A part of me wished I hadn't known he was coming. A part of me wished he wouldn't show. A part of me wished he'd see me dominate on the field, see the whole town cheering me on, calling my name, and hang his head in shame.

But he never showed. Or, if he did, he never showed himself. I heard later that someone ran into him later that night at a local hotel, coming out of some room with some woman, so I guess he had someplace else he needed to be. Just like there was always someplace else he needed to be.

We beat the Dreadnaughts that night, and it should have been a glorious moment, an exclamation point to my high school career, but all I remember is feeling disappointed, devastated, again. I ran out to the parking lot soon as I could after the game. I sat there, in the back corner of the lot, for the longest time. I sat and sat, couldn't bring myself to leave. Don't know what I was thinking in that moment, if I was thinking much at all, but I wasn't moving.

Finally, I stood to leave. The parking lot had mostly emptied. I was still in my uniform, thinking nobody would notice me, that's how lost I was inside my own head. But as I started to walk away, a man came up to me with a football in his hand.

He said, "Would you do me a favor, young man?"

I said, "What is that?"

He said, "Would you sign this football?"

He handed me the ball and a marker.

I said, "Why?"

He said, "I want to be the first person to get your autograph, son. Don't know if anybody told you, but you're 'bout to be a superstar."

I said, "Don't know about that, sir. I'm just trying to figure it out."

But I signed the man's football. Just my name—no date, no jersey number, no little saying or inspirational quote. Just my name.

It was the first autograph I ever gave, and if you're ever in

Lakeland, Florida, I can show you the exact spot where we stood, but I didn't take in the moment for what it was, not at the time. My head was someplace else. We still had a job to do in the playoffs. I still had a job to do on the wrestling mat. I wasn't done with this place. Not just yet.

FIVE

Welcome to Miami

Senior year of high school, I was a problem. I was a problem on the field. I was a problem on the mat. It was a lot, to have to deal with me. We made a lot of noise that year, me and my boys. Kicked up a lot of dust—nothing terrible, but there were a lot of distractions. Didn't get into any kind of *real* trouble, but I got close to trouble, let's just say that.

Real trouble—that kind of thing just wasn't allowed in my house. Only trouble I ever made, really, was stepping up in defense of somebody else. My cousins, my friends, whoever. I would sometimes step in and take the heat for them, but it was never a heat of my own making. I respected my mama's *brand* too much to embarrass that woman. Plus, she didn't even give us an opportunity to do anything wrong. We couldn't have people over at the house, couldn't stay out once the street lights came on. She had us covered, man.

College, I took it as a given. I wasn't really feeling it, though. Part of the reason for that was that my mother was in Memphis my last two years of high school. She'd been struggling down in Lakeland, and had taken up with another man, and we all packed up and went with him to Memphis, to try and make a go of it there. This all happened right after my sophomore year in high school, that summer. But I wasn't really *feeling* Memphis, either, and I kept pushing my mama to let me go back home, finish out my high school career in Lakeland. I worked it out so I could stay with my grandmother on the McKinney side, and that's how it worked out.

I said, "Mama, I'm gonna make a way for us."

She said, "How you gonna do that, Junior?"

I said, "Mama, I'm telling you. I will make a way for us. I'm gonna go to college."

Best I can remember, that was the first time we ever talked about college—and here I was just using it as a kind of bargaining chip, to convince my mother to send me back to Lakeland so I could be with my friends, my team. So when coaches finally did start talking to me about college, for real, when my friends on the team started talking about college, for real, my mother wasn't around for me to get her take. She was still up in Memphis with my brother and sisters, so I was kind of on my own in this.

Football was a way to get to college. That's all—at least, that's all it was at the time. College would take me the rest of the way, and back then I wanted to study business law. I had it in my head that this would be my ticket up and out, and I would get my degree, get a job, and find a way to help my family. I wasn't thinking of making football a *career*—that came a little later.

Meanwhile, I got a ton of recruiting letters, a ton of coaches calling me, but I still had my wrestling season. Back of my mind, I was still thinking wrestling was the way to go, so I was hearing from some schools wanting me to wrestle, some schools wanting me to play football, some schools wanting me to do both. About the only school that didn't really have any interest in me was Miami—wasn't all that far from home, but it could have been a million miles away, far as I was concerned. And me, I might as well have been from Alaska, the way the Hurricanes were scouting me.

End of the day, it came down to Florida State and Auburn. I was sold on either one, could have gone either way, only, the way it worked out, last game of our football season, the game that cost us the state championship, Dennis Erickson, from Miami, was in the stands with his offensive-line coach, Art Kehoe. They weren't there to see me. They were there to see a wide receiver named Jammi German, probably the number-one recruit in the nation at that time—definitely the number-one wide receiver. He was playing for Fort Myers, on the other side of the field, and Miami was making a push to bring him on board. Coach Erickson, Coach Kehoe, they came looking for Jammi German, but what they saw, corner of their eyes, was me. Turned out, I had some kind of game. I was *sizzling*—man, it was ridiculous. But the scoreboard didn't say so. The scoreboard said Fort Myers was sizzling, and we were sent home. I can still remember falling to my knees and crying after that game. We'd all been so hungry for that state championship. All season long, it was close enough to taste—and just like that, the taste was gone.

Now, just getting to this game against Fort Myers, it wasn't easy. It took a black-and-blue defensive war in the rain against Boca Ciega in the first round of the playoffs—with me scoring the winning touchdown on a ten-yard run off the left side, to make the score 6–0 as time ran out. Oh my goodness, it was one of the sweetest runs—ever, ever, ever. All these years later, I can still close my eyes and picture it—I can still *feel* the plant of my foot into that muddy field as I made my first cut. And against Tampa Jesuit in the next round, I was blessed to be able to score on an eighty-five-yard punt return—another game-winning touchdown, this one with just thirteen seconds left on the clock.

Off of these two games, they pinned me with the nickname "Mr. Everything," because I would beat you coming and going, every which way. But I didn't care about any nicknames. I didn't care *how* I beat you, only that I beat you.

So we were riding high, but then we ran into Fort Myers—and this game, it taught me a lesson. It taught me that you can picture a moment in your mind and get to thinking you can will it so, but there are other forces at play. You can *will* yourself to the door, but getting all the way inside, that's not *just* on you. Wrestling, maybe it's all within your reach. You're on your own. Football, there are so many moving parts, it's a different story, and this story didn't end how I'd pictured it. But this wasn't the great lesson of that game. No, the great lesson of that Fort Myers game was that we had let this moment get away from us. We'd started to think it was something we were *entitled* to, instead of something we had to earn. I made a promise to myself that when I got a chance to knock on that door again, I would push myself inside. Not because I'd willed it so. Not because I'd pictured it. But because I would not rest until I powered through.

The job ain't finished until the job is finished.

Coach Erickson, he must have seen something to file away for later, because Miami came calling eventually—but a whole lot happened before *eventually* came round. Early on, I set my sights on Florida State. It had been my childhood dream to play for the Seminoles. When you grow up in Lakeland, that's like climbing to the top of the rainbow. I just wasn't feeling all those other schools or coaches. One reason or another, there wasn't a good fit. Even Auburn wasn't getting it done for me, by the end of this process. But Florida State—I told myself it fit like a glove. Bobby Bowden, he'd spoken with Coach Joe, heard all about my game, my character, my commitment. All of that. And he must have liked what he was hearing, because he kept that conversation going.

There were times in there, my senior year, I could have

pinched myself. It was like a dream—another door I was about to step on through, but I was making this journey on my own. My mom had no clue about any of this college stuff. She wanted the best for me, always, but she wasn't taking me on these recruiting visits. She wasn't hearing what I was hearing, seeing how some of these schools roll out the red carpet. Girls, parties, gear, boosters. Whatever you want. It all starts to mess with your head—only, it was messing with *my* head, just. Wasn't anybody else taking it all in.

More and more, it was looking like I'd be going to Florida State. There was even talk I could keep wrestling—although, who knows, sometimes that kind of talk is just talk. You get there, the coaches tell you they can't afford to see you hurt. They want you in the gym. They want you working out on *their* program, so they start talking a different game. But for now, they were telling me what I wanted to hear.

The others schools, they all fell away. One by one, either they dropped from my board, or I dropped from theirs. Either I didn't show enough interest at the right time, or they didn't show enough interest at the right time. But with Coach Bowden and them, I was feeling it. Big-time.

So there I was, up in Tallahassee for my final recruiting visit. Coach Bowden was saying all the right things. I was saying all the right things. Everything was lining up *just so*. And then I went in to see Chuck Amato, who was the defensive coordinator at the time. That's how it goes on these visits—the head coach butters you up and does his thing and then he hands you off to the coach who'll be working with you when you join the program. It's like a job interview, I guess. You do a little meet and greet with the big boss, but you're hired by the head of the department. And Chuck Amato started out saying all the right things, too. *We really like you, Ray. We think you are an exceptional athlete.* All of that. But then he went and said something that set me off—he said, "We'd like you to maybe play behind Derrick Brooks."

Wasn't expecting to hear *that*—and, really, I couldn't think of a thing to say in response.

Chuck Amato, he must have seen I was stuck, so he kept on—he said, "You do know who Derrick Brooks is, son?" He said it like a question, but it wasn't a question. Of course I knew Derrick Brooks—the dude could *play*. He'd go on to be a first-round NFL draft choice, win a Super Bowl with Tampa Bay, play in a bunch of Pro Bowls, bust his way to the Hall of Fame. At the time, he was the Seminoles' top linebacker. You watched football, played football, lived in the state of Florida— of course you heard of Derrick Brooks. He was *all that*—and a little bit more besides.

I said, "Yes, sir."

He said, "Two years behind Derrick, you'll be ready to go."

I heard that and thought, *Two years?* I thought, *Is this man for real?* So I stood and said, "Mr. Amato, thank you, but no thank you."

Coach Amato tried to turn the meeting back around. He stood and said, "Now hold on there, Ray. Let's talk about this."

I said, "No disrespect, sir, but how you know I'm not better than Derrick Brooks *right now?*"

I said it like a question but it wasn't a question. I didn't give the man a chance to answer. I just walked out. Don't know that anyone had ever walked out of one of those meetings before at Florida State, but I was gone. I got it in my head that these folks were disrespecting me, so I collected my plane ticket home—and the whole time, I think Coach Amato was back in his office, wondering where our meeting went wrong.

By the time I got back to Lakeland, Coach Joe had already heard what happened. I went to see him, talked it through, and it was the first time I'd ever seen a grown man cry. He was a good, good man. He wanted the best for me. He said, "Ray, it was all set. You threw it away."

I said, "Coach, he told me I was gonna play *behind* Derrick Brooks. Not alongside him, *behind* him."

He said, "You've got to earn it, Ray. Nothing is handed to you."

I said, "But they've never even seen what I can do. I ain't even there yet, and already they've written me off."

Years later, Coach Bowden gave an interview and he was asked if there was anything he regretted in his long coaching career. The man had coached at Florida State for over thirty years, won two national titles, twelve ACC Championships—probably one of the most accomplished college coaches of our time. And what did he say? He said his one regret was that he let Ray Lewis slip away from his program.

Wish I could say it was mine, too. It was nice to hear, after all that time, but Bobby Bowden didn't give me a fair shake. That's the bottom line of it. They hadn't even put me in a uniform, and already they were telling me I couldn't play—so, better believe it, I slipped away from the program. Quick as I could.

Even so, Coach Joe had me feeling like I'd let him down, and I guess I did. All of them other coaches, they'd set their sights on other players, worked their way down their lists, so everything went dry for a while. I was nowhere. Just like that, all these doors were open for me, and now I'd walked through the wrong one, so I turned my focus back to wrestling. I still had that state championship to win. And every now and then I'd see Coach Joe in the locker room and we'd talk things through, see what was what. He went from telling me I'd thrown away my big shot to telling me there were still some schools I could look at—wrestling, football, whatever. He had me thinking I should concentrate on my SAT exams, worry about getting a good score, maybe building off of that.

Turned out, there were no other offers. Probably, I could

have played at any of those top schools who'd come calling earlier in the year, but there are only so many scholarships to go around. All the slots were filled, so these coaches were telling me they couldn't guarantee any kind of full ride. But we didn't have money for college. Without a scholarship, I was nowhere but the same place I'd always been.

Graduation was getting close—and, still, no colleges had come calling.

I kept busy with work—at a Ford dealership down the road a piece, on Memorial Boulevard, detailing cars. Every lunch break, I had about an hour, I'd sprint back home across the railroad tracks, a couple miles. I'd fix myself a cool something to drink and then sprint back. That was my workout—because, hey, I needed that job, man.

Coach Joe was helping me on the football front. Making calls and talking me through some of my options. Coach Poole was helping me on the wrestling front. But I was still nowhere, no idea of my next move—matter of fact, it was starting to look like there wasn't even a next move to make. Back of my mind, I knew something would work out. I knew I could walk on and play somewhere, probably get a scholarship. I knew I could wrestle, probably on a scholarship. So I wasn't too worried about things breaking my way. They took a while, breaking, but I was too busy with my classes, with wrestling, to worry too much how things would go.

And right about this time, Miami came calling. They'd given a scholarship to this one dude who blew out his knee before reporting. I never learned the full story—but the upshot, for me, was that a spot had opened up. Comes down to Coach Erickson remembering seeing me in that Fort Myers game and him and Coach Kehoe hearing through the Florida recruiting grapevine that I had yet to sign with another program. So they called Coach Joe. It made no sense to them, me up in the air like that. The season I'd just had, the high school career I'd just had, the interest I'd gotten from coaches. It made no sense. But Coach Joe explained my situation, and out of that call they offered me that open scholarship.

Coach Joe called me up all excited. He said, "Let's not let this one get away from us, Ray."

I liked that he said *us*. That's how much he had invested in me. We were in on the same deal.

This all happened so late in the game that the college football media guide had already been printed. The freshman recruits had already gotten together, met the rest of the team. It's like I showed up out of nowhere. Soon as I got the call, I packed my few things and headed down to Miami on my own. My grandmother arranged for me to ride in a four-door white Cadillac, so when I pulled up I would make an impression. I packed light, the way I remember it. I had one trunk, like a footlocker, and it was mostly filled with my football stuff. Also, two packs of paper, two folders (a red one and a green one), a pack of number-two pencils, a four-pack of pens, one pair of jeans, two Fruit of the Loom T-shirts, a few toiletries, one pair of shoes.

Oh, and twenty dollars' worth of food stamps. My mother pressed those stamps into my hand as I was leaving—said, "Just for you to have, Baby Ray."

I stepped out of that Caddy and it was the first time I'd set foot on that campus. I didn't know a soul. A lot of the guys on the team came out to meet me, a lot of the coaches, but nobody had any idea who I was, what to make of me. Freshmen, they already had a hard time, fitting themselves into a top Division I football program. There's all this hazing-type behavior going on, returning players giving you the once-over, the cold shoulder. But here it was set up like I was the freshman of the freshmen, so even the newbies were putting me through my paces. Folks went out of their way to give me a hard time. I'd hear, *I don't see no Ray Lewis in the media guide.* Or, *You ain't even s'posed to be here.* But I was okay with that. I understood it—told myself they would know who I was before long. They would have no choice but to treat me right.

It was a tough adjustment, but I didn't have time for any of that. I wouldn't allow it, so even though I started out as a kind of outcast, I worked my way in. I was a bit of a comedian, a cutup, so that helped. I was *hella* good at "yo' mama" jokes—that was like my *go-to* move. And slowly, on the back of all those jokes, I began to feel like a part of the team. Funny that it didn't happen because of football. It happened because I could do a killer "Jerome"—this character Martin Lawrence used to play. It just about took these guys out of their game, seeing this big old dude from all the way up in Lakeland, playing like he was some pimp from Detroit, talking in rhymes. They'd look on and try not to laugh—thinking, *Man, he wasn't even recruited!* Thinking, *Who the hell is that guy?*

But eventually, I wore them down and won them over.

And on the field? Well, I wore them down there, too. When I came in, I was playing behind a senior named Robert Bass—but I was more worried about James Burgess, our number-one linebacker recruit. He came from the Miami area, played his high school ball at Southridge, and people talked about him like he was the number-one freshman linebacker in the country. Nothing against James—he was good, but he wasn't *that* good. He wasn't the dude you could build your team around, and even in preseason you could start to see that. *I* could start to see that, so I wasn't just thinking of Robert Bass, blocking my path in the middle. I was also thinking of James Burgess on the outside.

First day we put on pads, I made my presence known, laid

into one of our running backs, James Stewart. James was a big old boy—six foot three, 235 pounds—and I just flattened him. Didn't feel good about it, didn't feel bad about it, but there it was. Truth be told, you weren't supposed to hit like that in practice, not on the first day, but I was the dude with the last scholarship, joined the team at the last possible minute. Those rules didn't apply, far as I was concerned, so when James came around on a toss, I lit into him, and when he finally got back on his feet after that tackle, I got in his ear—said, "Man, there is a new sheriff in town! Don't you *ever* think you gonna run the ball that freely around me."

Now, let me just be clear: In practice, you *hit*, but maybe not as hard as I hit James on this toss. There should be no letup, just because it's your teammate on the other side of the ball. The thinking is, *Hey, if you can deal with us, you can deal with anybody*. We weren't out there trying to put a hurt on our own boys, but there was no letup to the way we played. Practice or no, teammate or no—we played *hard*. We played *for real*. And here it's like I was shot out of a cannon, flattened poor James Stewart—left him seeing stars, just like in the cartoons.

After that, all them boys, they came runnin' round. All them amazing veteran players we had on that team. Rohan Marley, my very good friend to this day—Bob Marley's son, who went on to play in the Canadian Football League. Warren Sapp, who made it all the way to the Pro Football Hall of Fame, after a great career in Tampa Bay and Oakland. Dwayne Johnson—"The Rock"—who also played in the CFL before kicking butt as an actor, professional wrestler, whatever. Patrick Riley, who went on to play for the Chicago Bears.

All my brothers on D, they started jumping on me, clapping me on the helmet, and I heard somebody say, "That joker is *for real*."

Yes, sir. Yes I was.

• • •

Second game of the season, that same old theme music kicked back in, the story of my career: Robert Bass blew out his knee in a game against Virginia Tech, and right away there was all this talk on our side of the field about who should go in for him. All this scuffling. First name I heard was James Burgess. Don't know who said it, but it's the one name that popped out at me in all that confusion: "Somebody get me Burgess."

Soon as I heard it, I had to talk myself down from being pissed. Told myself it made sense, Burgess getting the nod ahead of me. He was the top linebacker recruit. He'd gotten all that attention. Me, I stood just a shade taller than a walk-on, wasn't even in the media guide. Even so, I wasn't too happy, hearing his name like that. But before I could get too down on myself, before I got to wondering who else would have to go down before I got the call, I heard the voice of our linebacker coach, Randy Shannon.

Now, Randy Shannon was a big deal. You grew up in Florida, you played football, you *knew* Randy Shannon. He'd played for the Hurricanes, played for the Cowboys in the NFL. He wasn't built like a typical linebacker—he was smaller, faster, *quicker*. I liked the way he played, man. I did. He had a different approach to that position, an athlete's approach. Me and him, we got along pretty well, those first couple weeks.

In fact, it was Randy Shannon who pinned me with my number—52. That number came with a story. You see, when I got to Miami, I had my eye on number 1. Jessie Armstead, another great linebacker, had done that number proud for the Hurricanes, but he was off to play for the New York Giants, and I thought the number was in play, but it went instead to one of our running backs, Danyell Ferguson. He was a year ahead of me, so he had seniority—that's just how it goes. But then

Randy came over to me one day in practice and said, "You look like somebody who's gonna start his own thing."

He knew I was fishing around for a number to wear—someone to honor, maybe put it out there that my game would be like this other person's who wore it before me.

I said, "What you mean?"

He said, "Why don't you wear a number not tied to anyone else? Make it your own."

I said, "What number you have in mind?"

He said, "Fifty-two."

I thought about it, some. And then I smiled.

Randy said, "Why you smiling?"

I said, "Fifty-two. That's seven. I'm good with that."

He said, "Seven?"

I said, "Five and two is seven. That's completion, man."

He said, "Hold on, Ray Lewis. You're spiritual? It's like that?"

I said, "Yes, sir. It's like that."

He said, "Boy, you alright. Your mama did a good job."

Completion. The Lord rested on the seventh day. I thought, *I can get with that.* But there would be no rest for me until I made that number my own, like Randy said, and here he was, calling James Burgess back before the dude could step from his place on the sideline.

Randy said, "No, no. Not Burgess." Then he looked at me and said, "Ray Lewis, you up."

So I grabbed my helmet and ran out onto that field, and right here I'll tell it the way old folks tell it when they spin a tale.

Here on in, the story has begun.

SIX

Hurricane Seasons

First game freshman year we drew Boston College. I got in late, scoreboard already lit our way, game in hand.

Four plays—that's all, just four plays. But it felt to me like I'd arrived.

I'll never forget those four plays—made three tackles and nearly got myself a pick on a pop-up pass. That near-pick, it was something. The quarterback dropped back, and I could see by his eyes where he was looking to throw, got my hands up, jumped, put my fingertips on the ball, tipped it up in the air. Oh my goodness. That tipped ball hung there for the longest time—time enough for me to backpedal, get myself under it, maybe make the grab, but the quarterback followed the play. Wasn't expecting that, but there he was, jumping up a beat ahead of me, batting the ball down. This was maybe the first time I realized I was playing at another level than I was used to. Nothing I couldn't handle, but something to adjust to.

Next game, home against Virginia Tech, the game when Robert Bass went down, I went from counting *plays* to counting *games* and *seasons*. That Virginia Tech game was a big deal, and not just for me. The Hurricanes had a big streak going at home—hadn't lost a game at the Orange Bowl since 1985, when I was ten years old. We were at fifty-one games and counting, and none of these guys wanted to be on the field when that streak came to an end. No way, no how. The older players, they'd had some time with this type of pressure, but for the freshmen, this was our first taste. Pressure like that, it didn't bother me—but the other guys, it was an extra something to think about, a weight we all had to carry.

You want to keep those distractions to a minimum. That's why we stayed as a team in a nearby hotel before home games—the way they do it at a lot of big-time programs. For us, this meant Shula's Hotel in Miami Lakes, where Coach Don Shula was one of the investors. Rohan Marley was assigned as my roommate, and he'd checked in ahead of me. I got to my room, threw my bags down, headed right back out to go hang with some of the other freshmen.

Rohan stopped me—said, "Where you going?"

I said, "Nowhere, man. Thought I'd go hang with the guys, one of the other rooms."

He said, "Hang here."

And so I did, and that was the first we got to know each other, me and Ro—Rat, we used to call him. We became close—like, right away. Wasn't nothing to our friendship at first, just two ballplayers doing our thing, thrown together like that, but we seemed to click. That first night, we got to talking. Football, life, family. Man, we just talked and talked. And as we talked, I went into my routines. I took out my deck of cards and started in on my push-ups and sit-ups. Didn't even give it a thought—I just went to work.

Rohan looked at me like I was plain crazy. He said, "What you doing?"

I said, "I work out before every game."

He said, "What?"

So I told him, showed him. I went through that whole deck of cards, shuffled 'em up, went through the deck again. I had my feet up under the bed for support to do my sit-ups, and Rohan kept looking at me.

Finally he said, "You know what, youngster?"

I liked that he called me "youngster." He was a big old sophomore, but that one year made him a wise veteran, compared to me. Before I flipped the next card I said, "What's that?"

He said, "You take the body, I'll take the mind."

Then he waited until I'd gone all the way through that deck a second time, handed me his headphones—said, "Listen to this."

It was one of his father's songs—Papa Bob, we all called him. I listened to the first couple beats and pulled one of the buds from my ear—said, "No disrespect, but I don't really listen to this type of music." I felt bad about it, since it was his father and all, but it just wasn't my thing.

He said, "No, no, no. It's not what you think. *Listen*."

I laid back down on the bed and gave the music another try, really started to *listen* to what Papa Bob was saying—all about peace and love and standing up to be counted. All of that. It was the difference between *hearing* and *listening*. Those words, they took me away, outside myself for a little bit. Where I grew up, the way things were back home, this type of music didn't find us. Who had time for music, anyway? I knew who Bob Marley was, of course, but I never paid him no mind—only, here in this hotel room, lying down on that big old bed, the words just lifted me up and carried me away. Next thing I knew, I'd drifted off to sleep. That's how at ease I was with myself at just that moment. Whatever distractions I'd had piling up for my attention, the weight of the young season—it all fell away.

Out of that, we found our Friday-night routine. Me and Rat, we'd hole up in our hotel room and start flipping through my deck of cards. Push-ups, sit-ups. We'd listen to Papa Bob. We'd get our heads around the game. We'd talk and talk—not *just* about football, but there was a lot of that, too. For Rohan, it was just a once-a-week type deal. That's as far as he went with those workouts. He couldn't understand at first that I was cut a little differently. He said, "You do this every day?"

I said, "Every day of my life."

He said, "For real?" He couldn't believe it.

I said, "Rat, I'm not like you. I'm broke, man. All I do is school and football. All I got time for."

Funny thing is, we didn't talk about it after that. Rohan just dropped to the floor and joined in, so this became our thing—Friday nights before games, flipping through that deck of cards, pushing each other like nothing else mattered.

Monday after we won that Virginia Tech game, I was feeling pretty good. We had our Sundays off, so this was the first time we were all together as a team, first time I went in to look at film with a real role to play. It wasn't a full-time role just yet, but it was better than being on the second string—maybe even on the third string, depending on who was calling the shots. James Burgess, some folks might have put him ahead of me on the depth chart, but I couldn't worry about that.

Anyway, it was a while before I started talking in these meetings, but I was taking it all in—believe me, I was taking it all in.

Another funny thing: the language was different than what I was used to at Kathleen. Everything had a different name, a different term, so I was trying to keep everything straight. The coaches, they had their own little shorthand. The players, we had our own way of talking to each other, too. And me, I was still figuring it all out.

That Monday was when we all heard that Robert Bass would be out for a while with a blown knee. We knew he was hurt, but we didn't know how bad. Coach Erickson, he took the opportunity to announce that I would be his starting middle linebacker, here on in. I heard that and thought, *It's my time now.*

That week, we played at Colorado, on national television. It felt to me like all eyes were on us and on *me*. And that Colorado team was *loaded*. Kordell Stewart at quarterback. Lamont Warren and Rashaan Salam in the backfield. Charles Johnson and Michael Westbrook at wide receiver. Christian Fauria at tight end. Offensively, they had a lot of weapons, a bunch of guys who'd go on to play in the league, but we came into town with some straight swagger. Our confidence—that was our weapon. It was through the roof. We didn't give a damn how many players they had. Our attitude was, *Hey, we're not only gonna punch you in the mouth during the game, but we'll meet you in the parking lot afterward and finish you off.*

The national television piece, it wasn't a distraction so much as it was a motivation—that's how I looked at it. Our motto was simple: big-time players make big-time plays in big-time games. Out of that came another motto: this is how we feed our kids. And this was just one of those games, how we made ourselves known.

Folks told me later that Keith Jackson took a shine to me up in the booth. He was calling the game for ABC, kept saying my name. I was in on so many tackles, there was no avoiding me—"Ray Lewis, a young kid out of Lakeland, Florida." In that folksy, singsong voice of his.

This was my first official game that I'd started, so I paid attention to my stats—but then, I *always* paid attention to my stats, counted my tackles. This was how I took my measure, same way a basketball player might keep track of his points. Ten tackles—that was always the magic number. You get to twenty points on a basketball court, ten tackles on defense, you were having a good game, so my whole focus was on getting to double digits, and here in this Colorado game I got to ten tackles by the end of the first half.

You get to ten tackles, everything else is gravy, right?

Randy Shannon was into it, too. He was keeping score right alongside me. He came over, end of the second quarter, told me I'd hit my number. I didn't need him to tell me, but I liked that he did; I *liked* that he knew what was driving me out there.

He said, "Already at ten, Ray. Already at ten."

And I said, "Ain't no stopping me, Coach."

And, really, there wasn't. Second half, Keith Jackson ended up calling my name a whole lot more. The young kid out of Lakeland, Florida, ended up with close to twenty tackles, a sack, four pass breakups. It was just a crazy game. A *statement* game. And you have to realize, we had an outstanding defense that year. We had Rohan, Warren Sapp, Patrick Riley—these dudes came to *play*, so it's not like I was running around out there all alone. No, there was help all around, and we held on to win 35–29, made ourselves a factor in the national conversation.

A lot of folks in college football watched that Colorado game, and the takeaway for them was that we were a handful. And, just being honest, that *I* was a handful. I'd come out of nowhere, far as a lot of people were concerned. I wasn't a top recruit, not by any stretch. Wasn't even in the media guide. And here I was, on a rampage, messing with Kordell Stewart's head, getting into his game plan. It set me up, that game—got me into a little hot water, even. After the game, a reporter came by to talk to me. He wanted to talk about the game, but he also wanted to talk about *my* game, and here I'd never been shy. Yeah, this was my first college start, but I'd just put up some big numbers, on a big stage. I'd just made a *statement*. So I said what I was feeling. I said, "By the time I'm through, I'll be the greatest player to ever play for the Miami Hurricanes."

And just like that, I was in the spotlight. Got a big response, a line like that. It was all over the sports talk shows. Columnists wrote their little pieces, left and right. Wasn't exactly a foot-in-the-mouth type moment, because I meant what I said—but if I'd known the firestorm it would set off, I might have kept quiet. At least until my *second* game.

Right away, I started getting calls from all these former Miami players—a lot of them giving me a hard time for pumping myself up like that. They'd say things like, "That's a tall order, son." Or, "Why don't you get a few more games under your belt before you start running your mouth?" It was mostly a good-natured hard time, don't think anyone was too upset, but it got people talking, I'll say that.

Best call I got was from Michael Irvin—who was still tearing up the league for the Dallas Cowboys, on his way to the Pro Football Hall of Fame. He said, "I like it, Ray. That's Hurricane football."

I had to pinch myself, that Michael Irvin was taking the time out of his day to call me—but it wasn't *what* he said so much as that he called. His message, I already knew, didn't need to hear it from him. Damn straight it was Hurricane football! Damn straight I would be the best player to come out of the U! I didn't need to hear from anyone else on *that*. An outcome like that, it was up to me and no one else. But just hearing from Michael Irvin *at all*, just hearing from all these other great players was something special.

Wasn't just my team that was now part of the conversation.

I talked for a while with Michael Irvin. Everybody called him "The Playmaker." It was a name he encouraged, so he knew as well as anybody what it meant to strut, to play with confidence. And I think he appreciated that same quality in me—that's why he called. And when it came time to end the call he said, "Now go out and do it."

Hurricane football—that's a phrase you hear a lot when you play for Miami. There's a certain style of football we play at the U. We're dead serious about our game, and I always appreciated it when someone picked up on that, and here we were three games into my freshman season, undefeated, on a nice little roll.

Fifth week of the season, we were *still* undefeated, headed up to Tallahassee to play Florida State, the number-one team in the nation. Another big game—for me, especially. Just a couple months earlier, I sat with Chuck Amato, the Seminoles' defensive coordinator, who told me I'd be stuck behind Derrick Brooks for two years, so a part of me had something to prove. Of course, it was only *part of me* with something to prove, because the validation wasn't for me. I didn't need Chuck Amato or Bobby Bowden or anyone else on that Florida State coaching staff to know they made a mistake, letting me slip away from their program. I already knew this myself, and that's all that counted. No, the real motivation here was that I wanted to make these people pay—told myself I would put a hurt on them they'd never seen coming, make them regret writing me off the way they did.

So, yeah . . . there was *that*.

Charlie Ward was the Florida State quarterback—a magician with a football in his hands. Charlie ended up winning the Heisman Trophy that year, and leading the Seminoles to their first national championship, and he was just lighting it up. It was a big rivalry, man. This was the first I knew what it meant, Florida State going up against Miami, and that stadium was thumping. We had our rivalries back in high school. Those games against the Lakeland Dreadnaughts were knock-down, drag-outs, so I knew what it was to hate on an opponent, and here there was some bad blood. All that week, leading up to the Florida State game, there were stories about how Charlie would hold up against the "Eye of the Storm." Already, that's what they were calling me—the middle linebacker on a strong Miami Hurricanes team.

The Eye of the Storm.

A young kid out of Lakeland, Florida.

Four games in—two and a half games, really—and I already had a nickname, already had a reputation, and I played to it. But that Florida State team, they were just too polished. They were stacked at every position, efficient, poised—just a solid, balanced team. And as much as I hated to admit it, they were well coached, too. We were dominant on defense, but we couldn't move the ball against the Seminoles, so we played to a kind of standoff, most of the way. The game was close, but then, Florida State got two picks late and turned the game around, and we wound up on the short end of a 28–10 score.

It was a disappointing loss for us as a team, but for me personally it was huge. In a good way. Don't mean to make it sound like I was a selfish player, because winning was everything. Forget those double-digit tackles, the nicknames, the calls from Michael Irvin. None of that mattered if it didn't come wrapped inside a win. But just to be on that field, in the middle of that rivalry, playing in front of all those fans, a lot of folks who knew me from my high school career—that was an important milestone. It told me I was playing with the big boys now. It told me that *Hurricane football* was serious.

A lot of my teammates, they didn't like how this Florida State game was called—the veterans, mostly. Truth was, the Seminoles outplayed us, deserved to win, but some of our guys wanted to hang it on the officiating. Some of them wanted to hang it on the coaching, even. They didn't like some of the personnel moves we made late in the game, and I don't want to call anyone out here, but the feeling was we might have had a better shot at moving the ball with a different package, a different look.

I was just a rookie, so it wasn't up to me to agree or disagree on this. I kept my mouth shut, but the veteran players were talking up a storm, got it in their heads that the thing to do was boycott our Monday practice. Far as I was concerned, it was just a bunch of noise, but I could only go along with it. When you're a freshman, you do as you're told. And besides, our Monday practices weren't much. We looked at film, went for a light run. So instead, the upperclassmen put on a barbecue at Thirty-Six—the dormitory-type suites where a lot of the guys lived.

Wasn't much of a protest—it was more of a party, really. There was a lot of talking, a lot of finger-pointing, a lot of nonsense, but do you know what? Out of that little piece of rebellion, we came together as a team, got a good dialogue going. The coaches, they didn't like how we'd broken ranks, but they let us speak our minds, and underneath all of that we began to feel like we were all in this thing together. It was *Hurricane football*, in a whole new way. Wasn't the way I would have handled it—because, hey, the Seminoles beat us fair and square. But there was some good that came out of this.

Out of that, we went on a little tear and won the next four games by big, big scores. Syracuse, 49–0. Temple, 42–7. Pittsburgh, 35–7. Rutgers, 31–17. Those Big East teams, they couldn't touch us, man, and on the back of those big wins we climbed to number four in the national rankings. It set us up for a Big East showdown at West Virginia—the Mountaineers ranked ninth in the country.

This was a game we should have won and, got to say, the

main reason we lost was *me*. Not because I got beat. Not because I didn't play well. But because I didn't play much at all. See, this was the game where Robert Bass came back from his knee injury—and, nothing against Robert, but he wasn't ready. He got his job back, but he wasn't up to it just yet. Forget that the dude couldn't match me on that field, that *nobody* could match me on that field—physically, he wasn't ready. He wasn't all the way healed. But he'd been cleared to play, so he played. He had seniority, so he played. That kind of thing, in the college game, it's just understood. I didn't agree with it, but I didn't question it.

Now, let me just be clear: I don't believe we were a championship team that year, but there's no denying we were in the conversation. Here we were, Week Ten, the number-four team in the country, going up against another top-ten team—so, yeah, definitely, we were in the conversation. But then I barely even saw the field, and we ended up losing a close game, 17–14. Would it have made a difference, me being out there instead of Robert? Well, it's not for me to say—but I'll go ahead and say it anyway. *Hell yeah it would have made a difference.* The dude was not a hundred percent, and West Virginia took advantage of that. They hurt us up the middle. On the six or seven plays I did get into the game, I made damn near every tackle, so it would have changed things up. Plus, we'd been on a nice momentum run, had a good flow going, a good energy.

Robert Bass could play—my goodness, he went on to play in the league, so of course he could play. But he was much bigger than I was, much stockier. He played a different type of game, gave us a whole different look. Me, I was quick, played with a ton of energy, tore through that line like a rifleshot. That afternoon in West Virginia, we let the air out of whatever mojo we had going on that midseason run, whatever version of *Hurricane football* we'd been playing.

We finished up our regular season with a big win against

Memphis, but I didn't get to play much, and I only got in for three plays in our Fiesta Bowl game against Arizona—a game we ended up losing 29–0—so in the end it's tough to look back on my first season as anything but a disappointment. And it was, but a lot of good came back to me underneath that disappointment. For one thing, I'd shown the college football world that I could play. For another, even more important, I'd shown my brothers on D that I could play. I won the coaches over, too. And I'd started to build some good friendships on that team, so that by the time my sophomore year rolled around, we were tight.

We were good.

We were ready.

Sophomore year, I came into camp ripped, pissed, hungry.

I was a full-fledged, card-carrying Hurricane by this point. I was *seasoned*, proven. When it started out, folks had their doubts about me, about my size. I joined the program late as a freshman, but I made my mark right away, so by now I was moving around campus with confidence. I even had me a serious girlfriend named Tatyana. We met freshman year and hit it off. From the very beginning, it felt to me like we were meant to be together, would *always* be together, so that's how I looked out at the world. Doesn't mean I was always the world's best boyfriend—but we were tight, solid.

My freshman year on the field, it left a bad taste—and not because I didn't play as much as I thought I should play. No, I was good with that. Robert Bass, he earned that starting job, didn't need no freshman lining up to run him off just because he blew out his knee. No, I got my chances, turned some heads. Really, the bad taste had more to do with how we didn't get it done as a team—which, in a lot of ways, was not at all where my head was at after we were trounced in the Fiesta Bowl. But that's how it goes sometimes, heat of the moment. When our season just kind of fizzled like that in Arizona, I wasn't man enough to hang my head and regroup with my brothers. I put the blame someplace else, told myself those last two losses weren't on me.

But that's not how you win as a team, is it? That's no winning mind-set, and here I came roaring into my sophomore year thinking we would not be denied—as a *unit*. Already, I knew full well that I could dominate, every which way. But football wasn't wrestling. Yeah, at bottom, when you break it down, it's just a one-on-one battle, same way it is on the mat. That's how I'd seen the game all along, since Pop Warner ball. But there are other elements at play. There are parts of the game you can't control. So my thing was to control what I could, and to *influence* everything else. To set an example.

Beginning of the next season I started running with the defensive backs in practice. You want to put me on the clock? You want to race? I wasn't running with the linebackers. I was running with the DBs, putting it out there that there was no stopping me.

However dominant we'd been on defense the year before, now we were dominant on top of dominant. Most of our guys were back from the year before, and it was clear early on that we would be a force. Other teams, they could barely move the ball against us. I'd line up behind Patrick and Warren, alongside of Rat, and we were like a brick wall. First game of the season, at home against Georgia Southern, we were *impenetrable*. We won that game going away, 56–0. In all my years in football, I'd never been on either side of such a lopsided score—but I'll tell you, it felt good to be on the *winning* side. A game like that, it's what we called a "stat" game—meaning, it was a chance for all of us to rack up our statistics, to pile on. To look at the scoreboard, you'd think all those stats were on the offensive side of the ball, but that's not how it shook out. Me personally, I got my tackles. They ran the ball a lot. They had this triple option play they tried all day to get to work, but it never even *came close* to working.

Let me tell you, it was a bad day to be a Georgia Southern Eagle. Oh, it was. It was. And it was a good day to be a Miami Hurricane. Coming out of that game, we were flying. We told ourselves nobody could touch us. We told ourselves the national championship was within reach. Wasn't about the score we'd just run up in that opening game—because, frankly, Georgia Southern wasn't a very good team. No, it was about *how* we'd run up that score. It was about how rock solid we were on D. It was about how the game was *slowing down* for us. *For me.* When you play behind someone like Warren Sapp, you learn to see the game in a whole new way. Warren was such a dictator on the field; the game moved to his will, and me moving in behind him, we had to be in sync. The more we played together, the more we moved together. We had our own language out there—didn't come from studying film, didn't come from the coaching staff. It came from studying each other, trusting each other. It got to where Warren knew that if he went *front side* he had to stay *front side*. If he tried to be an athlete and go *front side* and then come back to make a play, we'd be exposed. A dude like Warren, you've got to learn how to play off of him very quickly.

That front-seven box we featured on that 1994 team—man, I've been a part of a lot of great defenses, but I will take that Hurricane line against anybody. We were as solid as solid could be, and off that first big win we went out to Arizona State and grabbed another big win—47–10—sending us to number five in the national rankings.

After that, the talk just grew. Wasn't a team in college football could run with us, we kept hearing. Although, of course, this was what we kept hearing because it was *us* running our mouths. But I'm sorry, we were just too good to think of anything less than a title. So when we came home to face the seventeenth-ranked Washington Huskies the third week of the season, we were flying high. Better believe it, there was excitement all around. We had that home winning streak going full tilt—all the way up to fifty-eight games. Fifty-eight games! That covered almost ten years!

It was the first time our two schools had ever played, but we were *rivals*. Wasn't like the rivalry we had with Florida State, but there was history. In 1991, we'd both finished with identical 12–0 records, wound up sharing the national title because the bowl schedule was already set and there was no way to settle things on the field. *This* game came out of *that*—so, yeah, we were rivals. The personnel was all different, but the feeling was the same.

That whole week, we were vigilant, locked in. One of our coaches put up a poster with Napoleon Kaufman's picture on it—he was the Huskies' main threat, a beast. On the poster it had all his stats, how much he weighed, how much he lifted, how fast he ran the forty, yards per carry—all of that. And it set us off, looking at that poster all week long.

We were *fired up*.

And then, just like that, the streak was gone. The *national championship*, some folks were saying that was gone, too. Three weeks in and it felt to us like our season was over. It's like there'd been a death in the family, that's how knocked out we all were over this loss. To a man, we took it hard. The football writers started calling the game "The Whammy in Miami," making it sound like we were cursed—and it felt like that to us for a while.

The game went bad for us at the coin toss. People *still* talk about that coin toss. What happened was Warren Sapp went out to represent and the officials claim he "deferred" the call. It ended up Washington got the ball twice—to start the game *and* to start the third quarter. Of course, Sapp did no such thing. He elected to kick off in the first half and to receive in the second half, which is how Dennis Erickson liked to play it with our tenacious defense—you know, to set the tone early. But the officials heard it another way and it ended up costing us. (Who goes out there with any kind of football IQ and *asks* to kick the ball to start each half? It made no sense.) That opening drive in the third quarter, it changed the game. The Huskies ended up scoring twenty-two points in the first five minutes of the second half, and we were on our heels. That game also changed the way they do these coin tosses, because after that they had microphones out there, so everything was clear.

It just wasn't our day, man. No excuses, but it was a big wake-up call for our group. We got burned on a couple big plays, both sides of the ball—and we looked ahead to the rest of our schedule knowing we couldn't afford another stumble.

That loss at the Orange Bowl, the whole world watching, it left me thinking of what folks mean when they talk about an *upset* in sports. It was an *upset*, a big one, but we couldn't let it *upset* us if we wanted to make some noise the rest of the way. Anyway, it would not *upend* our season. We needed to set it aside, start a new winning streak at home. And we all felt that and wound up just going off to make up for that loss.

We *shut down* those Big East teams, man.

We *destroyed* Florida State, to make up for the year before.

We ran the table, closed out the season with eight straight wins—some of those teams, we downright *embarrassed*—and next thing we knew we were back on track to be the national champions. At least, that's how *we* saw it. A lot of folks, they saw it another way. See, we finished out the regular season ranked third in the nation. We were set to play number-one-ranked Nebraska in the Orange Bowl. Penn State was ranked second, and they were playing Oregon in the Rose Bowl. Nebraska and Penn State were undefeated, and we had that one loss against Washington, so there was all this talk that even if we knocked off Nebraska we'd still be behind Penn State if they won their bowl game. In those days they didn't have the BCS format in place, so there were a lot of years like 1994 when there was no consensus national champion.

The BCS bowl system they have now was a long time in coming. It's great for the game, great for the fans. We could have used that kind of tournament setup, would've taken away some of the distractions we all felt, leading up to this Nebraska game. It would've settled the matter *off* the field, so we could focus our full attention on settling the matter *on* the field.

We didn't buy into this talk, of course. Our thing was, Hey, if we're already ranked third and we beat the number-one team in the country, that makes us the number-one team in the country. End of discussion. Far as we were concerned, the Orange Bowl was the national title game—didn't matter what the so-called "experts" had to say. Didn't matter what the Penn State folks had to say.

It was our title to win—and if you had a problem with that . . . well, you could just take it up with us after the game.

But all that talk, it turned out to be beside the point because we couldn't get it done. The Cornhuskers came in—to *our* house!—and took it to us. Tommie Frazier, Lawrence Phillips—those dudes came to play. They *game-planned* us. We jumped out to a 10–0 lead, but they came clawing back. They took our strength and found a way to make it a weakness. And as good as we were on defense, I had to admit, that Nebraska team had a strong offensive line. Best in the country, people said, and I didn't doubt it. Wasn't enough to shut us down, but they did manage to slow us down a little bit, in spots. And—now this was the *game-planning* part—they knew how to pick those spots and jump on them. Really, the reason we lost that game, it came down to just a couple plays. Tommie Frazier found a soft spot in our defense at a key time. Warren Sapp was so fast off the ball, he penetrated so fast, that Tommie was able to spin out and hand off to Cory Schlesinger, who rolled behind our defense on a trap for a fifteen-yard touchdown run early in the fourth quarter—after the two-point conversion, it tied the score at 17–17. Then, those two came back late in the fourth and did us the same way—another trap, this time for a fourteen-yard touchdown run.

We got the ball back inside our own twenty with a little less than three minutes remaining, but we couldn't get anything going. We moved the ball on a short pass on first down, but then Frank Costa was sacked twice, Nebraska got a pick on fourth down, and Tommie Frazier took a knee the rest of the way while the clock ran out on our season.

Final score: 24–17, Nebraska. And we could only look up at that scoreboard and fall to our knees, too.

Hurricane football. The winds blew another way after that 1994 season. I stayed to play another year, but it felt to me like I was the only one. Sapp was gone. Rat was gone. Patrick Riley, gone. Even Dennis Erickson announced a couple weeks after my sophomore season that he was leaving to coach the San Francisco 49ers, so we got *real* young in 1995.

Our new coach was Butch Davis—one of Jimmy Johnson's boys, he'd followed Coach Johnson from Miami to the Dallas Cowboys, where he was the defensive coordinator. Me and

Butch, we didn't get along. Felt to me like he was always out to teach me a lesson, make an example of me in front of all these young players. In fact, he called me out right away—only, not by name, not directly. He took the whistle and made his presence known. One of our first practices, he called the team over for a talk—said, "There's gonna be some changes round here."

Those changes? No celebrating on the field. That was it—his big contribution to *Hurricane football.*

I heard that and thought, *Damn!* I thought, *You can't come in and do us like that.* It was part of the culture, man. The right celebration, at the right time, was spontaneous, joyous, infectious—and it could spark our whole team. And the thing of it is, I heard this as a knock on me—because, wasn't no secret, I could get into it better than anyone out there.

I just kind of filed that away, told myself we'll see what happens. And sure enough, first game of the season, we were out in California against UCLA, and at some point early in the game Karim Abdul-Jabbar took the handoff and I shot the gap and flattened him for a loss. So what did I do? I stood up and started doing my thing, same as always. It just kind of happened. The way I played the game, with so much emotion, so much energy, it spilled out in all these ways I couldn't always control—only here, got to admit, I was looking for a moment to show Butch he couldn't keep us from doing like we'd always done.

Right after that, he pulled me out of the game, and I didn't think anything of it at first, just assumed he was putting in a new package, giving me a blow, but on the next set of downs, I was still out. I went over to Randy Shannon and asked him what was up, me sitting out like that.

He said, "Butch told me to pull you."

I said, "Seriously?"

He said, "For celebrating."

So I grabbed my helmet and said, "Man, the hell with him!"

And I ran back onto the field. Wasn't like me to go against a coach like that. I'd been raised to respect authority, but I got it in my head that this man didn't deserve my respect. To come in to *my* house! To change *my* program! To take the joy and passion from *my* game! Yeah, he was the head coach, but this was *my* team. That was my attitude—not saying it's right, not saying it's wrong, but there it was.

Butch Davis, his hands were tied. But it set me off, man— it did. Already, I was on tilt. Losing that game to Nebraska. Losing my boys like that. It felt to me like the torch had been passed, and this was how I chose to carry it.

It ended up we lost that game to UCLA—by a big score. But I told myself I didn't care. I told myself I was gone.

When we got back to Miami, Butch called me in to his office for a dressing down. He told me how things were gonna be on his watch. But I cut him off before he could get all the way through his talk. I said, "It don't matter. I'm going anyway."

I'd been thinking about declaring for the NFL draft, going pro. Wasn't anything left for me to prove at this level—and, now that my boys were all gone, wasn't any reason to stay. But this was the first I talked about it, put it out there, and I was surprised by Butch's reaction.

He said, "You're going? You're going where?" He knew what I meant, but he wanted to push me, make me spell it out.

I said, "I'm out. End of the season, I'm going to the league, man."

He said, "You're making the biggest mistake of your life." Like he was *scolding* me.

I couldn't believe it. All my life, I'd been around coaches who worked to lift their players up and out and on to the next thing. My dreams were always their dreams—my success, theirs, too. And here was this man, bitter, full of himself, probably a little angry that his best defensive player was telling him he had a foot out the door, shooting me down like I was some punk kid who'd just stolen the family car.

I said, "Wow. You *really* believe that?"

He said, "Yes, I do."

I had something to prove to this man, so I piled it on thick—said, "You won't find a more dominant college player than me. Right now, I'm the man to beat."

Here Butch went into a long-winded rant about his friends around the league, who'd assured him I'd go in the fourth round—said that was about the best I could hope for. And here, too, I couldn't believe it. Even if this was *true*, even if the NFL scouts had concerns about my size, my stature, my ability to play at the next level—why would this man go out of his way to shoot me down like that? What was in it for him, to do me dirt? And why was he even asking around the league, if he didn't already think I had one foot out the door?

I hadn't known for sure, going into his office, but as soon as I stepped away from that man, I knew. I was gone.

My thinking wasn't just about what was going on down on the field. My mind was also on what was going down at home. It had a lot to do with my mom, really. She'd been struggling since I went away to school—got to where she was flat broke. Wasn't even enough money coming in to keep a roof over her head, so I did what I had to do. At the end of my junior season, I brought my whole family down to Miami to stay with me. I fixed it with a friend who let us use a two-bedroom apartment off campus, in a little complex called the Grove, and we squeezed in and made the best of it—my mother, my sisters, my brother. It was a tight setup, hectic. I stayed there, too, a lot of the time, but I also kept my place in student housing, with my roommates. All of a sudden, college was nothing at all like it had been my first two years—but then, a lot of my buddies were gone anyway, and I was happy to be able to spend all this time with my family.

We were doing okay—really. We still didn't have enough money, so I was scrambling to keep ahead of our bills. I'd load up on food from the dining halls, from our training table, and bring some of it home. I'd take odd jobs here and there, just so my brother and sisters could have some walking-around money. It was only a short-term setup—once I'd made up my mind that I was declaring for the draft, I knew it'd just be a couple months before there was *real* money coming our way, so the goal here was to just get by. That's not always so easy for a college athlete—not when you're in season, not if you want to take classes. We were amateur athletes—that was a big deal to those NCAA folks—so we could not get paid to play, and we could not participate in any of those television deals the schools and conferences sign. I understood that. We all understood that—that's the deal we signed up for. But then, a lot of times, there were local car dealerships, local restaurants or clubs who wanted to slip us some cash for some kind of endorsement deal, maybe an appearance fee, but we weren't supposed to do that, either. And for a lot of us, there were agents lining up left and right, just for the chance to represent us, and a lot of those guys were flashing money around, trying to get with you—another big *no*, as far as the NCAA was concerned.

Still, there was money to be made in a sidelong way—decent money, once the football season was over. And like a lot of the guys I played with, I *needed* to make money, man. Life was just too damn expensive, especially down in Miami—and now there were five other mouths for me to feed. The whole time, I was meeting with agents, and they were promising me the sun and the moon and everything in between. Each time out, I made my position clear—said, "I will sit down and listen to what you have to say."

Said, "I will keep you in mind."

And I was good to my word—I kept them *all* in mind.

But money became more and more of an issue in those few months I had my family with me, more and more of a worry. Even before Butch Davis took me out to his woodshed like that, this was how I was leaning, so I found the time to talk to my mother about it. A decision like this—I couldn't make it without her blessing.

Turned out that blessing was hard to come by. I went to her one day, not long after I put it to Butch that I was leaving, and told her what I was thinking. I said, "Mom, I'm coming out."

She said, "You what?"

I said, "I gotta go."

She said, "Go where, Junior?"

I said, "To the league. Ain't nothing for me in Miami. Ain't nothing for us, as a family."

She let this sink in for a couple beats—said, "What you gonna do, Junior? What happens if you get hurt? Ain't nobody gonna pay you then."

I said, "I won't get hurt. That's all." Then I put the same argument back on her—said, "What happens if I get hurt playing for Miami? That happens, where's the money gonna come from then?"

She had no answer, so she moved on to the rest of her argument against me leaving—said, "What about college? You can't leave without your degree."

I said, "I'll come back and get my degree. I promise."

We went back and forth like this for a while, circling around our one real option. I would declare for the NFL draft and leave school after the spring semester. Like I said, it was the only way, and after a long talk, I was able to persuade my mother that it was the only way.

But the thing is, that talk should have been a little longer. There was another piece to my thinking that I wasn't ready to share—and this was a piece of news I'd just gotten from my girl

Tatyana. I was going to be a father. Didn't think my mother wanted to deal with a bombshell like that, on top of me leaving college early, so I let that one lie. Plus, Tatyana and her, they never really saw eye to eye—maybe because mama saw something in Tatyana I'd yet to see, or maybe because she wasn't ready to share her Baby Ray with another woman.

Anyway, it was a glorious piece of news, but it was a little too big to share. Still, I added everything up in my head and it all came out to the good: I was going to the league, I was going to be a poppa, I had my family together, and there'd be money coming in. All good things.

SEVEN

Draft Day

Underneath all that good stuff, there was sadness. There was struggle. The way I grew up, it doesn't leave you. No father. No steady paycheck. All these men, some of them abusive, in and out of our life. No clear path I was meant to follow. And that doesn't even include the tragedies that happened all around—the violence, the dysfunction, the desperation. The older we got, the kids I was running with, playing football with, the bigger the trouble—the bigger the *consequences*, anyway. By the time we got to high school, in and around Lakeland, we all knew too many people who'd fallen to drugs, to gang violence.

I carried those folks with me, *literally*. Had a black panther tattooed by my right shoulder, to remind me of my high school teammate Timmy Moore, murdered just after my junior season at Miami. Had another black panther on my chest, to remind me of a man named Raymond King, who was like a mentor to me when I was growing up. Shot dead by the police a couple years earlier—caught in the middle of a bank job gone wrong.

What all this meant, when I left for Miami, was that I didn't know what *normal* looked like. *Normal*, as in how other folks grew up or how you see on television or in the movies. I didn't know what it was to grow up without people getting shot left and right. I didn't know what it was to have a refrigerator full of food, to fill a car with a full tank of gas instead of ten dollars' worth, twenty dollars' worth, whatever. I didn't know what it was for a family to sit down at the same dinner table every night, all together. I didn't know what it was supposed to be like on Christmas morning. In our house, maybe there'd be one gift, and we'd all have to share it, but that's just how it was. We were okay with that. We were. But now it was looking like my life was about to pop in a whole new way.

Football, I knew. Wrestling, I knew. Faith, I knew. And faith helped me through it all. But what it was like to raise a family, under one roof, everybody tied in to the same goal, everybody *on the same page*? These things were all the way outside my experience, so what did I know, after all? I only knew there was no going back. Staying in school, maybe getting hurt, not getting my chance to make it in the league—none of that was an option for me. I couldn't let that happen. I mean, what did I have to fall back on but the game? My daddy being gone? My mama being broke? Me living in the projects and about to be a father?

That deck of cards I kept flipping, it sure wasn't stacked in my favor. And now, after *all that*, it started to feel like things were about to change. There was money coming, a baby coming, a whole new chapter about to start.

Coming from where I come from, going to the league was like going to the promised land. This was the NFL, the pot of gold at the end of the rainbow. This was hope and glory. If I played it right and smart, it meant that all those worries that had been dogging my family would just disappear. Just hearing my name called on draft day, it would change everything, so that was my thinking, spring of my junior year. It wouldn't bring back those folks I lost—no way, no how. It wouldn't put all those Christmas presents we never had back under the tree. But it would set things right, here on in. That was where I was coming from, and one of the great joys of being on the verge like that was the chance to experience it with my great friends—because, let's be honest, life was about to change for a lot of them, too. The people I was running with at that moment, the people I was playing football with right then, they had a shot, same as me.

It was *all good*, all around.

Probably my closest friend at Miami was Marlin Barnes— we roomed together freshman year, stayed joined at the hip from that point on. He played linebacker, same as me, and we were cut in a lot of the same ways. Junior year, we were living with Earl Little, one of our cornerbacks, and Trent Jones, one of our running backs. We were set up the same way as freshmen, as sophomores. Why mess with a good thing, right? We were a wild group—only, we weren't *reckless* wild, like most everyone else we knew. No, we were just plain wild. Had a lot of good times together. We stayed home a lot, played a lot of cards— only, we didn't play for money. We played for push-ups. The loser had to *work*.

One of the first things we bonded over, me and Marlin, was this idea that football was a game changer for us. Already, it had gotten us into college—something we had no reason to count on, no reason to even think about when we were growing up. Yeah, we were just freshmen, backing up the first string, but we knew our time would come. We knew the game could take us someplace special. So we made a promise to ourselves: whoever made it to the league first, the two of us would get a truck, take a ride to Black Beach Week in Daytona, and celebrate together.

This was the size of our dreams, back then—but, one thing you have to realize, to us, Black Beach Week was the pinnacle. Black Beach Week was just an all-out party. But who had time for that sort of thing when we were playing ball, trying to get by? This year, me declaring for the draft like that, it was time to make good on this promise. I'd already gotten myself a big old truck—a black Chevy Suburban, first real set of wheels I'd ever owned. I already had a big old pile of cash—an "advance" on my future earnings. So me and Marlin, we started making plans.

I said, "Red, I got the Suburban ready."

(Don't know why, but he was always "Red" to me—to a lot of the guys on the team.)

I said, "I got a couple cases of Heinekens and a pocketful of money. Let's go."

He said, "What time you want to head out in the morning?"

Now, it was just me, coming out that year. Red, he was planning to come back to Miami for his senior year. He still had some things he needed to do on the football field, wanted to get his degree. He had *plans*, man. So this road trip, it was on me. I was spending all that money I was about to earn—livin' large, before I had a *right* to it—which was how I got the truck.

We set a time, but Red said he had something he had to do over at his mama's house first, so he wanted me to pick him up over there. First, I went and gassed up the truck, did a couple other things to get ready. Next thing I knew, Red beeped me on my pager—yep, in those days, that's how we stayed in touch. I called him back and he said he was running late. Said there were still some things he had to do over at his mama's.

Wasn't anything for me to do but wait, so I told him I'd wait. It was just the two of us. We were only going to kick back, let off some steam. There'd be plenty of time for that.

This was all on a Friday morning—April 12, 1996. The plan was for us to stay the weekend, then head back home and get ready for draft week. There was a lot going on, there'd *been* a lot going on, but we had it all figured out.

After another while, there was another page from Red. This time he said, "You go ahead without me, man. I don't want to hold you up."

I said, "Hold me up? What's the matter with you, Red? I

don't even need to go to Beach Week. This is just something we always talked about. If there's a problem, we can find something else to do, maybe go another time."

He said, "No, man. I really want you to go. For both of us, I want you to go. We been talking about it for so long. It's important."

I said, "Bro, you sure?"

He said, "You always had this plan. You should go."

He was right, you know. I *did* always have this plan. It *meant* something. So I went—headed off, anyway. About an hour or two later, I was riding north on I-95, my beeper went off again. It was Red—couldn't think why he'd be calling. I pulled over first chance and called him back. Turned out he was looking for this tight white shirt I used to wear, wanted to borrow it for a party he was planning to go to later that night. No big thing.

I said, "Party? What party?" This was the first I was hearing about a party.

He said, "Louis Oliver, he's having a party at the beach. I'm thinking of going through."

Louis Oliver was a safety for the Miami Dolphins, went to school at the University of Florida. We had some friends in common, so it sounded like a good time. But me and Red, we had a rule. We never went out in Miami without each other. Why? Because there was trouble round every corner, man. Freshman year and sophomore year we'd had some problems. Nothing major—just knucklehead problems. Dudes kicking up some dust, talking trash. Dudes jealous of how the girls would all seem to line up for us—because, can't lie, we had it going on. Oh my goodness. We were fit as hell, big men on campus, all of that. Going out to the clubs, we always had each other's backs. A private party like this—that was another deal, but we all knew how these private parties went down. You'd start out one place and end up another, probably at a club.

I said, "Louis Oliver, for real? If you're going to that party then I'm turning around. You know how it is."

He said, "I know how it is, Ray. And how it is, you should go to Daytona."

I said, "I'm coming back. I'm going to the party with you."

He said, "Up to you, man."

So I got off at the next exit and doubled back to Miami—but then, about an hour later, Red paged me again. It was crazy, him calling and calling like that. Something was up, but he wasn't saying. All he said this time was, "Bro, I ain't gonna make it. Why don't you turn back around and hit Beach Week?"

By this time, I was almost back to Miami, but Red was pretty clear he wasn't up for a party, so I just figured I'd turn around, start all over again for Daytona. I was like a yo-yo, man. Up and down I-95.

Finally, I made it to Daytona. I had my two cases of Heinekens and a couple thousand dollars in crisp hundreds in my glove compartment. I was good to go, ready to kick back. Remember, there was all this good stuff about to happen. Draft day was coming. I'd been working out, talking to a couple teams. So there was a whole lot to celebrate. Trouble was, I didn't really know anybody at Black Beach Week. Oh, there were folks I knew to say hello, but none of my good friends were there, so I sat in my fine new truck as the sun was setting that first night, sipping my beer, checking out the scene, thinking things through. After a while, I got out of the car, started walking around, and sure enough there were some familiar faces up and down the beach. Folks from Lakeland, from Miami. All over. I wasn't really feeling it, was thinking about turning around and heading back to Miami that night, but I'd been drinking a little and it was a six-hour drive, so I knew this wasn't a good idea.

It ended up, I ran into one of my homeboys, he said I could just chill in his room, so that's what I did—only, I *still* wasn't feeling it. There were these cute girls hanging around with our group, everybody was messing around, but I was kind of hanging back, you know. My head was someplace else. One of the girls finally said to me, "Baby, what's wrong?"

I said, "I honestly don't know. Something's not right with me."

Midnight came, and I was still on the outside looking in. One o'clock passed, then two o'clock. Same thing. By three o'clock, everybody had kind of paired off or fallen asleep, and I was just sitting by myself, sipping my Heinekens, wondering why I was in such a funk. This was supposed to be the time of my life, right? I was about to turn twenty. I was about to get drafted. I had my family all set up. We were in a good place, finally. There was money coming my way, a baby coming my way. But I couldn't loosen up for trying.

Then my phone started ringing and my first thought was, *Dang, Red! It's five o'clock in the morning!*

But it wasn't Red. No, it was Randy Shannon.

I called him back—said, "Randy, what you doing up at this hour?"

He said, "It's Red. He's no longer with us."

I said, "Red get himself kicked off the team? What the hell did my boy do?"

He said, "No, Ray. You're not hearing me. It's Marlin. They found him dead this morning in your apartment."

I didn't think I'd heard Randy straight, but of course I knew I had. Deep down, I knew. Oh man, I knew. Whatever happened, it was tied in to the funk I'd been in all night long. It's like my head wasn't on straight for a reason.

Still, I fought the truth. I said, "Wait a minute, Randy. Hold on. My roommate Marlin? My boy? This is what you tellin' me?"

He said, "This is what I'm telling you, Ray. I'm so sorry."

I couldn't think—couldn't think what to *say* or what to *do*. But also, couldn't *think*.

I stormed out of that hotel room, busted a hole in the wall on my way out, headed straight for my truck—I'm telling you, I lost it. Like, completely lost it. Somehow, I had the presence of mind to pull into a gas station on my way out of town. I hadn't been drinking all that much, but this call from Randy, it sobered me up, straightaway. I was clear, wide-eyed, awake as hell, and full-on *grieving*. My phone, it kept ringing. My beeper, it kept going off. But I wasn't picking up. I just drove. Only time I reached for my phone was to call Red. It made no sense, but I kept dialing his number.

That whole ride back to Miami, it passed in a blur. I remember getting on the highway, setting up in the slow lane, putting the car on cruise control. Turned the radio all the way up. And then I cried and cried.

It's been twenty years, and I still can't think back on that day without tearing up. But I'm pushing myself here because I want the world to know we lost a good man that day, in a senseless way. I want the world to know the tug and pull that finds you when good things are about to happen—because when good things are about to happen, the bad things can't be too far off. Joy and sorrow. They're two halves of the same whole. If you hope to celebrate, you had better expect to grieve. I'm sorry, but you can't have one without the other. You just can't. Because that's not living.

Like I said, I didn't know what *normal* looked like. I'd lost too many people close to me. And other people close to me, I never even had them to lose.

Wasn't just Red we lost that day—no, it was Timwanika Lumpkins, too, his good friend since just about forever. Me and T spent a lot of time together. She was a special spirit, a special person. We dated for a while—but T and Red, they weren't together like that. In fact, Red had just started seeing this other girl, Lisa, and things were starting to get serious. But T had a history, she did, and it was that history that came into play that Friday night. She'd had a baby by this man named Labrant Dennis, and he was out looking for her. Don't know why he was looking for T, what set that in motion, but there he was, and how it shook out was he beat them both to death with the butt end of a twelve-gauge shotgun. The report said Labrant Dennis struck Red twenty-two times, and then he turned and did T the same way.

It was Earl Little who found them. He came back to the apartment, late, noticed his tires had been slashed, raced upstairs to get his keys and see what the deal was, but when he tried to open the door it wouldn't go. He pushed it open a crack and saw Red laying there, all covered in blood. Then he saw T.

For the longest time, me and Earl, we tried to figure out what went down. The police kept saying there was only one man involved, that Labrant Dennis was acting alone, but this made no sense to us. If you knew Red, you knew he didn't back down. He was a big dude. The only thing that would have stopped him was a gun—but if it was just that one bad guy, acting alone, Red would have taken his chances. A punk like that puts a gun on you, that time of night, that kind of spot, only way it ends is you getting killed. Ain't no talking. Might as well take your chances. So there had to be someone else in that apartment. *Had* to be.

But we'll never know.

I was tore up, man. Beside myself. Outside myself. I couldn't get my head around what happened. So what did I do? I left. Not right away, but I don't remember how we passed those terrible hours on Saturday. Talking to Red's family. Talking to the police. Talking to my roommates, my teammates. It was another blur. But then at some point I was back in the truck, headed to Lakeland. Don't know why. To this day, I can't think what I was looking for back home, can't remember what I did while I was there. Only thing I know was I shut off my phone, shut off my beeper.

I checked out, man.

Meanwhile, there was the draft, peeking out of this dark cloud. All these years, it was something to look forward to, but now that it was here it didn't much matter. Red, he would have wanted me to get into it like we'd always talked about, but my heart was just shattered. It felt to me like maybe I was cheating on Red's memory, looking for something to celebrate so soon after he'd been killed—even though, I knew, Red would have told me I'd worked too hard *not* to celebrate.

So I went through the motions. All those weeks, leading up to Black Beach Week, there was a lot of talk. Teams calling, folks wanting to know about my character, my conditioning. I didn't go to the scouting combine, didn't think I had anything to prove in that kind of setting, but I did work out for a couple teams. I went to the weigh-ins, all these little procedures they had set up.

A lot of the talk had to do with my size, because by NFL standards I guess I was a little short, a little light. But that was the knock on me when I started at Miami, right? Made no difference in how I played, but it made a difference to these experts, these coaches. I went to one of those meat-market weigh-ins, and Bill Cowher walked by—the head coach of the Pittsburgh Steelers. He stood in front of me as I took off my shirt and stepped on the scale—said, "Wow." Meaning, you know, that I was cut, ripped, whatever . . .

Then I stepped up to where they measure your height, and the person calling out the measurements said, "Six foot w-w-w . . ." You know, like they were caught between saying six foot even and six foot one.

Coach Cowher, he looked on and kinda smiled. He caught my eye and said, "That's a little short."

So I smiled back and said, "Ain't nothing tall ever won no championship."

He said, "What you mean?"

I said, "We'll see, Coach. We'll see."

He started to walk off, but he turned back and said, "I'll remember you, Ray Lewis."

At the U, they did this thing where all these former Hurricanes would come back and watch you work out. It was like an alumni ritual, and the older players would take the time to encourage you, tell you how things would go. And then, some of the scouts around the league, they'd come by to check you out—like our own little combine.

In those weeks leading up to the draft, before we lost Red and T, I was going back and forth, talking to all these folks—folks from Green Bay, most of all. The Packers had the twenty-seventh pick, and they were looking at me, hard.

There was a lot of talk about my speed. I ran the forty so many times, it felt like a hundred miles of auditions. Back of my head, I had to clock a 4.5 or better to cut down all that talk about my size. Told myself a 4.5 would put me solidly in the first round. But each time out, I was off by just a little bit: 4.55, 4.52, 4.61 . . .

I was determined to beat the number, so every time a scout asked me to run, I took off. The guy working me out from Green Bay, he said, "Man, you're the only one ain't scared to run."

I said, "Because it don't matter."

For him, I finally got my time: 4.45.

But that was when I was riding high, headed off to Daytona with my boy Red, headed off to the league, knowing I was a lock for the first round. That was when I was running in the light.

It worked out that the day of the draft was the day of Red's funeral. The whole time we were burying Red, I don't think I took my sunglasses off, not once. There were too many tears, man. Just too many tears.

All through that day, I kept those glasses on, even when I got to this little suite my agent had set up for me at Dolphin Stadium, which back then was known as Joe Robbie Stadium. Wasn't that I was embarrassed to be crying—because I had every reason to be crying. No, it's just that I didn't want to lock eyes with anyone. You make eye contact, then that person has to say something about Marlin, something about T, and I didn't want to go through all of that, just then. I wanted to keep what I was feeling to myself—to keep what I was feeling to a *minimum*. That's the only way I could get through this low, low time, to shut those feelings all the way down—kept telling myself there'd be plenty of time for *feelings* later.

So I sat there through that first round, all these people coming through the suite, hearing all these names called out ahead of me.

Keyshawn Johnson, wide receiver out of USC, to the New York Jets.

Kevin Hardy, linebacker out of Illinois, to Jacksonville.

Simeon Rice, lineman out of Illinois, to Arizona.

Jonathan Ogden, offensive tackle out of UCLA, to Baltimore.

That was a big draft for wide receivers, the way it played

out. But I wasn't counting wide receivers. No, I was counting linemen and linebackers, and there were six of them taken off the board by the time we got to the twentieth pick, which belonged to the Miami Dolphins—six guys who went ahead of me because of size. (And just so you know, not one of them lasted in the league longer than seven years.) Each name was like a dagger, but something told me I was destined to fall to this twentieth spot. I mean, I was sitting right there in their stadium. I'd played my college ball right under their noses. The Miami fans, they loved the way I played. I was a Florida boy, through and through. So I told myself it was all good, all those defenders going ahead of me, because it set me up.

But then, the Dolphins drafted Daryl Gardener, a defensive tackle out of Baylor. Let me tell you, the boos that came on the back of that call were like sweet music to my ears. These Miami fans, they had no interest in Daryl Gardener. Jimmy Johnson, he was the Dolphins' new coach, and he had that whole Miami connection going on. It made no sense, and a lot of folks thought that pick should have been me. They were counting on it, and at just that moment, if I was being completely honest, I was counting on it, too.

But that's just how it goes on draft day. There's no time to sit and fuss, because those picks just keep coming. Every couple minutes, there's some twist and turn, and all around me people were speculating, wondering where I'd end up. The first round was about to run out on us, but I wasn't worried. I knew if I fell to the Packers, I'd be going to Green Bay—they'd already told me I was their man, so that was as far as I would fall.

After that Miami pick it went:

Pete Kendall, offensive tackle out of Boston College, to Seattle.

Marcus Jones, defensive end out of UNC, to Tampa Bay.

Jeff Hartings, guard out of Penn State, to Detroit.

Eric Moulds, wide receiver out of Mississippi State, to Buffalo.

Philadelphia had the twenty-fifth pick, and for a beat or two we all thought they would call my name, but they went to the other side of the ball and grabbed Jermane Mayberry, an offensive lineman out of Texas A&M–Kingsville. So at this point we all thought Baltimore would pass me up and I'd wind up playing for the Packers.

Matter of fact, we had the television on in the suite, and we were listening to Mel Kiper do his analysis, and he was talking about all these holes they needed to fill up in Baltimore. They'd already taken Jonathan Ogden with the fourth pick, so the feeling was they'd go with a skills position–type player, someone to maybe get the fans in Baltimore excited about their new team. Remember, this was the year the Modell family moved the Cleveland Browns franchise to Baltimore, and the city had been hungry for a team since the Baltimore Colts left town for Indianapolis in 1983.

Just then, the phone rang in our suite. It was Ozzie Newsome, director of football operations for the Baltimore Ravens. He said, "Is this Ray Lewis?"

I said, "Yes, sir. What's going on, Mr. Newsome?"

He said, "Son, your name is about to be called."

I said, "By who?"

He said, "Baltimore."

I said, "Okay, I know, Baltimore. But Baltimore *who?*"

A lot of folks forget, but when Mr. Modell announced he'd be moving the Cleveland Browns to Baltimore, the plan was for the team to be known as the Baltimore Browns. That's what was in all the papers, all over ESPN. But then there was all this legal nonsense I didn't really pay attention to—it ended up the team name, the team colors, all the team records would stay in Cleveland and a new ownership group would come in. I wasn't really paying attention, because the fight had nothing to do with me. And now that it *did*, I honestly didn't know what this team was called.

To be honest, my head was a mess to begin with, with everything else that had gone down. Burying my best friend. Talking to his family, to the police, to our teammates. In some ways, it was like the draft was beside the point. But then I'd catch myself thinking about what this moment would be like with Red at my side, told myself he *was* at my side, still. Told myself Red would have wanted me to celebrate this moment, maybe even find a way to laugh about it—me going to the league to play for this brand-new team that didn't even have a logo, a uniform.

The Ravens name wasn't announced until a couple weeks before the draft—and it would be *another* couple weeks before the team had its colors and a uniform design. So this was just another example of me not knowing what *normal* looked like. *Normally*, on draft day, you get selected, you put on your team's hat, maybe a jersey, and you pose for a bunch of pictures, but that's not how it happened.

Normally, on draft day, you don't run from burying your best friend up the road to a quiet little draft party in a stadium suite, just to hear your name called by a team that doesn't even have a jersey, a logo, a name that anyone outside their own front office can remember. And it's not like I really cared, with everything else going on—felt to me like this was maybe appropriate. This was maybe Red's way of telling me to hold on just a minute, make sure this moment didn't get lost.

But it was something to notice—something to laugh about. Ozzie and me, we laugh about it to this day, because this was how that phone call went down—me saying, "Baltimore *who*?"

As moments go, this one was bittersweet—but it was a new day.

EIGHT

Ride That Train

The Ravens front office finally got the team colors and logo all set, but my uniform didn't look right. Something didn't fit. I was used to wearing 52, ever since Randy Shannon pinned it on me at Miami, but here they gave me 53. Pepper Johnson was wearing my number—he'd been wearing it all the way back to his days at Ohio State. He was also slotted in as the starting middle linebacker. I could see that, I guess. Pepper had won a couple Super Bowls with the Giants, played in a couple Pro Bowls. He'd been a veteran presence on the Cleveland Browns, so of course he came to Baltimore and was expected to fill that same spot.

I was just a rookie, didn't think it was my place to say anything, so I kept quiet. For a time. First couple practices, I ran with the second unit, made my presence known with my game instead of my mouth. And I must've made some noise, because, middle of training camp, our defensive coordinator, Marvin Lewis, came up to talk to me. He said, "Ray, we like how you get to the ball. We're thinking of starting you at weak-side linebacker. I know you're used to playing in the middle, but we've got Pepper."

He said it like he was expecting me to be excited he was putting me on the starting unit, but I heard it another way. I heard it like I was back in high school, sitting in Chuck Amato's office on my recruiting visit to Florida State, him telling me I'd have to play behind Derrick Brooks for two years.

I said, "I can't play no weak-side linebacker."

We talked about it some. I wasn't trying to be difficult, but I wanted Marvin to get my thinking. A lot of guys, to go from middle linebacker to weak-side linebacker, it might have been an easy transition. You go from seeing the whole field, covering every which way, to just focusing on one side, with a lot less ground to cover. For some players it might be no big thing, but it went against my strength, against my nature. The weak-side linebacker really had just one job—to get to the ball, but a great middle linebacker can cut an offense in half, just by dominating the line of scrimmage, just by seeing the play before it takes shape. In the middle, you have to react off the guys in front of you, the guys to either side. You have to quarterback the defense, which worked for me because I was like a dictator on the field. It fit with my personality.

He said, "You can play middle, you can play weak side. All you need to do is dial it down."

I said, "No disrespect, Mr. Lewis, but I'm not cut that way. You put me out there, weak side, I'll just run over everybody. I'm not the *less involved* guy. I can't *dial it down*. That's just not me."

He heard me out, but I wasn't done—figured I'd take the opportunity to press him on my number, long as we were talking. I mean, your number is your identity, man. It's how you're known. And here I'd taken Randy Shannon's good advice and found this meaningful number and made it my own. Wasn't about to let it go without a fight. So I said, "One more thing, fifty-two is my number. The shirt you gave me, it says fifty-three. The dude wearing that, I look in the mirror, I don't recognize him."

Marvin Lewis looked at me and tried not to smile—don't think he'd ever heard a rookie talk in such a brash way. But

I didn't know any other way to be. I was all about what was mine, based on what I knew I could do. And I wasn't shy about putting it out there, so he flashed me this look that said, *Okay, well I guess we'll see about all this, youngster. We'll see.*

Next day—the *very* next day!—I got to training camp and there was a 52 jersey hanging in my locker with my name on it.

Whatever I was expecting to come out of the talk with Marvin Lewis, I wasn't expecting *that*. Not right away.

There was no one around to ask about it, so I just put on that jersey, thought maybe Marvin Lewis had gone to Pepper Johnson and asked if he'd give up his number for this brash kid out of Miami. Didn't know what else to think. So I went out to the field for our walk-through—on that team, we always did a walk-through before we started running drills. But the whole team was lined up, first-string defense, and there was no middle linebacker. I looked this way and that, couldn't see Pepper Johnson.

Didn't occur to me that I had anything to do with Pepper not being here—the jersey, yeah, but not his absence. Never in a million years would I have thought the one followed from the other. Then, after a couple beats, Marvin Lewis came striding over to me—said, "This is your team now."

Turned out, Marvin went to talk to our head coach, Ted Marchibroda, told him he liked what he was seeing out of me in practice, hearing out of me on the sidelines. Turned out, too, that the coaching staff was looking to make some changes, maybe move the team away from how things were in Cleveland, the culture of losing they had on that team, so they went and gave Pepper Johnson his release. Wasn't a knock on Pepper. The dude could still play—he'd led the team in tackles the year before, would go on to play another couple years in the league. But that Cleveland Browns team that packed up and moved here to Baltimore was Bill Belichick's team, and this brand-new

Ravens team was Ted Marchibroda's team, and this was one way to shake things up.

Still, I couldn't believe it, wasn't really following—said, "Pepper's gone? For real?"

Marvin Lewis said, "For real. So tell me, how good do you want to be?"

I said, "The best to ever play the game, sir."

He said, "Are you willing to work for that?"

I said, "All I know is how to work."

He said, "Well then, get to work. Already told you, this is your team now."

Can you imagine *that*? I hadn't played a *down* for this man, and already he'd seen something in me to treat me in this way. It was the most remarkable thing—about the last thing I was expecting—and it wasn't just Marvin Lewis. No, it was Coach Marchibroda and his whole coaching staff. It was Maxie Baughan, the linebacker coach, who'd seen something when the team was working me out before the draft. Maxie was an All-Pro linebacker in the 1960s, for the Eagles and Rams, so he could *play*—and he knew what it meant to roam the middle of that field on defense. He knew what it was to *hit*. He came up to me one day in training camp and said, "Ray, I've been around a long time. I've seen a lot of put-together athletes. Ain't seen too many *put together* like you."

I took it as a compliment—but it wasn't really. What Maxie meant, when I pressed him on it, was that I might have been ripped and in tremendous shape—and I was—but that it wasn't enough. He said, "You won't last three years in this league."

Just like that, he went from a compliment to a knock.

I said, "What are you talking about?"

He said, "You need to put some meat on your bones if you want to survive in this game, the type of pounding you're about to take."

There was a lot I had to learn—and the very first lesson was that I had a lot to learn. That's how it goes when you're young—you think you're invincible. You think the game will keep coming to you. But no, you reach a certain level, you have to take a different approach. This was the NFL. I was going from playing with teenagers to playing with grown men who knew their game. I was going from figuring out these other players, learning their tendencies, to studying coordinators, to playing against these big-time coaches. I was going from a game to a career, from a college campus to living on my own in a strange new city. Only time I'd ever been out of Florida was for road games back in school, so it was a big adjustment, me living on my own, learning my way around.

Some of the veteran players, they took a liking to me. I was blessed in this way. Bennie Thompson, a defensive back out of Grambling, came up to me one day in training camp and pretty much asked me the same thing as Marvin Lewis, and I gave him pretty much the same answer. He said, "You want to be great? Meet me in the gym every morning at six to work on the StairMaster."

I said, "Every morning?"

He said, "Every morning."

I said, "I'll be there." And I was—*every* morning. Bennie saw that I was serious about my game, about my conditioning, and soon some of the other guys started to notice. Stevon Moore, defensive back out of Mississippi. Anthony Pleasant, defensive lineman out of Tennessee State. Antonio Langham, defensive back out of Alabama. Eric Turner, a free safety out of UCLA— may he rest in peace. One by one, these guys took me in and helped me out and taught me what it was to be a professional athlete. Eric Turner used to stand over me in the weight room saying, "Lordy, Lordy, Lord, you gonna be rough." (*Rough*— that was like the highest compliment.) To a man, they took an interest in me, poured so much energy into me, and I tried to do the same thing after I'd been in the league a while, whenever a young player joined the team showing some promise, looking for guidance.

A lot of times, you're new to the league, coaches throw you out there on kickoffs, and that's how we lined up for the first couple practices. It's like a trial-by-fire situation—they put you on special teams, see what you can do. Bennie Thompson was the L5 and I was the L4, and I would just take off down that field and do my thing. But once they released Pepper, once it was clear to Coach Marchibroda and his staff that I was meant for this other role, they pulled me back. Marchibroda, he was like Dennis Erickson. The man did not want me on special teams. He didn't want me running up and down the field like that, hurling my body at full speed, scrambling for field position.

This is your team now.

For the first time, I didn't have to wait for the guy in front of me to go down with an injury. I'd earned this spot on my own. It didn't fall to me, the way it always had—and it felt good, like I'd finally arrived.

Things were coming together at home, too. For the first time in a long while, we were all living under one roof—my mother, my sisters, my brother, and me. I'd always been the man of the family, in a certain way, but as soon as the Ravens called my name on draft night, I was able to provide for my family, too, so I moved everyone up to Baltimore with me. I found a three-bedroom apartment in a nice part of Reistertown, just outside the city. My older sisters were able to finish high school there, and Kadaja and Keon were set up in school as well, so we were all set as a family. Mama didn't have to worry about money coming in, and my brother and sisters didn't have to worry about coming home to a tense environment, an uncertain environment, so it felt to me like this great weight had been lifted off my shoulders—a weight I'd been carrying since I was a small boy.

Caught myself thinking, *This is your home now.*

Only thing missing in this family picture was Tatyana and the child we now shared—our son, Junior. Somehow, I went from thinking we'd find a way to be together as a family, always and always, to shuttling everybody back and forth between Baltimore and Florida. See, her family was from the Orlando area, and that's where she wanted to be, and try as I might I could not convince her to give Baltimore a chance. To give *me* a chance. It broke my heart, to see our brand-new family broken up by this long distance before we even had a chance to make our way in the world together, but this was how Tatyana wanted to play it for now—and it felt to me like I had no choice but to let her call the shots. We weren't *separated*, necessarily, but at the same time we weren't *together*, so I tried to put all of that out of my mind and focus on football.

It worked out that I made some big noise the very first game of the season—so I was blessed in this way, too. We were at home against the Oakland Raiders. In those days, we played our home games at Memorial Stadium, which was where the Baltimore Colts used to play. Oh my goodness—it felt like that rickety old stadium would come tumbling down on us, all those Baltimore fans crammed in there for their first taste of professional football in over ten years. The place was a madhouse—64,000 people. I'd never played in front of that kind of crowd, and it wasn't just the *number* of folks that got me all stirred up, but the way they were screaming for this new team of theirs. This new team of *ours*. We hadn't done anything but show up to play for them, and they took us in, so it wasn't like it was just me and Jonathan Ogden and the other rookies making their debut—no, we were *all* making our debuts, on this grand old stage.

Those fans were *hungry*, man. And we fed off that hunger. Sadly, we weren't a very good team. I'm sorry, but we just weren't. But for this one day, at least, we were able to put up a decent fight against another team that also wasn't very good. They were up by a touchdown at the half, but we shut them down the rest of the way, tacked on a couple field goals in the third quarter to make things close. Then, fourth quarter, Earnest Byner ran it in from the 1-yard line to put us ahead. At this point, the scoreboard said we should go for a two-point conversion, push the lead back to a touchdown, but we couldn't get the ball back in the end zone, so with time running out we were sitting on a 19–14 lead.

This was where I first got to show Marvin Lewis and the rest of the Baltimore organization that they had backed the right guy. My first big play in a Ravens uniform. Folks *still* want to talk to me about this play. Oakland was driving, and the Raiders tight end, Rickey Dudley, came off the line on an up and out. He tried to do a little shake route on me, but I was able to read it early and stay on his hip. And as soon as the ball hit his hands, I reached out and made sure it hit my hands, too—it ended up I just kind of ripped the ball from Rickey's clutches and grabbed onto it for myself, right there in the end zone.

Let me tell you something—the roar that rose up from that hungry crowd was like nothing I ever experienced. I couldn't hear myself think. That place just erupted. First real football game in that stadium in just about forever, and this rookie out of Miami seals the deal by ripping the ball from the enemy at the last possible moment.

That interception, with time running out, it was the AFC Play of the Week—made all the highlight packages, sent a message around the league that we were in business. Told all those scouts and general managers who'd looked past me on draft day that maybe they should have paid a little less attention to how tall I stood and a little more attention to how big I played.

My Ravens teammates went a little crazy, too. We were a veteran team full of a lot of journeyman-type players and a lot of players who'd been *all that* in high school and college but hadn't won anything in a while. And in that one play there were all these waves of emotion up and down our sidelines, because this brand-new team in this brand-new city meant a fresh start. Fans, players, coaches—it was a new day for all of us. A brand-new day. And we were all caught up in it.

Off of that one play, Bennie Thompson hung a nickname on me. He started calling me UPS. Why? Because I *always* delivered. Because I was *always* on time. Before long, every time I saw Bennie he'd say, "UPS! What you got for me today?"

Down in that end zone, the game in my hands, Memorial Stadium about to burst, a T-shirt with a picture of my buddy Red pressed close to my chest beneath the 52 on my new Baltimore Ravens jersey—it felt to me like I'd arrived. All those years, all those drills, all those push-ups and sit-ups, all those hours in the gym, all that time studying film, learning the game from every possible angle all led me to this first big spot of my professional career. So what did I do? I *celebrated*, man. I'd always been big into celebrating these big-time plays, and here it just came pouring out of me. Didn't even have to think about it. Just happened. There was a song out at the time—"C'mon 'n Ride It," by the Quad City DJs. It was playing all over, and it had this great *Woo-woo! Choo-choo!* lyric, so I just started chucking my fist like I was pulling on a big old train whistle.

C'mon ride this train!
Hey ride it!
Woo woo!

And the crowd was all the way into it. *Everybody* was feelin' it. The stadium was *thumping*, man. We were bringing light to the city. We were all riding the train, excited to see where it would take us.

That first year, the train didn't go very far. We only won three more games the rest of the way, but each week the culture of that Ravens team moved a little further from what it had been in Cleveland, a little closer to where we needed to be here in Baltimore.

Week Two, we got into it. We went to Pittsburgh to play the Steelers, and for the first time I got what it meant to make your mark as a team. Over the years, we would have a great rivalry, Steelers versus Ravens, but it wasn't a rivalry yet. No, it was just a team with all this history going up against this team with no history at all. But it gave us a *taste*, man. It was a motivating thing, an inspiring thing, to walk into Three Rivers Stadium and feel all that history. It was in the air, all around. We were inside the Steel Curtain, and that building just reeked of defense. That's how it goes in the league, I was learning. You develop a reputation as a team, you play a certain way, and it stays with you—and here it was on us to figure out how we'd be known. And the thing of it is, that first year, we had one of the top offenses in the league—Vinny Testaverde passed for over 4,000 yards. Our defense wasn't much. In fact, our defense was pretty terrible. But ask someone to tell you what the Baltimore Ravens stood for back then—what the Ravens continue to stand for—and they'll tell you it's defense. But that didn't happen for us that first year.

No, that first year it was all about these grudge matches taking shape, about making an impression. For me, it was staring down Jerome Bettis two times a year in that Steeler backfield. Eddie George two times a year at Houston. The next season, it'd be Corey Dillon two times a year at Cincinnati. That AFC

Central division, it was fierce, hard-nosed football, all the way. When I was a kid, starting to watch football, they called it the Black and Blue division, and that description still applied. We were a division of *bruisers*—we kept taking turns putting a hurt on each other, but now it was on us to start dishing out some of that hurt. It was on *me*. So we got all these rivalries going, and the seeds of those rivalries were laid down that first year. It got to where you'd go in to one of those divisional games and you'd be thinking, *I'm gonna knock somebody out today*. That was the mentality, and you couldn't see it on the scoreboard just yet. You couldn't see it on the stat sheet. But we were making strides, moving toward something, and looking back I think it came out of that first draft, before the Ravens had their colors. We would make our mark in the trenches—Jonathan Ogden on one side of the ball, me on the other. A lot of teams, that situation, they might have looked to build around a quarterback, a running back, a headline-type player, all flash and flair. But Art Modell, Ozzie Newsome and them, they went another way. They went gritty. They went down and dirty. And it just worked out that Jonathan wasn't a *voice* the way I was a voice. He was a cornerstone, a future Hall of Famer, a game changer, but it wasn't his style to play to the crowd, to rally his teammates. Me, I was primed for that role, and it just kind of fell to me as that first season played on. It started in training camp, and it built from there, and after that opening-day interception in the end zone, me pulling on that big old train whistle, it got built up even further.

I got along great with Ted Marchibroda, but my relationship with that coaching staff was really with Marvin Lewis. He took to me those first couple years in Baltimore, called on me away from the field to talk about the team. He even had me coming to his office every morning to talk through what we needed to be doing on defense, to look at some of the personnel moves he was considering, because he was determined to brand our team as a defensive force and he saw me as the dude who could help him do it. Don't know why, but he trusted my take, wanted to hear from me how things were going in those trenches.

So that whole first year, you couldn't really call it a disappointment. Yeah, we only won four games. But we lit up the crowd. We moved the chains a little bit on how we wanted to be known around the league—we even beat up on the Steelers, second to last home game of the season, so we were putting it out there that we meant to be a force. We weren't there yet, but we were on our way. Slowly, the culture of the team started to change, and Marvin Lewis kept coming to me with all these free agents he wanted to add—guys he was just plucking off the scrap heap. He talked to me about guys he was looking at in the draft. More and more, folks around the league were taking us seriously—taking *me* seriously. I even got myself an invitation to the Pro Bowl, my second year in the league, and this was a real initiation. In the bar at the Ihilani hotel in Hawaii, where everybody stayed, that's where you made your bones. That first year, I remember sitting on the fringes, a little bit off to the side. I was like a kid being let into the grown-up party, and I was careful not to overstep, and at one point, me sitting there, Derrick Thomas—one of the greatest pass rushers to ever play the game—called over to me.

He caught my eye—said, "Home Team, don't you bring your young butt over here. You ain't earned your stripes."

Home Team—we were both from Florida, so we were connected, but even though we came from the same place, Derrick was telling me I hadn't earned my way to his side of the room. He was just razzing me, but there was a truth to what he was saying. I'd gotten my foot in the door, but I wasn't ready to step all the way inside.

The Pro Bowl, that's where we took our medicine. Forget the

game. It was in the bar of the hotel, where we sat at the feet of these great legends and soaked in what it meant to play at the highest level, what it meant to be great—not just for this one season, but for all time. And it took a couple years for me to feel like I belonged. On the field, back in Baltimore, that was my turf—very quickly, I *owned* that team. But here in Hawaii, among these giants, I was in awe, intimidated, still feeling my way. And yet somehow, that first trip to Hawaii, I started to feel a little more at home among this group, a little more like myself, to where I finally went up to Junior Seau—may he rest in peace as well—and started to give as good as I was getting. I said, "I'm coming for you, Fifty-Five. You know I'm coming. I ain't coming to no more Pro Bowls as your alternate."

Running up to that first Pro Bowl, me and Jonathan got a lot of play in the Baltimore papers, the two of us representing our new-look Ravens. Right around then I started to see the effect around town, away from the stadium. I had a routine in those days where I'd stop in for lunch at this great crab place on the water by the Inner Harbor—by myself, usually. They had this dish they used to make, a nice piece of grilled fish, a lump of crabmeat on the top, and I thought it was just the greatest meal in the world. I would have eaten it every day if I could, and I used to love sitting there, on my way to the stadium, on my way back home, and treat myself in this way. For the first time in my life, I could sit down at a nice restaurant, order up a nice plate of food, and not worry what it cost.

So there I was, sitting down for an early lunch, and the place was mostly empty when I sat down. But then, when I got up to leave, there was this mad crush of people off in the corner— kids mostly, pressing into the doorway. I'd never seen so many people crammed into such a tight space, couldn't think what was going on. What happened was, word had gotten out that I was inside, and this little crowd had started to form. And then it got a little bigger, and a little bigger, and finally there was this mass of people—hundreds, probably. I looked through the window of the restaurant and could see the crowd was for me, so before I stepped outside I called my mama.

I said, "Mom, you'll never believe what's going on out here."

She said, "What's going on, Junior?"

I said, "All these people. I'm just here having lunch. And outside, there's a whole crowd gathered to see me."

She said, "Well, what do you know . . ." Her voice trailing off, like she was giving this some thought, what it might mean.

And just then, I couldn't know what it might mean, couldn't know I'd never again be able to walk through the streets of Baltimore without drawing a crowd, without folks turning their heads. All of that, it didn't happen overnight. It had been a slow build, over those first couple seasons. But this was the first time I realized that my world was forever changed.

With my father, Elbert Ray Jackson, and my mom, Sunseria Smith, at the Ravens' Ring of Honor induction on September 22, 2013. It took quite a journey to get to this moment. (*Michael Greene*)

One of my first team photos, with the Lakeland Patriots. That's me, wearing number 40, kneeling at the far left.

A head shot from my sophomore year at Kathleen High School. Guess you could see the fire in my eyes even then.

Here I am running back a turnover in a 1993 game against Virginia Tech at the Orange Bowl in Miami—my freshman season. I'd come into the game for Robert Bass, who went down with a knee injury, and I found a way to show that I belonged on that field. (*Photo by Collegiate Images, LLC/WireImage*)

A shot of me and all my Hurricane brothers on D: (*from left to right*) Corwin Francis, C. J. Richardson, Rohan Marley, Warren Sapp, Ray, and Pat Riley. (*Bill Frakes*/Sports Illustrated/*Getty Images*)

With my heroes, at a practice during the 2000 season: (*from left to right*) Jim Brown, Joe Frazier, Spike Lee, and Hank Aaron. (*Baltimore Ravens/Phil Hoffmann*)

On Draft Day, getting a hug from my grandmother Elease McKinney while talking with my lifelong team, the Baltimore Ravens. *(Associated Press)*

In Tampa, January 28, 2001, savoring the Super Bowl XXXV victory over the New York Giants and being named the game's MVP. *(Getty Images)*

My comeback dance on January 6, 2013, to open the Ravens' Wild Card game versus the Colts. *(Baltimore Ravens/Shawn Hubbard)*

Sacking Tom Brady during the Ravens' 2012 playoff win versus the Patriots. (*Baltimore Ravens/ Shawn Hubbard*)

At the Superdome in New Orleans, February 3, 2013. Holding up the Vince Lombardi trophy after we won Super Bowl XLVII over the San Francisco 49ers in my last game. (*Baltimore Ravens/ Shawn Hubbard*)

With my children at Diaymon's sweet sixteen: (*from left to right*) Diaymon, Rayshad, Rayvyn, and Rahsaan. (*Judith A. Dixon, RDJ Photography*)

Surrounded by my kids right before the Cowboys game in October 2012 where I got injured: in the front row (*from left to right*) are Junior, Rahsaan, Ralin, and Diaymon, and in the back next to me is Grady Jarrett, who I'm proud to say calls me uncle. (*Baltimore Ravens/Phil Hoffmann*)

At my final home game with my brother and sisters (*from left to right*) Keon, Laquesha, Lakeisha, my mom, and Kadaja. (*Michael Greene*)

A nice moment at the Ravens' Ring of Honor day with Dad and my daughter Kaitlin. (*Michael Greene*)

At my fortieth birthday party, May 15, 2015.

The amazing day when the Ravens unveiled a statue of me outside the stadium, September 4, 2014. (*Baltimore Ravens/Shawn Hubbard*)

NINE

Atlanta

Four seasons in, my career was going good. Every year, we inched a little closer to competitive. First year, 4–12. Second year, 6–9–1. Third year, 6–10. Fourth year, 8–8. Led the team in tackles every year. Led the *league* in tackles twice, put it out there that the Baltimore Ravens defense was a force. Those first few years, we might not beat you on the scoreboard, but we would *beat you down* on the field.

The word they use in football to describe an 8–8 team is *respectable*. I always hated that word—left me thinking you've been wracking your brain to come up with something nice to say and this was about the best you could do. So on the one hand it was a good thing, to have fought our way back to *respectability*, but on the other hand it was a knock, because it told us how far we still needed to go—in people's minds, at least. End of the day, we were average, middle of the pack. We were *nowhere*. But we told ourselves nowhere was okay, long as we were headed somewhere. As long as we were *rising*. And we were. As a team, we were on the move—just look at how things were about to pop for us that next season.

Me, I was headed out to Hawaii for my third-straight Pro Bowl, but the plan was to fly from Atlanta, right after Super Bowl XXXIV—which was being played there in the Georgia Dome. Tough to keep track of all those Roman numerals, but that was the year the St. Louis Rams beat the Tennessee Titans 23–16, time running out as Kevin Dyson was tackled just a couple inches short of the goal line. Folks *remember* that Super Bowl, man—but that final drive was just one reason they remember it.

What a lot of folks *don't* remember about that game was that there was a major snowstorm up and down the East Coast. That whole week—January 25, 2000—flights were being canceled every which way. The day I was supposed to leave Baltimore, it was bad upon bad. You couldn't get out of that airport for trying. I had a good mind to cancel my trip, to just sit tight, but I had a week's worth of commitments lined up—an "NFL Experience" event, autograph signings and all these different appearances I had to make. I hated to cancel, because I needed the extra money, and because I'd given my word. Folks were counting on me to show. All these wheels were in motion.

I remember talking on the phone to my mother as I was scrambling to leave Baltimore, find another flight. She said, "Don't go to Atlanta, Junior." Three times, she called to tell me to stay put, ride out the storm, head out to Hawaii from Baltimore after the game. It's like she had a premonition, and she said it clearly: "Junior, it's crazy out there. You don't need to be going nowhere."

No, I guess I didn't.

But I'd made all these commitments, set my mind to it. Trouble was, my mind couldn't put my flight back up on the board, so I called my driver at the time, Dwayne, asked him to check on the roads. The driving was tough, a mess of snow and ice, but he put some chains on the tires of his black Lincoln Navigator and we were good to go. We stopped in North Carolina to pick up my boy Kwame King—just a little detour, because his flight had been canceled, too.

The weather was nasty the whole way to Georgia. Wet,

cold. Just *nasty*. But we made it there, eventually. Got there in time to settle in at the hotel before my first event, so I went up to my room and started in on my outfits. One thing you should know about me: when I travel I have my little routines. For Super Bowl week and those different events I needed about ten different outfits. I'm sorry, but this is one of my quirks. I like to look *good*. I had a daytime outfit, a nighttime outfit. I had a formal outfit, a casual outfit. I had something to wear for the day of the game, something to wear to the clubs, something to wear on the flight to Hawaii. I've been told I'm obsessive about this, and I guess I am. The way I do it is I set everything out beforehand and as the week goes on, every couple days, I pile up all the outfits I already wore and ship them back home. Who wants to think about all this with everything else going on? Who wants to deal with all that mess? Who wants the hassle of carrying all that stuff around if you don't have to? So this was the system I'd worked out—I still do it everywhere I go.

I called my mama, told her I'd made it to Atlanta safely, laid out all my clothes, headed to my first event—left the inside of my room looking like a trunk show, all these clothes set out *just so*. Came back, stepped into another outfit, went out to the next event. The long drive had set me back a bit, but now I was good. I was into my routine, doing my thing, and as the week wore on the city began to fill. That whole Super Bowl vibe, the circus atmosphere, it started to take over, and it was a good time for me to be in the middle of all that. A lot of years, your season ends in a disappointing way, you don't make the playoffs, you lose a first-round game, you go to all these Super Bowl events and you're torn. You feel like it should be your team out there, playing for the championship. But this year didn't feel that way to me, because we hadn't *earned* the right to be disappointed. Not yet. We'd just had a good year. We were on the rise. Things were coming together for us, so this time in Atlanta was a chance for me to look ahead, check in with my friends around the league, reflect. Good things, all.

And it was a chance to be with my kids. My two oldest sons were meeting me in Atlanta with their mother, and then traveling with me out to Hawaii for the Pro Bowl, where my mother was fixing to meet us, so this was another good thing—a *great* good thing.

Let me tell you, that Super Bowl week was shaping up to be a sweet little exclamation point, and it came around at just the right time. There were good things to celebrate, good things to come—at least, that's what I thought.

Day of the big game, I went to a party at my boy Marty Carter's house. Marty played for the Atlanta Falcons at the time. Wasn't one of those *off the chain* parties, where nobody pays attention to the game. No, Marty did it up just right. The catering, just right. The dancing, just right. The people, just right—a nice mix of guys in the league, guys from college ball, friends, family. Nothing crazy. Even so, I did catch myself dancing on the pool table at one point—got myself into a little dance-off with this girl, and we were moving pretty good.

Folks were scattered around the house, but here in this one room there were maybe ten or twelve of us. We were sitting on the bed, on the floor, all over. And as the game got going, I caught myself getting a little sick in the head, a little jealous, because there on the field were the Tennessee Titans, one of our division rivals. Seeing that team, in those familiar jerseys, got under my skin. Even though I didn't view our last season as a disappointment, once I saw these guys that I had been going up against all year long on this grand stage, doing their thing, it started to tug at me. So a part of me was watching that game thinking, *Dang, Eddie George! What's he doing out there on that field?* Thinking, *That should be me.*

Like I said, we were *rivals*. And I respected Eddie—I did. We had our problems, but we were cool. Still, I didn't like that his team was playing and my team was not. It got to me. We had some wars, man. Me and him, we played each other hard. There's a lot that goes on between a running back and a linebacker that doesn't come across in the stands, on television. You're connected in battle, all game long. For one to survive, the other has to falter, so we had our history, and that history reached up and grabbed me while I was watching the game.

And it was some game. Better believe it, folks will be talking about that Super Bowl for generations to come—it was one for the ages. The Rams jumped out early, but the Titans came clawing back, and midway through the second half Eddie ran it in from short yardage for a touchdown. The Rams had him stopped, dude had his hand on Eddie's helmet, but Eddie just kept fighting it and fighting it until he burst into the end zone.

At just that moment, I heard one of Marty's actress friends call out, "Oh man. Eddie George is a beast!" It was almost like a scream.

She was a fan. That's all. She was excited—Eddie had just made a great play in a big spot. But I heard that voice and it set me off. Again I thought, *Dang, Eddie George!* I thought, *I got to get into this game!* Of course, the only way to do that was to get to the *head*. Only road to the Super Bowl, in our division, was through Tennessee. That's how it had been my whole time in Baltimore. When I came into the league, they were the Oilers; now they were the Titans, and Eddie George was a monster. That's just facts. He was the force at that time—the force *I* had to deal with, anyway. So that's what I mean when I say we had to get to the head, because that's how you cut down a beast like that. You get to the head.

Now, that history we had, me and Eddie, went all the way back to college, when he was at Ohio State. We had some words—and not even *on* the field. What happened was we were both named College All-Americans, and they flew us all to Los Angeles for some press events and appearances. A bunch of us became really close, went on to big careers, and back then we *knew* we were going on to big careers, so this was a special time, a special trip, our lives just kind of unfolding in front of us. It ended up that one night we were at a party at a nice house in Hollywood. Eddie got us playing a game called "Smashers"— said he played it all the time at school. The deal is you take a vodka, mix it with a soda, and then you shake it up and smash it against the table. Then, when it explodes and fizzes, you have to drain it—easy enough, right?

After a while things started to get a little competitive. We were competitive dudes. Add a little vodka to that and what do you expect? So at one point, I was going up against Eddie, and he looked across to me and said, "Man, you too small to *see* me." Like he was calling me out, giving me attitude.

I said, "Hold on, brother. Let's not go there. We just playin' a game."

What he meant was that us Big East players couldn't touch Eddie and his Big Ten boys. *You too small to* see *me.* We were small-time, he was saying, so we went back and forth on this for a while. Some of the other guys joined in, and it was all in good fun. I was giving as good as I was getting—but then Eddie pushed a little too hard. He said, "Man, I'm telling you, you don't never want to *see* me." Meaning, once we got to the league.

All night long—the whole trip, really—the talk had been about what we would do to each other once we got to the league, how we would strut, find a way to dominate like we'd dominated in college. At Miami, Ohio State, wherever we went to school, we were all masters of our little domains, big men on campus, and now we were getting ready to amp things up, play with the best of the best.

I got my back up—said, "Eddie, if I *ever* see you, I will end your career."

It was just something to say, but the heat got turned up after that. Eddie, he wanted to throw down. He kept saying, "We can go on the grass right now. We can go on the grass right now."

Eddie was all riled. He even ripped off his shirt and started making like these other dudes had to hold him back from jumping me—you know, just a bunch of testosterone nonsense, locker room nonsense, but I was getting all riled up, too. Usually, I let this kind of thing slide. It doesn't bother me. But we kept pushing it and pushing it, to where the two of us were getting ready to go at it, and that's when our host came by to diffuse the situation. Duane Martin—a sports agent, trying to sign a bunch of us, it was his place. He became a good friend to a lot of us on that College All-American team. He was married to the actress Tisha Campbell from the show *Martin*, and last thing he wanted was for this gathering of the nation's top college football players to end in a brawl, so he brought out these paintball guns he just happened to have lying around the house.

He walked over to me and Eddie and handed us each a paintball gun—said, "Y'all need to chill out. Whatever it is, we can settle it with these."

Turned out to be a genius move, because after that the tensions seemed to die down. There were no apologies, no handshakes. We just shrugged, drifted away, and that was the end of it, but that's why it set me off, hearing that actress scream Eddie's name like that. *Eddie George is a beast!* We had this history, see. We had this rivalry. And it lit something in me, seeing

Eddie in this big spot, scoring this big touchdown, hearing his name called. It got me thinking, *I've got to get into this game, man!* Thinking, *I need to be on that field!*

Yeah, I know. It was just a Super Bowl party. It was just a game some dudes I sometimes played against were playing on the television. But something was lit in me that night. I told myself that next year it would be me. I told myself that next year there'd be some other dude sitting on this bed, watching me and my teammates in the Super Bowl, listening to some other pretty actress scream in amazement, *Oh man. Ray Lewis is a beast!*

So it was like that.

After the game, I went back to my hotel room to change clothes. This was my routine—a different outfit for each stop of the night.

My postgame look was all about style. I put on a suit, a long mink coat. I put on some bling, too—a Piaget watch, a bold lock chain, a jammin' set of earrings. All that jewelry, plus my mink coat, I must have been *wearing* about a quarter-million dollars, but those were heady times, man. This was how we rolled, me and my boys, and when you come from nothing like I did, step into all this money like I did, you're bound to strut a little bit. I was over the top, I'll admit. *Way, way* over the top. I get that. I'm sorry. Frankly, I'm a little embarrassed about all that now, but this was the mentality, and I only mention it here because it became a part of the story.

All around the league, this was how dudes were dressing. Young players today, I tell them to lean another way. I tell them not to call attention to themselves—because, clearly, I made myself a target, dressing like this. It's like I had my chest out. That doesn't mean you can't enjoy nice things. But if you're gonna wear a $100,000 Piaget watch, make sure you're rolling with other people who've got nice watches, too. Make sure it fits with where you are. That mink coat—same thing. Make sure you're not the only dude in fur.

But other than the mink coat, I wasn't flashing all that money around. My jewelry wasn't on display, the way you'd sometimes see. No, I just had a taste for some fine, creative pieces. Some of them, I helped to design. And that watch—man, I've always been a watch guy, and that one was just a beautiful thing to see.

Another thing it helps to know here is the way people latch on to you in that kind of setting. Kwame and me, as the week went on, we pulled in all these different folks. A couple of gorgeous young females, who started hanging around with us—four or five, by the time we left Marty Carter's house. A couple other guys we were just meeting at these parties, these events. A friend of a friend. Somebody's cousin. We put together this loose little entourage—and some of these people, I couldn't even tell you their names. There were just along for the ride—and, got to say, we were happy to have them. Everybody knew somebody. Together, we were in on the same good time.

This type of thing, it was just a reflection of the times, how I came up in the league. And Super Bowl week, in a city like Atlanta, there was a lot going on. People cut loose in a different way, almost like you were in this big old bubble and the rest of the world was put on pause.

It ended up that we stepped into a club called Cobalt. All the after parties in town, this was the place to be. We didn't know this, going in, but it worked out. We found the right party. It felt to me like every athlete and celebrity in town for the game had found their way to the Cobalt.

My drink at the time was Remy VSOP—wouldn't touch nothing else. So I had the bartender pour me one and I went to check the place out. The music, it was thumping. The people, they were jumping. It was a good, good time, all around, and I'd shaken all that Eddie George jealousy, now that the game had ended. I'd shut down all those thoughts about our season running through Tennessee. The day wasn't about rivalries anymore. Wasn't even about the big game. It was about celebrating with my friends, being young, on top of the world, all of that. Back of my mind, I was thinking, *Baby Ray, life is good.* And, really, it was. I was twenty-four years old, making good money, a good name for myself, looking ahead to a time when folks would be dancing and celebrating after one of *my* Super Bowls—a time that was close enough to taste. And the next day I'd be heading out to Hawaii with my kids, meeting up with my mom flying in from Baltimore.

It would be a great week—another bunch of events and parties, all of us together, in the sun, a long, long way from how things used to be.

So that was my mind-set at the time, and as the crowd at the Cobalt started to thin, we made our way outside. We still had some of those folks from our loose entourage with us, and we all talked about keeping the party going back at the hotel. We weren't ready for the night to end, for all this good feeling to fall away, so we gathered our things and started making our way out to the limo, which was parked just down the street—and this was when the night started to turn.

As we left the club we ran into this one girl, looking like she wanted to make an impression. She had on this sheer turquoise top. She was a beautiful girl, tough not to notice, and as we walked past I saw these other dudes starting to hassle her, harass her. Wasn't anything, really, but it was something to notice. She was with this other girl, said it was her sister. So I turned to the girl with the sheer top and said, "Probably ain't good for y'all to be walking out here, just the two of you, looking like that. Lemme give you a ride."

And just like that, our loose entourage got a little bigger. Wasn't anything planned. Wasn't anything to discuss. These two girls just decided to roll with us, and I walked the rest of the way to the limo with one sister on each arm. We were having a big old time, all of us, and who knows how the rest of the night would have gone if it weren't for what happened next.

Instead this other bunch of dudes came up to our car as we were piling in, making a bunch of noise, roughhousing. Six, eight, ten of them. I couldn't tell how many, wasn't really paying attention. Dudes like this, we see them all the time when we're on the road during the season. Making noise, making trouble. They were just hanging around outside, hassling, harassing. At the time, I just saw them as trouble—nothing we couldn't handle, nothing we hadn't seen before, but trouble just the same.

I got to the car first and held the door open for our group, waiting by the curb while they piled inside. Can't say how many *we* were, either, but a bunch of people climbed in. Then, just as I was about to set down myself this one dude from the group ran toward me. He was all worked up, agitated. He turned to his friends and said, "Man, f*** Ray Lewis! Kill that nigger, dawg!"

It took me back, hearing this kind of ugly talk—from a black dude, no less. But I could see him and his gangbangers starting to circle, so I said, "Hey, look man. Ain't nobody doing all this right now. Let's just move on." Right then, I took this as my signal to get everybody out of there, and all hell broke loose from that moment. Remember, I was dressed out, had my jewelry on, my fine mink coat. I wasn't about to start mixing it up looking like *that*. That's a general rule of thumb when you're doing the town and looking good. The nicer you're dressed, the less inclined you are to get in a fight—that is, if you're even inclined in that way to begin with. Anyway, we'd all been down this way before, knew enough to know it was just a bunch of noise, just a bunch of nonsense, so the thing to do to diffuse all that noise and nonsense was to show each other what you had. It was like a standoff-type situation, and there really wasn't any more to it than that. Only thing flying around was words, but at the same time there was trouble in the air. You could kind of *feel* it.

This dude talking trash, he had this Moët bottle in his hand—just kind of hanging off to the side. One of the people with me, Reginald Oakley, the dude must've thought he stepped a little too close, moved in on his personal space, because he drew back that hand with the bottle in it and came down hard with it on the top of Reginald's head. None of us saw it coming, Reginald least of all, but there it was, and it was *on*. Reginald's head was just split, and he was bleeding all over the place, and people were yelling and menacing and scuffling. Those next few moments—maybe thirty seconds, maybe a full minute—were just crazy on top of crazy, but I didn't engage with these dudes. No, sir. I tried to *disengage*, pushing the girls back in the car, and we all piled inside. Reginald was able to separate himself from the mix and join us; we started to drive off.

I remember there was this big old oak tree on the sidewalk where we'd been parked, and I looked out the window and saw these dudes—four or five or six of them—pushing each other around underneath that tree, still going at each other, mixing it up, jawing. I could hear them, too, but then their voices faded as we shut the door and started to pull away.

Reginald, he was in a bad way. He was bleeding all over the backseat, talking his own trash, wanting to go back outside and deal with this dude who hit him with that bottle, but just as we started to put that big old oak tree in our rearview mirror, we heard these shots ring out—*pop, pop, pop!* Wasn't clear to me straight off what they were, but then I knew. Very quickly, I

knew. First, there were just a few, then a whole bunch more—
pop, pop, pop, pop, pop, pop! And they weren't just ringing out.
No, they were hitting the trunk of the car, the side panels.
Everybody got down in their seats. Folks were screaming. My
driver, Dwayne—he stomped on the gas. It was a terrifying
thing, and the shots came out of nowhere—*pop, pop, pop, pop,
pop!* And then, just like that, it stopped—almost like whoever
had been shooting at us had emptied their clips.

One of those shots ripped into one of our back tires, it
turned out, so we were rolling flat—but Dwayne, he kept us
moving. We weren't stopping for no one, no reason. We rolled
for about a mile, past a Holiday Inn, so Dwayne just eased the
limo into the driveway and came to a stop, figured we could
take care of the tire and take care of Reginald. But instead of
all of us spilling out of the car and helping out, most everybody took off in all these different directions. Those two sisters?
Gone. The other girls who'd been running with us? Gone. The
other dudes in the car? Gone, gone, gone. Even Reginald Oakley took off—bleeding all over the place, still.

Only ones left were me and Kwame and Dwayne, and we
couldn't figure out what the hell had just happened or what the
hell we were supposed to do about it.

First things first, we needed to take care of the car, so we called a
tow-truck company. I stepped into the Holiday Inn lobby with
Kwame and the few folks left from our loose entourage. We
were shell-shocked, man. *Stunned.* So we sat there and tried to
figure out what had just happened, where things went wrong,
why. And the thing of it is, nobody thought to call the police—
not because we had anything to hide, but because there was
nothing to say. Where I come from, you don't call the police,
tell them shots were fired, until you know the deal.

Nobody'd been hit, far as we could tell. Nobody'd been hurt, other than Reginald upside the head—and he'd already taken off. So we waited on the tow truck with Dwayne, finally made our way back to the hotel around three o'clock in the morning, and as I walked through the lobby I caught a glimpse of myself in one of the mirrors. There I was, all dressed out in my mink coat, my fine suit. Dude dresses like that, he's not looking for a fight. Matter of fact, he's doing everything he can to stay away from a fight. How I was dressed, it made no sense with what went down, those shots being fired, all of that. Forget what kind of statement my clothes might have made. Forget that I might have been a little loud, over the top. Point is, when you're dressed like that, you're off to the sidelines, and here were these gangbangers stepping to us from the shadows, looking to make trouble—but it was a trouble we drove right past.

I was *wired*, man. Couldn't sleep. Turned on the television when I got to the room, thought I could maybe fall asleep to *that*, but as I was flipping around I caught a local news report saying the cops were looking for a black Lincoln Navigator that had been involved in a shooting outside a local club—*my* Lincoln Navigator! I shot straight up in the bed. I had all these racing thoughts, kept coming back to the one that said these gangbanger dudes must have clipped somebody—only thing that made sense to me. But there was no more information on that one channel, so I kept flipping around, looking for another local station, finally found one telling me the cops were looking for a black Lincoln Navigator that had been involved in the stabbing deaths of two young men.

I heard that and I couldn't believe it. *Stabbing deaths?* I hadn't seen a knife, seen any kind of scuffle other than that hit to the head with the champagne bottle. When we pulled away from that mess, it really wasn't all that much of a mess. Yeah, there were those shots fired, but we were already on our way by then.

That was in our rear view. Wasn't anything in my full-on view to suggest anyone had been stabbed. It was just crazy, scary, impossible. All of that. At the time, I didn't know anything but these few details, so I was caught between thinking of the whole thing as a sad tragedy for the families of these two dudes who'd been killed and thinking we'd just stepped into some serious trouble. Last thing in the world I would have wanted was to bring trouble to my family or to the Ravens, or to myself.

I couldn't think of what to do—like I said, my head was bursting. So I called my girl Tatyana, who was staying at her aunt's house in town with our two boys. Couldn't say what time it was, but it was early morning—*early*, like before the sun. I said, "Look, there's some crazy business going down here. Give me your address so I can find my way over to you."

Tatyana said, "What crazy business, Ray? Tell me."

I said, "Don't you worry about it. Don't even know myself, but I wasn't involved. We were caught up in some stuff, is all. I'll explain when I get there."

Next, I called my driver—said, "Dwayne, you awake?"

He said, "I can't talk to you right now."

I said, "What you mean you can't talk to me right now? Yes, hell, you can talk to me. You watching the news? You see what's going down?"

He said, "No, I can't *talk* to you right now. I'm with the police."

I said, "Right now? You with the police right now?"

He said, "They're right next to me, asking questions."

I said, "Let me talk to them. Put someone on the phone."

Dwayne handed his phone to the lead detective.

I said, "Detective, this is Ray Lewis. What's going on?"

He said, "Mr. Lewis, where are you?"

I said, "Wherever you need me to be."

We went back and forth a couple times, trying to come up

with a good place to meet, so I gave him the address of Tatyana's aunt—where I was already headed. The deal was we were supposed to head to the airport from there, but looking back, other than not calling the cops right away after all those shots had been fired at our limo, this was the big mistake of that long night, because it set it up so this next encounter would play out in front of my boys. I hadn't thought things through to this point, because I hadn't done anything wrong, hadn't even *seen* anything done wrong, other than these shots being fired—and that type of thing, the world *I* was living in, it ain't nothing unless somebody's hit.

Far as I was concerned, I was just a witness—a witness who hadn't *seen* anything—so why would I even think to keep my boys from this little meeting with the cops? It played out, I *should* have thought this way, but there was no basis for it. I was just fixing to tell what I knew—which, like I said, wasn't much.

Can't remember if I got to the house ahead of the cops or if they were waiting on me when I pulled up, because these next moments are just a blur. What I do remember is standing on the lawn in front of the house, daylight already, one of my sons clinging to my leg, the other in my arms. Tatyana's aunt lived in a nice suburban neighborhood, on a pretty little cul-de-sac. I can still picture that moment in my mind—probably the most defeating, most deflating moment of my life.

This cop crossed over to where I was standing with my boys, stepped to me in this superior way. Looked at me like I was dirt before we even started talking.

I tried to keep my cool, mostly because I had my boys with me, but also because I knew how ugly things could get if I didn't check myself—like I said, when you poke at me, I'm a different dude. And this police officer, he was poking at me, hard. Threatening me, hard.

He said, "I guarantee you'll fall for this one."

Those were the first words out of his mouth.

I guarantee you'll fall for this one.

I said, "What?"

Like I needed this man to repeat himself—but he did. He elaborated on it, too. Told me it was *people* like me, with money, thought we were above the law, *better* than the law. That we were to blame for what was wrong in the world. There was all kinds of ignorant nonsense coming out of this hateful cop's mouth. And it set me off. I'm sorry, but I got my back up. I knew better, but there it was—in front of my kids, even.

The cop said, "Who else was in the car with you, Mr. Lewis?"

I said, "Man, I don't know everybody in the damn car. How the hell am I supposed to know everybody in the damn car?" This was the truth, but I could have said it without yelling, getting up in this man's face. I could have just told how it was.

And the *interrogation*—because that's what it was—just went on from there. The cop said, "You mean to tell me you've got this Navigator limo, you're out at a club, and you don't know the names of the other passengers in the vehicle?"

I said, "Hell no! How am I supposed to know everybody's names?" Yelling, still—even louder. Oh man. I was fuming.

Months later, after everything went down, after I had no choice but to cop to *something*, this was what they nailed me for—this stupid conversation with this stupid cop on the front lawn of my girl's aunt's house. What they nailed me for, specifically, was obstruction of justice. Go ahead and read the court documents, pull up my records, check the papers—this is what you'll see. *Obstruction of justice.* This is what that looks like, apparently. Because I didn't take down the names of everyone who was riding with us that night after the Super Bowl. Those sisters we'd "rescued" outside the club. Those other girls, those other dudes—what was I supposed to do, check everybody's ID, take down their personal information before letting them ride with me? It was just a party, man—had nothing to do with whatever happened to those two young men. And at this point I *still* had no idea what happened to them.

After a couple beats, the cop got out of my face, and I turned to take my boys inside, get them away from this ugliness. I didn't want them to see me all agitated, to see me on the receiving end of this kind of treatment. But as I was walking to this house, this other cop came up to me—said, "Hey, brother. I'm with you, man."

He was black, of course. Right away, I could see what was going on. They were pulling this black cop/white cop move. Good cop/bad cop. Playing one off the other—me in the middle, getting yanked every which way.

The black cop said, "You just need to tell us everything that happened, brother. Just tell us what you know." Trying to keep me calm, trying to keep me talking.

The whole time these cops were going after me, I was thinking of my mom. You talk about getting in trouble? You talk about the law? My entire life, growing up, she was the law in our house. I lived in fear of letting that good woman down—going all the way back, for years and years, before I was even old enough to make any kind of real trouble. This right here? Police procedure? Holding out until my attorney was present? Whatever was going on with these two cops on that front lawn? I had no frame of reference for it, no *mind* for it. I'd never been in trouble in my life, so I didn't know to keep quiet. Oh, I *knew*. But not enough to lawyer up and chill.

So I kept walking into the house, running my mouth the whole time—said, "I'll say it again, officer. Ain't nothing to tell."

We took the conversation inside, my boys by my side the entire time. They were little, too little to understand what was going on, but their eyes were wide. Their faces worried. They could see their daddy was getting agitated. They could see these other men being aggressive, challenging. But I didn't have it in me to hush. I didn't have it in me to listen politely and then say my piece. I was *irritated*, man. These dudes were *on* me.

The black cop said, "Just talk to us, Mr. Lewis. We can figure this out."

I said, "Like I told you, ain't nothing to figure out."

The white cop said, "It don't matter. People like you, this is what you do."

This set me off. *People like you.* Better believe it, this set me off. We were standing in the hallway, my boys at my side, but I turned to this man and spoke my mind—said, "I'm telling you, I will slap the taste right out of your mouth."

I probably shouldn't have spoken like that to a police officer—I *get* this, now—but then, he probably shouldn't have spoken that way to *me*. You get what you give, only here it was an unfair trade. These cops, they had their weapons, and at this point the white cop put his hand on his pistol. He didn't draw but he was ready. However this confrontation was gonna go, he was good and ready.

I said, "You do what you gotta do. I'm good. I'm good with *me*. I guarantee you, I'm good with me. And if you pull that trigger in front of my sons, I guarantee you, they will remember me."

Those words can come across in a passionate way, like I was making some kind of emotional plea. But it wasn't like that. No, I was angry—emotional, yeah, but *angry*. Felt to me like I was being violated—in front of my girl, in front of my children. My boys were crying, because they'd never seen me this way, so I went to comfort them. Tatyana, she went to comfort them. But there was no one to comfort *me*.

This confrontation with these two officers, it went on for the longest time. The house was just a big pile of commotion, all kinds of yelling, all kinds of crying, so I slipped into the next room—a little room they had off the front door. I sat down, took a deep breath, tried to keep myself from myself.

I didn't know to panic. I didn't know to worry. It never occurred to me that I was in trouble with *the law*—just with this one dude who seemed to have it out for me. That's all. I had no knowledge of what happened to those two young men. I hadn't been involved in any altercation other than that business with the Moët bottle just before we drove off, other than those shots fired at our car. In the light of day, I was realizing I should have called that in, but that was on me. *This?* These hateful fools, judging me, convicting me, telling me I would fall for these stabbings even though I knew they couldn't have the tiniest piece of evidence against me? This was something else, man.

He wasn't about to arrest me, I could see that. He had no call to arrest me. So we sat there for a while, and I gathered myself, swallowed my pride, tried to get past it. I said, "Look, we all have a flight to make. We need to get out to the airport."

These two cops, they just kind of stepped back a bit, put up their hands to say, *Hey, we can't stop you.* So me and Tatyana, we got the boys ready, got her things ready. The plan was for her aunt to drop us off. Usually, that type of situation, I'd get behind the wheel and drive. But here Tatyana stopped me— said, "Probably not a good idea, Ray. They'll pull you over for nothing."

She was right, of course, so I walked back around to the other side of the car and Tatyana's aunt got behind the wheel. The boys were in the backseat just crying, crying, crying. They'd been holding it together pretty good back in the house, trying to be big, brave men in front of those police officers, but now that it was just me and their mom and their auntie, they let loose. It got so bad, we had to pull over, and I got in the back-seat with them, tried to comfort them, tell them everything was gonna be okay. And I honestly believed that at the time, that everything was gonna be okay, because I hadn't done anything wrong except maybe show some poor judgment, maybe run my mouth a little with these cops. But I was no criminal.

And then the craziest thing happened—like a car chase, in reverse. Tatyana's aunt rolled onto the highway and started to drive at the speed limit. We were late, thinking we might miss our flight, so she was trying to hurry us along, but then these two cops pulled up alongside. They'd been following us all along, we could see them the whole time, but now that we were moving at a good clip they kind of sidled up against the driver's side of our car—like, drifting into our lane. We were going fifty, maybe sixty miles an hour, and they just came up and started boxing us in, cutting us off.

Tatyana's aunt was freaking out—she didn't know what to do.

Tatyana, she was freaking out, too, because our boys were still crying, and these two cops were trying to push us off the road.

I said, "Just slow down some. Let 'em win this one."

So we slowed down some, and then we slowed down some more, but the more we slowed down, the slower they seemed to want us to go. Got us all the way down to twenty in a fifty-five zone—these two cops half in our lane, pushing us onto the shoulder, messing with us. Don't know what they were trying to accomplish, except to set it up so we would miss our flight, and that's just what happened. We were cutting it close as it was, and at twenty miles an hour there was no way—just, no way. So we pulled up by that little drop-off area they have at the airport, and I got out and looked at the monitors, saw our flight had already boarded and was fixing to take off, so I got back in the car and we drove back to the house.

Those two cops, they followed us most of the way, but then at some point they peeled off, and when they were finally gone from our rearview mirror, when the boys were finally quiet, Tatyana turned to me and said, "Ray Lewis, what in the world was *that*?"

I got back to the house and called my agents—Roosevelt Barnes and Eugene Parker. Told them what was going on, but they didn't need to hear about this from me. It was already on the news—me being questioned in the case. They'd already been getting calls, already had a lawyer lined up to help me out.

I went to see the lawyer that afternoon, walked him through the whole story, same way I'm doing here. He'd been in touch with the police by this point, and he told me they wanted to come back and talk to me some more, have me make a statement. It didn't feel to me like I had much choice in the matter, but I said that would be fine, long as he would be with me. You need to have your lawyer present, right? Especially with the way I'd been running my mouth over this. So I kind of filed that away, told myself I'd set aside that nonsense with those two cops, put this whole thing behind me.

My mom, she'd been trying to reach me. She'd heard about it, too. Wasn't anything to it, but it was a big story. She was at the airport, headed to meet up with us in Hawaii—in fact, she was already on the plane when she finally reached me on the phone, while I was sitting with this lawyer.

She said, "Junior, what is all this business?"

I said, "Don't worry none. Whatever happened, I wasn't involved."

She believed me, of course—but she believed the television, too. Her generation, you see something on the news, something in the newspaper, it must be the truth, so we went back and forth for a while—me telling her what she already knew, deep down.

Finally, she said, "We gonna be okay then?"

I said, "We gonna be okay."

She said, "I will see you in Hawaii then?"

I said, "Tomorrow. I'll be on a flight first thing in the morning with Tatyana and the boys."

Already, we'd gotten ourselves booked on another flight. Wasn't any reason to think we would have to miss out on this trip—we were all looking forward to it, and after everything that went down after I left the Cobalt, I was itching to get out of this strange hell.

Then, before I could finish with my mother, there was a knock on the door—the police, come to take my statement. But it wasn't just one or two cops. Wasn't three or four. No, sir—nine police officers came barreling into the house. Nine! It made no sense, such a show of force, just for me to make a statement. I'd watched a lot of television, seen a lot of cop shows, but I'd never seen anything like this.

The lead detective on the case—a man I'd never seen before—walked over to where I was sitting on the couch, talking on the phone. He said, "You need to put down the cell phone, Mr. Lewis." His voice was cold.

I put my hand up, my index finger out, to show him I would just be a minute. Just then, I had no reason to think this visit from the *entire police force* was anything other than what my lawyer had just led me to believe. They were here to take a statement. That's all. I had my mother on the phone, and she was upset, confused about what was going on—and now with this new commotion, nine police officers barreling into the house, she heard all of that and was even more upset, even more confused, so of course I wanted to make sure she was calm.

She said, "What's going on, Junior? Who are all those people?"

I started to answer her, but the lead detective stepped in closer and said, "You need to be off that phone, Mr. Lewis." His tone was menacing, hateful—like *I* was the one out of line.

So I held up my hands, to show I meant no harm, no disrespect, but he kept coming—said, "Mr. Lewis, you are under arrest. You are being charged with the double murder of Jacinth Baker and Richard Lollar. I need you to put the phone down and come with me."

Of course, I lost it. Of course, I went off—started yelling, fussing. This was not supposed to happen. My poor mother was still on the phone, and in the middle of all this yelling, all this fussing I put it back to my ear and said, "Mom, these folks are arresting me."

I didn't know what all she'd heard.

Tatyana came over and took the phone from me, and as she did these other officers just surrounded me. It was like a swarm. I was in shock, couldn't understand what was going on, or why. I needed a moment for this new reality to set in. I just needed to *breathe*, was all. But these officers couldn't wait, not even a moment, so they moved in, and as they did the lead detective said, "That's how it's gonna be, huh?"

These dudes, they were grabbing at me. Muscling me. Treating me like dirt. Two of them put a pair of handcuffs on me. Another one stood me up. Another one said, "You a big man now, huh?"

Mocking me.

Taunting me.

It felt to me like I was outside myself. Like this terrible business was happening to some other dude, and I could only watch. Didn't matter how powerful I was on the football field—I was powerless against this right here. And so I let these men do what they had to do. I let myself be dragged from that house—my boys crying, my girl frantic, my mother on a plane waiting to take off for Hawaii, doors closed, no way for her to reach back out to find out what was going on.

Guess I ached for her most of all.

Those officers dragged me, cuffed, across that front lawn, and pushed me into a tiny gray Chevy Cavalier. Shoving me every which way. When I got into the car, I did a foolish thing—I said, "I cannot ride like this, back of this little car, my hands behind me, these handcuffs so tight."

Why was this a foolish thing? Because it seemed to rub a number of these police officers the wrong way, set them off. Off of that, a bunch of them were out to teach me some kind of lesson, and here I don't want to honor these few rogue cops by detailing their mistreatment of me, so I will just say this: in a civilized society, you don't treat *animals* the way some of these officers treated me.

These kinds of cops, they have their tactics. They don't hit you where it will show. You learn to brace yourself for hits, flex, absorb the blows. You learn who the bigger man is, this type of situation, and it got to where I told myself these blows were like taps from a mosquito. Told myself these men could not touch me.

After a while of this, another cop stepped in for me—said, "Y'all know this man didn't do this." He got in the backseat with me, took off the cuffs so I could have my hands in front of me. When I thanked him, he said, "Ray, the word over the radio is you had nothing to do with this fight."

We drove for a while, stopped somewhere so they could switch me into another vehicle—like a paddy wagon. They fixed my cuffs to a hook in the ceiling, so I had to ride a half hour with my hands in the air, the cuffs already tight to begin with, digging into my wrists every time we turned. Dude at the wheel making tight turns, at speed, just to get me leaning this way and that, knowing he was snapping my wrists each time.

Finally, we pulled up to some kind of courthouse, photographers everywhere, folks yelling my name, telling me to look here.

Inside, waiting, somebody brought me something to drink. I'd been asking. They sat me at a table, hands cuffed behind my back. One dude put a can of Sprite on the table, opened it, then tipped it over so the soda started to run out the mouth—said, "Here, drink that."

So I did—got down on my knees like a dog and slurped at the soda as it fell off the table.

I kept running my mouth. That first lawyer my agents found for me? He was nowhere, man, so there was nobody there to save me from myself. I was livid, fuming. Talking a good game to make up for the way they had me bound, humiliated— saying, "You take off the badge, I guarantee most of y'all are cowards." Saying, "Y'all gonna have to deal with me someday."

Like that.

They put me in an orange jumpsuit, moved me to another facility. Hands fixed tight to the roof of the car, again. Driver making those tight, fast turns, again.

Next day, the district attorney went on television and said he could prove without a shadow of a doubt that Ray Lewis stabbed and killed these two young men. The police did not have a shred of evidence against me. There was no motive, no timeline. They couldn't even put me on the same street as the victims. All they had on me was that I had left this club and gotten into this limousine and that shots were fired. What was I doing, running through the streets of Atlanta with my full-length mink coat, doing these stabbings, then running back to my car without being seen?

The charges made no sense. Told myself, that district attorney, he would suffer for this. Told myself, *Ray, you got praying folks in your corner.* That was my mind-set at the time. I came at this thing from a place of rage, a place of revenge. But in the end *I* would be the one to suffer. These poor boys, they paid the ultimate price, how things went down for them that night. But me, I was made to pay for their deaths. In the court of public opinion, I was made to pay. In the detention facilities of the city of Atlanta, Georgia, I was made to pay.

I was crucified, man.

Those praying folks in my corner? They couldn't help me. I could only help myself. I could only reach down and call on my own faith to see me through. These police officers, they had to know they had nothing on me. The district attorney, he had to know. Only way they could make me pay for these crimes was to provoke me while I was in custody. And so they provoked and provoked, again and again. They kept at me, man. It was all I could do to keep calm, hold my fire. Here I could only hold my tongue, take whatever they were dishing out. And they kept dishing it out. Every night I'd hear this loud clang, telling me one of the guards was unlocking my door, telling me another group of cruel, racist cops was coming for me. Three or four o'clock in the morning, the lock rattling on the door to my cell, I just had to deal with whatever garbage they sent my way. Every night it was the same thing. They came to rough me up, so they roughed me up. Time and time again, they roughed me up. They violated me in every way. But they could not break me.

Let me tell you, your faith can be tested in all kinds of ways. And that's just what happened here. *In all kinds of ways*, I was tested. I didn't need faith to tell me I was innocent, only that justice would be served. Only that my name would be redeemed. Only that whatever these men would do to me—whatever this *system* would do to me—I would rise above it.

That first night in jail, I cried so much my hands were full of tears. Sweet Jesus, it was like somebody poured water into them, and I could only take that water and grab at it, all pooled in the cup of my hands, and toss it into the air. I just threw those tears away—said to myself, "I ain't looking back."

I heard God's voice. I did. He came to me from somewhere in the darkness of that holding cell—said, "Can you hear me now?"

And underneath this voice, in the middle of that darkness, there was a message—came in clear and loud and true.

The message: whatever muck and mire I had to slog through in that jail cell in Atlanta, it would strengthen me.

Whatever shadows there were now hanging over me and my family, it would strengthen me.

Whatever dirt these people in law enforcement were determined to do to my name, my standing, my pride, it would only strengthen me.

Can you hear me now?

Oh yes—yes, I can hear you! Yes!

I wanted to shout it out, but if I raised my voice they would come and beat me down. And so I raised my voice in silence. I sang to Him in silence. Wasn't any other way to play it. For two and a half weeks, this was how it went. For two and a half weeks, I would drop to the floor of that jail cell and do my push-ups and sit-ups. For two and a half weeks, I would drop to my knees in prayer. All night long, until they would come for me. I would not be beaten down by this terrible weight. I would survive on nothing but orange slices and faith and sheer iron will.

Orange slices? Yep, that's all I had to eat—except for but

one time. They'd send around these dry bologna sandwiches on moldy bread, but that was just too nasty. That one time, it was a feast from Long John Silver's. It was brought to me as a kindness by a childhood friend of my cousin Tony who just happened to be working in detention. He'd heard I was there, came to see me one night, asked how I was doing.

He said, "You hungry?"

I said, "I'm starving, but I won't break."

He said, "Let me bring you something. There's a Long John Silver's, not too far. What you want?"

So I told him: two orders of fish and chips, some hush puppies. That's all. Only problem was I had to eat it all in sixty seconds, so the kindness wouldn't be found out, and I scarfed down that mess of food in no time flat. Good Lord, I went through it all so fast I don't even remember it.

The way I was treated in custody, it was a low-down shame. This day and age, you would think there'd be some checks and balances in place to keep any kind of racist, abusive, arbitrary cruelty from raining down on folks they've got in custody. Innocent or guilty, it shouldn't matter. But then you look at the headlines, past fifteen years, you see this type of thing still going on. New York. Miami. St. Louis. *Baltimore*. This black mark won't go away, but there's no call to treat people like dogs—hell, I was treated worse than any dog. Some of the things these police officers did to me, these corrections officers did to me, I won't ever speak of them again. Not from my lips. I will not reduce myself to revisit this ugliness. I'll just say it was demonic, the way I was treated. It was pure evil.

The Baltimore Ravens, they stood by me. They *knew* me. The entire organization, from Art Modell all the way to the clubhouse attendants, the folks in the ticket office knew it wasn't in me to fight, unless it was on the football field. I was a warrior, but only on the field of battle, and so they lined up behind me, testified on my behalf, supported me in what ways they could.

For all the negative forces lining up against me, there were positive forces all around—but it wasn't so easy to see them from the darkness of that cell. For the first time in my life, I couldn't see outside. For two and a half weeks, I had no idea if it was day or night. My whole world was darkness. Once, I stood up on a small table they had in my cell, craned my neck to an up-high window, desperate to see the moon. I said, *Lord, if you let me out of here I will cherish every sunrise, every sunset.* My children, I've burdened them with the same promise. Whenever we're together, we stop what we're doing to watch the sun go down.

I'll say, "What's that?"

And whoever I'm with—Junior, Diaymon, Rayshad, Rahsaan, Ralin, Rayvyn, Kaitlin—they'll come back with the same answer. They'll say, "That's Heaven."

But those two and a half weeks, in the middle of that hell, I could only close my eyes and picture my Heaven. I could only take it on faith that it was out there, up there, waiting for me.

The Good Book says, "Touch not my anointed and do my prophets no harm." I speak these words and tell myself my enemies will find their judgment, in this life or the next. Their day will come. These people, they know what they done. *I* know what they done. And that is enough.

And then, after everything, after running me through the mud and vandalizing me every which way, the district attorney comes out and says he's dropping the charges. After *all that?* It was an outrage. But there it was. And in place of those two murder charges, there was a new charge: obstruction of justice. And to this, I had to plead guilty—that was the deal.

Time served—that was the deal.

Thirty-three percent of the court costs—that was the deal. Just for everything to go away. But, of course, nothing went away. Those poor young men, they were still gone. Their families, they were still grieving. Nobody's been brought to justice, and they're still gone and grieving. The stain on my name, it's still there. The stain on my heart—always.

There was a civil suit, too. I answered that the way God laid it on my heart. I *settled* that matter, and how I settled it was how I was asked. I could not bring those young men back. I had no hand in their deaths, I could not ease the suffering of those families. But I had so many blessings in my life, I told myself I could use some of those blessings for these good people. They were hurting. I was hurting. It was not an admission of guilt—it was an expression of love, of sympathy. I gave because I had it to give. I knew that money would never bring back what the families wanted most. But they asked for it and so I gave. But that was just money—it didn't matter. It only mattered that I was down and now I'm out. I was despairing and now I'm free.

My mama, she had some scripture of her own to share with me when I was in custody, when it was looking for a time like I might never find my way out of this mess. She said, "Put your trust in no man, Baby Ray," she said. "Put your trust in God."

So I did, and as I did I came to see that my greatest challenge was to be a light in this darkness. And I told my mother how it would be—I said, "I'm gonna do something the world has never seen. I'm gonna flip it. Everybody who hurt me, I'm gonna walk away. I ain't gonna argue. I ain't gonna fight. I ain't gonna curse."

And I haven't. I stopped cursing at the age of twenty-four, right there in that jail cell. Told myself I was done with it. I changed my walk, right there in that jail cell. My walk became a walk of love.

I was done walking in that darkness. I was tired of it. So I stepped outside and walked in the light.

TEN

Resurrection

Before I could move past those low moments in Atlanta I had to go through the trial put on by a district attorney who had me in his sights, for whatever reason. Maybe he had it in his head that the way to light up his name was to blacken mine. It started in May, almost four full months from the night of those stabbings. I was holed up in a hotel room close to the Fulton County courthouse in Atlanta. I was alone, a lot of the time. The trial was a wearying thing, emotionally draining. I felt for the families of these two victims, Jacinth Baker and Richard Lollar. I truly did. I *prayed* for them. But underneath all that feeling and praying I was tore up, broken. I'd been beaten down by this mess—*literally*, and every which way besides. And now I was desperate to win back my good name.

I thought back to the man who gave it to me and my promise to him.

I will make it great.

I thought back to the sweet, noble woman who raised me, and my promise to her to walk every day on His path, in His light—to make my family proud, to be a light unto others. All of that.

I had some work to do to keep good on my word, but first I had to get past this trial, and here I mean a *trial* in every sense of the word. Because it was a trial, man. It was a test—not necessarily a test of my faith, because that was unbreakable, unshakable, but a test of my character, my strength as a man to endure whatever hatred and nonsense came my way on the back of these charges. And then, on top of *all that*, I had to find a way to get back to how things were.

I was helped in this by two angels who appeared before me in the strangest, most wonderful way. I walked into a local Houston's restaurant one day after court, just to get something to eat. I sat down at a table in the corner by myself, across from another table with about five or six women, out for a good time. They were laughing, talking, enjoying each other—and, tell you the truth, I didn't mind looking on, wishing I could find a way to pass the time like that. Really, I couldn't remember a time when I was at ease, joyous, carefree, without the weight of this trial pressing down on me, so I was soaking in their gentle energy.

One of the women at the table kept looking at me, smiling at me. Finally, she came over—said, "Why are you sitting over here all by yourself?" Just as nice as could be.

I didn't really have an answer, so I shrugged my shoulders and said, "Been a long day. Just getting something to eat." It was something to say. That's all. I had no reason to think she knew who I was, what I was going through—and, even if she did, I had no reason to think she was with me on this.

She said, "Well, there's too many people praying for you. It won't do for you to be sitting all by yourself."

Then she took my hand and pulled me over to her table—and next thing I knew I'd met her sister, her aunt, her friends. They made me feel welcome. They let me laugh with them, unwind with them. And out of this one small kindness, a great friendship was born. These two sisters, Mona and Lisa, they saved my life—and now, all these years later, they're still in my life. I tell people I've got *two* sets of twin sisters—my biological sisters, Laquesha and Lakeisha, and my Atlanta sisters, Mona and Lisa. From this one chance meeting at Houston's, they started picking me up each day after court, bringing me back for home-cooked meals. They'd sit in court during the trial—just so I could see a couple more friendly faces and know that folks were pulling for me, praying for me. They'd review the trial with me, as it was unfolding. One sister was a doctor, the other a lawyer, so they knew a thing or two about human nature, helped me to see the case in a fresh way, with each new development.

With them, through them, I knew where I stood.

You find people like that in this world, you come away thinking there's a way out of this darkness—and it set me up to where I started to feel at home in Atlanta. This surprised me, got to say. All along, I couldn't get out of there quick enough. As soon as bail was set, I was gone—back to my house in Baltimore. All that ugliness been coming my way since the Super Bowl, all that tension and hatred and brutality, I'd come to connect it to the city itself. I wanted no part of Atlanta—*none*. I had to get out of town and wash all that ugliness off of me. But then these good women came along and made a place for me in their homes, in their hearts, and I started to soften. I did. And as soon as that trial ended, as soon as I copped to that obstruction charge, I decided to stick around in Atlanta for the rest of that off-season.

Hard to believe, but there I was, in the belly of the beast—because I could not let a few dark souls poison that whole city for me. Because I could not lash out at every individual who did me dirt. I could only find strength in kind souls like Mona and Lisa, who helped me to see that there was goodness all around.

It was another great kindness that kept me in Atlanta—and this one came from my friend Shannon Sharpe, the Hall of Fame tight end who'd just signed with the Ravens as a free agent. Me and Shannon, we'd known each other from sitting around the bar at the Pro Bowl, from playing each other, had a bunch of friends in common. I was excited to hear he was joining our team, because we needed another threat on offense—

and, frankly, I needed another good man in my corner. (Can't ever have too many of *those*.) Shannon was one on a long list of guys all around the league who'd reached out to me following my arrest. Oh, I heard from almost all of my teammates, almost all of my Miami teammates, almost all of my coaches, a lot of the guys I'd played against. Shannon, though, we made a connection. He lived in Atlanta, so he knew full well what was going on; he knew how folks could be down there, so we got to talking, and out of those talks a great friendship came to be.

He stepped up, man. He came through. He said, "Ray, whatever you need, just let me know." Wasn't like me to ask anybody for anything, but I was down and out. Money was tight, just then. I'd made a bunch of money in the league, had a bunch of money coming, but this trial was putting a squeeze on me. I hadn't had to pay out all those court costs just yet, but the meter was running. That kind of money, I just didn't have it lying around. On top of that, I'd been paying child support—probably $20,000 a month in those days. I could stay out in front of my own living expenses, I could pay off those court costs, give a little something to those grieving families, but Shannon helped me out with some of those custody payments that first year after the trial. I couldn't thank him enough, hated to have to ask, but he was happy to do it—and I was happy to be able to pay him back, as soon as I got out from under.

But Shannon Sharpe did more than just help me out financially. He also opened up his home to me, and I ended up staying with him the rest of that off-season. We worked out together, and this was huge, because coming off of those two and a half weeks in prison, all that time sitting in court, I was out of shape. Out of my mind *and* out of shape. I don't think I'd lost too much in terms of strength, but I was behind on my cardio, didn't know how I'd get my wind back. Plus, my nutrition was shot. Wasn't just that I'd had to live on those orange slices for all that time, but I'd never paid that much attention to what I ate. Food was fuel to me, man. When I was hungry, I fed the machine. Without a thought, I fed the machine. When you're young, you can get away with that type of thing, and I was still young, just turning twenty-five, but it was time to start paying attention to my diet, so Shannon helped me out in this way as well. Guys who find a way to stay in the league a long time, to keep playing at that high level, at some point they have to start thinking seriously about their nutrition, because it's all tied in. And here, with Shannon, it was tied in to me staying with him. It was one of those *do as I do* deals, so since I was living with Shannon, I started to eat like him. Dry lima beans. Half-cooked chicken. No food after eight o'clock at night. He had a whole system, and I was meant to follow it.

Shannon was like my life coach, man—a true godsend. A year before, we only knew each other to say hello, talk a little football in those weeks leading up to the Pro Bowl, but circumstances threw us together, and now we'd been thrown together as teammates, and more than anyone else he helped me set aside the stress and struggle of these past couple months and start focusing on football. At the time, he used to work out with this guy everyone called Ropeman—a former bodybuilder who lived in Atlanta and trained a lot of professional athletes—so he designed a program for us. The dude's real name was Ty Felder, and he knew his stuff. Folks came in from all over the country to train with him, and he had us doing a mix of cardio, weight training, nutrition. The whole deal. Me and Shannon, we went at it, hard. Ropeman, he was *relentless*—no letup. We'd go to the track and get our speed work in. We'd hit the gym—although Shannon had most of what we needed for our workouts in his gym at home, so we'd do a lot of our sessions right there. Then we'd get up the next day and do it all over again.

Little by little, I was back into football mode.

• • •

This time in Atlanta after the trial, it's like I was rehabbing from an injury—I wasn't *hurt*, but I was *hurting*. And the scars from that hurt would never leave me. I carry them to this day. I carry them proudly, because they remind me of what I was put through. But they would get worse before they got better—really, it took a while for those wounds to start to heal, because all these new hurts started piling on the ones I was just getting used to. I didn't know the vitriol that would find me once the season got under way and we started to make our way around the league. The venom, the evil—oh, I'd gotten plenty of hate mail. I'd heard my share of taunts on the street, on talk radio. My name was in the mud, all over. The worst things you could say about a man, the worst things you could *think*—folks were saying and thinking those things about me. But it took hearing all this hatred rain down on me from inside enemy territory, from opposing fans, for me to really *feel* what people were saying and thinking. The same way these Atlanta cops had prejudged me in this case, that's how folks were prejudging me in Pittsburgh, in Cincinnati, in Tennessee. And they were using it like die-hard fans, to get me off my game.

Pittsburgh was already a rival town, and those fans kicked off the 2000 season with the most intense hatred I've ever experienced. I was prepared for this, on some level, but you can never steel yourself against the kinds of things those Pittsburgh fans were shouting at me as we walked through that tunnel at Three Rivers Stadium to take the field.

Murderer!

Nigger!

Child killer!

Each taunt was like a dagger, and my teammates, they picked up on it. They were right there with me, man. Our head coach, Brian Billick, he was right there with me. In fact, I was walking side by side with Coach Billick when we passed this one kid, couldn't have been more than thirteen, fourteen years old. The kid caught my eye as we were walking through the tunnel, stepping to the field—said, "We're the only ones round here who murder niggers."

Coach Billick could only look at me—what do you say to *that*?

And when we got to the field, he was still looking at me, so it was me who finally said something. I said, "They don't know what they just woke up."

And it was in those low moments that I came up with a new way to approach the game, to approach what my life would become. I kept telling myself, *My smile represents my past. My heart represents my future.* And in those words, I lifted myself up, up, up—past the evil that found me in that stadium. In *all* those stadiums.

With Ravens owner Art Modell and Shannon Sharpe. They both stood by me and were great support when I returned to play after the low times in Atlanta.

Oh, and there was also this: that was the year that movie *Gladiator* came out, with Russell Crowe. I must've seen that movie fifty times by the time the season started, no exaggeration. And then, fifty times more, once we got going. I fell into this routine: every Saturday night, before every game, I'd watch that movie, straight through. There was that great scene, where this wise, old gladiator, Proximo, played by Oliver Reed, is training Russell Crowe's Maximus for battle.

Proximo says, "I was the best because the crowd loved me. Win the crowd and you will win your freedom."

And in response, Maximus says, "I will win the crowd. I will give them something they have never seen before."

That scene, it *inspired* me, man. It sent me back into battle with a whole new focus, and it took hearing this hatred from these Pittsburgh fans, it took hearing this cold, racist nonsense from that young kid leaning over the tunnel, for me to put that inspiration into play.

Win the crowd and you will win your freedom.

So this became my game plan, and as that 2000 season wore on, my rallying cry. I would win the crowd. I could not respond to every racist idiot who went after me. But I could get back at them in this one way. I could play my game, all out. I could win the crowd. It got to where I worked things out with the folks on the PA system at our brand-new stadium, got them to cut up some footage from that movie and play it on the big screen at an important spot in the game. We grabbed that scene where Russell Crowe is about to head off into battle and says, "At my signal, unleash hell."

Up until that season, I didn't know that kind of racism still existed in the world of professional sports. Those stories guys like Muhammad Ali and Jim Brown used to tell. And what Hank Aaron and Jackie Robinson had to go through. I thought that kind of evil was behind us. But here it was, in my face, at every turn.

After that first game, Coach Billick finally sought me out to talk about what he'd seen. He said, "I *get* it." That's all. And in those three words, I knew this man had my back the rest of the way. The entire Baltimore Ravens organization, they were *all* behind me. And the city of Baltimore was, too.

As for the game—well, we took it to the Steelers, set the tone for the season, shut them down 16–0. Held them to just thirty yards rushing—so we put it out that we would not be denied.

At my signal, unleash hell.

I had this new fire blazing inside of me, to quiet this new hatred, and in this I was joined by fifty-two men in battle. My teammates, they stood with me. We were dug in together, riled up together, *pissed off* together. So we set about it, and this season opener against the Steelers, it sent a message.

Trouble was, we couldn't always put points on the board. We had a *shutdown* type defense, a monster defense—there are a lot of folks who study the game who'll tell you that this 2000 Ravens team was the fiercest, most tenacious, most dominant defensive team in the history of the game. Not *one of* the fiercest—*the* fiercest. Hands down, second to none. And I have to agree with them on this. We posted four shutouts that year—the most since that famous Steel Curtain defense in Pittsburgh in 1976. We allowed the fewest points ever in a 16-game season—165, a record that still stands. We allowed the fewest rushing yards, too—970, which works out to about 60 yards per game, also a record. You just couldn't run on us.

But we had a tough time scoring. We were inconsistent. There was one stretch, in October, when we didn't score an offensive touchdown for almost a month. It cost us three games in a row. We lost 10–3 at Washington, 14–6 at home against Tennessee, and 9–6 at home against Pittsburgh. That string put us at 5–4 on the season—not exactly the kind of record that wins championships.

In response, in frustration, a group of us went in to see Coach Billick in his office. There was me, Shannon Sharpe, Tony Siragusa, Rod Woodson, and Rob Burnett—the most vocal leaders on the team. We had the respect of our teammates, the fans, the coaches. And our message to Coach Billick was simple: let's get back to basics. We were having quarterback problems, turnover problems. The thing to do, we said, was run the ball—thirty-five to forty times a game. Let us play defense.

I said, "We don't need but ten points, Coach. And if you give it to us early, the whole game will change."

Now, Brian Billick was an offensive-minded guy. This was his first head-coaching job, but he'd come to Baltimore from Minnesota, where he'd been the Vikings' offensive coordinator for a long time, back when they had one of the highest-scoring teams in the league. So he knew we were in trouble, on that side of the ball, and I think he appreciated our take. No doubt, he appreciated our passion. And halfway through the season, he could see how dominant we could be when we were in control. It was just a different way of looking at the game—wasn't *just* about scoring, it was about positioning yourself, playing chess, setting it up so the team could find a way to succeed.

And that's just what happened. We didn't lose a game the rest of the way. We switched things up at quarterback, from Tony Banks to Trent Dilfer, started playing more of a ball-control game, more of a pounding game. You've got to play to your strength, right? Jamal Lewis started touching the ball twenty-five to thirty times in the backfield, with Priest Holmes backing him up, getting *his* touches. And some of these games, we won by big, big scores. Only close game we had in there was a 24–23 win over our archrivals, the Tennessee Titans, handing them their first-ever loss in their new stadium, after sixteen straight wins. And we almost let *that one* get away. We were up by a touchdown, late in the fourth quarter, but then Perry Phenix intercepted a Trent Dilfer pass and ran it back eighty-seven yards for a touchdown. Luckily, the Titans missed the extra point, and we were able to answer with another drive, helped by a couple big pass-interference calls, and Dilfer found Patrick Johnson on a two-yard pass play for the score, and the extra point gave us that one-point lead.

The win put us at 7–4 on the season, and it set us up for a grudge match against the Titans in the playoffs—but we didn't know that just yet. We still had some work to do.

Win the crowd and you will win your freedom.

I was still hearing it, all around the league. The Baltimore fans, they couldn't have been more welcoming—it wasn't *them* I needed to win over. No, it was the folks in Cleveland, in Cincinnati, in Tennessee. All over. But as we imposed our will on these rivals, as we dictated and dominated and had our way, it wasn't about winning the crowd so much as it was beating those teams into the ground.

It was around this time I started doing "the dance"—this on-field celebration that became a real signature for me and for the entire Ravens organization. It came about like no big thing. You see, when I got to Baltimore, it was a different time. Players were starting to pump up the crowd, their teammates, themselves with these joyous, raucous routines after a big-time play. These days, the league has put in all these restrictions on this type of thing, but back then players were free to express themselves in this way.

Now, we used to do this dance back home called "The Squirrel." In high school, in college—it was just a fun, crazy dance, and once I started playing in the league, I used to go back home to Lakeland in the off-season and folks would come around to say hello, check me out. There was this one dude, Kirby Lee, and whenever we'd get a party going he'd start in on this squirrel dance. And the joke between us was that, one of these days, I'd take that dance back with me to Baltimore and do it in one of our games. It was like he was challenging me to do it—and folks in Lakeland knew I was up for *any* challenge, so I kept telling him I'd find a way to do it.

He'd always say, "Oh no you won't."

I'd always say, "Oh yes I will."

And we'd go back and forth like that for a while.

Finally, a couple years into my career, it just came out of me one day on the field, during the introductions before the game. I came out last—and let me tell you, the crowd just lost its mind. People went crazy for it. Had nothing to do with football, but it had everything to do with rallying the crowd, letting loose. And as our team started to grow, as we started to strut, play with a little more confidence, we were all trotting out these little dances—during the introductions, after a big play, whatever. It got to where we were even choreographing these moves, setting them to music, to movie clips—like I started doing with the scene from *Gladiator.*

A sack, a big tackle, a turnover—I used to run and jump and do all these crazy things, but then I started mixing in these moves I copied from Kirby Lee. The Squirrel, man. People just loved it, and it was mostly this wild romp, but underneath all of that it came to hold a lot of meaning. See, with everything I'd been through that year, that trial in Atlanta, the taunts that were finding me at every away game, I started to look on this dance in a spiritual way. It was my war cry, absolutely. But it was also my prayer. When I slid to the left, that was for the Father. When I slid to the right, that was for the Son. And when I came down the middle, that was for the Holy Spirit.

And out of all that, a *phenomenon* happened.

• • •

We were playing with such confidence, such drive, it didn't matter to us who we faced, here on in. There was this one moment, last game of the regular season, Chris McAlister picked off a pass from our old friend Vinny Testaverde, who was now playing for the Jets, and ran it back ninety-eight yards for a touchdown to give us our first lead of the game, time running out in the first half, when we were all starting to feel invincible. We *still* couldn't get out of our own way sometimes on offense, but our defense was *crazy*, and once the postseason matchups were set, we kept hearing that the one team you did *not* want to meet in the playoffs was the Baltimore Ravens.

No, sir. We was *problems*, man. You ran into us, it was a bad day for you.

We drew Denver in the Wild Card game, at home. A *problem* for the Broncos, you can be sure. There are some games, you just know. There are some games, you see how things line up, and it's there for the taking. Our front seven? Against *that* team? Are you kidding me? This was *our* game. In *our* house. We told ourselves, *We can bang these boys.* We told ourselves, *This is no contest.* And it wasn't. Held that Denver team to just forty-two yards rushing. Kept them out of the end zone—the first time *ever* that the Broncos didn't score a touchdown in a playoff game. In team history. Established our ground game early, got our points early, and *took* that game, 21–3. Really, we put such a beating on those Broncos that I'm sure there were folks in Denver switching off their television sets by the end of the third quarter.

One of the things you're not supposed to do in postseason football is look ahead to your potential matchups. You're supposed to take it one game at a time, because at this level, day of the game, anything can happen. But we had no time for *supposed to* with this Bronco team. We looked right past them. We did. Because the Titans had that first-round bye and they were waiting for us in the divisional round. It was the rivalry of rivalries, and we all knew our season would come down to this right here.

The road to the Super Bowl, it ran through Tennessee, so we couldn't wait to get there and get cranking.

Eddie George is a beast!

Those words still rang in my head. They *rankled.* And as we strode into Adelphia Coliseum I had but one thing on my mind—to get to the head of that beast. I thought, *Eddie, I'm at your crown!* This six-foot-three, 240-pound bruiser was the roughest back in the league, no question, and my one thought going into that game was to run into him at full speed, find a way to hit him so hard it would change his whole thought process. Eddie George, he played with *confidence.* That same swagger we all had on the other side of the ball. If we hoped to win, we could not let that confidence stand.

There are certain spots you look for in a game, certain moments, that change the whole conversation. Sometimes, it comes down to just one play. Sportscasters, they have a name for these moments—they call them *game changers*, and that gets us pretty close to it.

Me, I had my own name for these moments. I called them *mine.*

I'd gotten to a point in my career where I'd started playing against coordinators—meaning, it wasn't enough to line up across the ball and outhit, outhustle, outrun my opponents. No, I had to *outthink* the other team's coaches and coordinators, too. I had to predict what they would do, to get and keep an edge. You have to realize in football, it's all about finding that edge and laying claim to it, so here I knew there was this one play the Titans would be looking to run, and if I could read it, anticipate it, I could put myself on that edge and change the game.

Already, in our last regular-season matchup against the Titans, I'd gotten to the head—laid the groundwork for how this playoff game would go. I had it all figured out, all the way back in November. Don't think the offensive coordinators are the only ones drawing up a game plan, predicting how things would go. No, a lot of us players do plenty of studying. Plenty of planning. Up in the press box, these coaches think they're so smart. They think, *Just last week, we ran this play against this other team, it worked so well, let's run it again.* For real? Come on, man. Nobody catches me napping. I even pulled Rod Woodson aside and told him it was coming, told him I was laying in the groundwork. He'll tell you the same story. I said, "Paco, I've studied it." (For whatever reason, I called him "Paco".) I said, "They run this one play, Paco, this game is *ours*. They run this one play, Eddie George is *ours*. Every time we see him, here on in, Eddie George is *ours*."

This one play in that final regular-season game was a flare screen to Eddie. Second and ten, third and ten, this was their deal. Frank Wycheck, the tight end, runs to the middle. If he turns to face the quarterback, the ball isn't coming to him. That's the tell, the way he turns on that route. If he runs right at my middle linebacker spot, if he pushes up to me, hard, tries to get some separation, it's a different story—the ball's coming to him. But if he simply turns his back to me, it's going to Eddie.

So I was looking for this spot in the game, same way I knew the Titans' coordinator was looking for this spot in the game. Steve McNair—rest his soul—was looking for this spot in the game. Eddie, too. Eddie *loved* to get his hands on that ball. I was *dialed in* during that Week Eleven matchup. I was ready. And here it was. Frank Wycheck lined up, and I could see it in his eyes that he was coming to me, so the key to the play was in the way he'd run his route. Eddie was in the home position. There were two wide receivers, back side. Here it was . . . *Here it was.* And sure enough, Frank Wycheck came through the middle, stopped just short of my spot, and turned his back to me. He couldn't *sell* the play, because he'd never needed to *sell* the play, because all season long they'd been running it at their own will. But they hadn't been running it against *me*, so I knew, as soon as Frank Wycheck spun and showed me his back, that Steve McNair was throwing this little screen to Eddie.

And just to be double sure on this, I could see the offensive tackle lined up with his right leg fully open, which told me he was ready to sprint in the other direction. He wasn't coming toward me—he was headed to where Eddie was going.

All of this came to me in a split second—that's how fast you have to read a play like this. *Boom, boom, boom . . .* you snap all these pictures in your mind, line everything up, take it all in. I was *on* it, yes I was. Frank Wycheck started to turn his back, but before I could read his name on his jersey, I took off. I ran to a point on the field, and I ran hard. It was all in the timing. I had to get there at the same time as Eddie, same time as the ball. I wasn't looking to bust up the pass—no, that would have been *easy.* I was looking to bust up Eddie—not to *hurt* him, but to *rattle* him. To make him think twice about touching that ball if he knew I was anywhere close to him.

That's how you play the game. You put some *doubt* in there, you make him *hesitate,* the beast can't help but stumble.

So I ran to that spot, and Steve McNair tossed that little flare to that spot, and Eddie spun to that spot. And we all arrived at *exactly* the same time. And it ended up that I put a hit on poor Eddie that folks still talk about. Eddie, he probably dreams about it. And not in a good way. I hit him in a place no running back likes to get hit—by the side of his head, over the ear. A hit like that, everything goes silent. A hit like that, in the cartoons, you see stars, hear goofy music, waddle off. A hit like that, in a game like this, you can only peel yourself up off that turf and shuffle back to your teammates.

Oh, he caught the ball—held on to it, too. That's what beasts do. But he *paid* for it. He did. And I stood up over him and looked at his teammates and said, "Come get him!" I said, "It's over!"

And it was, man. Better believe it, it was. I was in Eddie George's head after that big hit. For two months, I was in his dreams. For two months, I was lurking around every corner. For two months, I was at the end of every play he ran in scrimmage, every play he ran in games. I was. And here in this playoff game, coming off of that one hit, Eddie George was *still* rattled. I was *still* in his head. The battle between us, it was *still* over. I'd gotten to the head, man. I'd slain the beast—and there was nothing for those Titans to do but fold.

That divisional-round game against the Titans was probably the most intense game I ever saw. Forget games I actually *played in*. This was a grudge match. This was war. And it had already turned on this one teeth-rattling play. Those Titans, they put up a fight, but the heart of the team wasn't in it. They went through the motions. But it had taken the life out of them, that one play. It took the life out of Eddie, that's for sure. He was shaken, playing scared. Of course, we weren't able to do much with the ball. Trent Dilfer had a difficult time that day, only completed five passes on sixteen attempts. We couldn't move the ball, couldn't score, and we were deadlocked at 10–10 to start the fourth quarter. But this was where our special teams got *special*. This was where our defense started to *defend*. Anthony Mitchell grabbed a blocked field-goal attempt and ran it back ninety yards for a touchdown to give us the lead.

Then, Tennessee took over and began to march, with about eight minutes left in the game. Steve McNair moved the chains on back-to-back first-down tosses to Derrick Mason, so the Titans were driving. They were *on the move*. And that's when that monster hit to Eddie came back into play. That's when the groundwork I'd laid a couple months earlier started to win this playoff game for us. I had changed his whole thought process. So here in this game, when he came out of that backfield, second and long on the Titans 47-yard line, and Steve McNair tried to hit him with a short toss, I was good and ready. And Eddie could *sense* it. And the ball hit his hands, but he kind of took his eye off of it for a moment, because it bounced free, and as it bounced, I grabbed it, and galloped with it fifty yards to the Tennessee end zone.

The crowd had been into it at the start of that drive, trying to get their Titans going. Man, that place was *rocking*. But as loud as that stadium was, it was now deathly quiet. You could hear a rat piss on cotton, that's how silent the stadium was, all of a sudden. As I ran, my head was filled with every possible thought. I covered those fifty yards in no time flat, but it was all the time in the world for me to think back on everything I'd been through that season, going all the way back to Atlanta. I was churning, and churning, running to glory, thinking, *God is amazing*. All those thoughts, they folded into just this one. *God is amazing*. And as I crossed that goal line, He spoke to me. He did. He said, "Don't say a word." Of course, I listened. When He tells you to hush, you hush. So I brought my finger to my lips and made a grand old *shhhing* gesture to the crowd.

Say nothing.

Let your actions speak.

Win the crowd.

Unleash hell.

And in that one small gesture there was a powerful message. It said, "Don't judge a book by its cover. It might just surprise you."

The AFC Championship Game wasn't much—not on the field, anyway. Going in, there was all this talk about the Oakland Raiders and their top-ranked passing game, their top-ranked running game. They had one of the best offenses in football that year. Rich Gannon was playing out of his mind. Tyrone Wheatley was a force. Tim Brown was a potent deep threat. They were riding high, and the talk in Oakland was how the Ravens could *ever* hope to win in "the black hole"—that's what all these die-hard Raiders fans called themselves, picking up on the team's silver-and-black colors. *The black hole?* Like that was supposed to get us thinking. *Please.* I heard all that talk and thought, *They can't be serious.* I even said as much during one of those press conferences they made us do leading up to the game. I said, "We don't give a damn 'bout no black hole, 'cause we got enough money to buy flashlights."

So there was this war of words going on, back and forth, on both sides. We were all having fun with it, getting into it. But then, we walked into the Coliseum on game day and what did I see? There in the stands, stretching across an entire section, covering about fifteen rows, was a giant banner—a picture of me, a knife in my hand, fixing to cut the necks of two babies. It took the wind out of me, that banner. The same way I'd gotten into Eddie George's head in Tennessee, these idiot Oakland fans had gotten into mine—only, not in a good way *for them.*

Yeah, it stung. Yeah, it put me on my heels. But I was used to all that by now. I'd heard all those taunts, all those slurs. Wasn't anything new here—only, I couldn't believe the Raiders front office didn't make these idiots take that banner down. I'm not saying the Raiders were *behind* this attack, and there's no way to control what kinds of things your fans yell down onto the field—but *this*? This was a little much, left me thinking the Raiders, the league, everyone was looking the other way. This was the AFC Championship Game. The whole football world was watching. And here was this giant banner, taunting me, disrespecting me, calling me out.

All I could do was rise above it. All I could do was think, *They just woke up a sleeping giant.*

It put me in mind of a line from scripture, Psalm 23: "You prepare a table before me in the presence of my enemies . . ."

So I thought, *Okay, so they want to watch, huh?*

It was fine with me, because we were about to shut those boys down. And we did. Once again, we couldn't do much on offense—but the Raiders, they could do a whole lot less. We forced four interceptions—five turnovers in all, including a fumble I recovered in the fourth quarter that led to our final score. We held them to just seventeen rushing yards. And Tony Siragusa knocked poor Rich Gannon clear out of the game with a ferocious hit.

Wasn't the most exciting game, but it did the job for us—and it sent us to the Super Bowl, only here, too, this game against the Giants was a bit of a letdown after that war with Tennessee. *That* was the real battle for us. These final games, they were just something to get past on our way to the championship.

The Super Bowl was in Tampa that year, twenty minutes up the road from where I grew up, so that was a personal thrill, to be playing on such a big stage, so close to home. A lot of athletes talk about these big moments and say they're surreal, but that's not how it was for me. No, this was as real as it gets, and I savored it, drank it all in. Couldn't quite believe, after the year I'd just had, the *trials* I'd just had, that I was standing on this field, at this moment.

Those two weeks leading up to the Super Bowl, we made a highlight video of our team on defense, watched it every day. It got us going, that video, and as we watched it, as a unit, we made up our minds that the New York Giants would not score. Kerry Collins? Are you kidding me? Tiki Barber? Are you serious? It was a joke to us, this game. It wasn't even an issue, this game. And we *bashed* these boys. We dominated. The final score was 34–7, so the game was never in doubt. That one touchdown for the Giants came on a ninety-seven-yard kickoff return, so we were good to our word on defense. They didn't score *on us*. And we answered right back with a kickoff return of our own—eighty-four yards, courtesy of Jermaine Lewis, a wide receiver out of Maryland. First time in Super Bowl history there were back-to-back kickoff returns for touchdowns, and *that* got started because Duane Starks, my fellow Hurricane, had himself a pick-six off a Kerry Collins pass intended for Amani Toomer, so you had this flurry of three touchdowns in about thirty seconds and not a one was scored on offense—got to think *that's* some kind of record, too.

I'm sorry, but that game was never in doubt. From the moment the matchup was set, it was never in doubt. We won that thing going away, in what was basically my hometown stadium, and it worked out that I was named the game's Most Valuable Player, which was an important validation for me, coming off the year I'd just had.

But then, before I could celebrate, before I could reflect on the suffering of that season, this happened: as my name was called for MVP, I saw the film crew that had set up on the sidelines to capture footage for Disney World. Remember those ads they used to run at the end of every Super Bowl? They'd show the MVP, all that confetti showering down on him, all that noise and celebration, and in the excitement of the moment someone asks the champion, "What are you going to do next?" And Joe Montana, Emmitt Smith, Tom Brady, John Elway— whoever was the star of the game, whoever was the MVP would answer, "I'm going to Disney World!" They'd been doing those spots for over fifteen years, it was a Super Bowl tradition, but when my name was called the folks on this crew just kind of spun on their heels and turned away. They didn't want anything to do with me. That tradition? It would end with me. The Disney people went and pointed their cameras at Trent Dilfer instead. Trent Dilfer? Nothing against Trent, a good guy who'd just quarterbacked his team to a Super Bowl championship, but he wasn't the MVP—not even close. But with the taint of those charges against me, with the public perception that I had somehow gotten away with murder, those Disney people wouldn't go anywhere near me.

That's just how it was—my new reality.

One of the production assistants had the decency to double back and tell me what was going on—said, "I'm sorry, but they don't want to use you. There's too much controversy."

Too much controversy?

Well, I guess that's one way to look at it. And I guess there was too much controversy for the Wheaties folks, too, because they checked in the next morning and told my manager they didn't want my picture on their cereal box—another Super Bowl tradition that didn't quite fit with my new reality.

Some people would say it was bittersweet, that victory. But not me. I say it was as sweet as it could get—because, hey, I was standing on that field, twenty minutes from where I grew up. Redemption is *sweeter* when people got to watch it. It means so much more that way, don't you think?

You prepare a table before me in the presence of my enemies.

I hadn't realized this was enemy territory. The Super Bowl

is meant to be played on neutral ground, but what I was realizing was that *everywhere* outside of Baltimore was now enemy territory for me. It went beyond football, beyond Super Bowls. I would have to live up under these new shadows for the rest of my life.

It made no sense to me. But there it was.

ELEVEN

I Feel Like Going On

I can't say for sure when I got the itch to call my father, but I can say for sure when I first scratched it. I was in North Carolina, headed to speak at a conference during the off-season. I knew that my father lived somewhere in the state, so this was the right moment to reach out. I was thirty-three years old, established in the league—a father myself, six times over. It was time.

I got him on the phone, told him where I was, told him I had some time if he wanted to hook up.

Of course, he did. My father wasn't a bad man—just a bad father. He didn't have the tools. That's all. He didn't have the frame of reference. He could be a daddy, because that was just genetics, biology, whatever. But a father? He didn't have it in him—basically, because *his* father didn't have it in *him*. And my granddaddy's father, he didn't have it in *him*, either.

The man hadn't been in my life in just about forever—so, yeah, it was time.

Now, I wasn't expecting to call on this man. I wasn't holding on to his phone number, waiting for the right moment to reach out to him. I just knew I was near where he was, and I found a way to connect with him, and next thing I knew he was coming up to see me at the hotel where I was staying. He pulled up in this little van he used to drive, and as he stepped out I caught myself looking at him, up and down. He was checking me out, too, and he crossed to where I'd been waiting on him. We didn't hug, didn't shake hands, didn't do much of anything, really. We just kind of stood there, checking each other out, not really saying much. What was there to say? Finally, he said, "What else you got going on?"

I said, "I'm done for the day. Wide open."

He said, "Want to take a ride?"

I couldn't think of a reason *not* to take a ride with him, so I shrugged, made a loud exhale, like I didn't really care either way. Don't know what had come over me, because I'd wanted to see him—hey, it was me who'd made the call!—but I was putting it out there that there were like a couple dozen places I'd rather be.

After a while I said, "Alright. Got nothing else going on." Like I was doing him a favor.

We ended up driving over six hours. He never told me where we were going, and I never asked. I don't know that I could have, because the man was talking a mile a minute. I didn't say a word, except to nod my head every once in a while, maybe offer up a one-word answer to a two-word question. ("You hungry?") The man wasn't interested in what I had to say, but at the same time he expected me to be interested in what *he* had to say. He told me his life story: women, drugs, ball, everything.

He said, "Son, I've thought about you every day."

I sat there in the front seat thinking, *Really?* Thinking, *Every day, huh?* I didn't say anything—what was there to say to *that?*

The whole time, I never once asked where we were going, and he never let on. We were just going. For a while, I thought he only wanted to drive, to keep me trapped like that, a captive audience. Finally, we pulled up at this small green house in the shade of an old oak tree. We got out of the van without saying a word, and I followed my father inside, where we were met by a man older than my father who looked kind of familiar.

My father pointed to him and said, "Ray, this here's your grandfather."

I said, "What?"

He said, "Say hello to your grandfather."

I'd never met this man in my life, never had any reason to even think of him—and here he was. It was a little too much for me to take in just then, felt like I had to lie down for a bit. A moment like this, I could have used a heads-up. It set me off, more than a little. Both these men, they weren't fathers. Yeah, they were *dads*, but that's where the relationship ended. Me, I was a *father*—other men, *fathers*. I didn't care to walk through the muck with these two, telling me why they were the way they were, how they never had what my kids now have. No, that wasn't how this would go.

No way.

For the life of me, I couldn't figure out why my father had driven me all this way. I mean, on the surface, it was good to lay eyes on my grandfather—Shadie Ray Whitehead. But I couldn't shake thinking there was something else going on— you know, a way for my father to justify his absence, to show me that this man had not been in *his* life, and that this would in some way explain why my father had not been in *mine*.

I liked my granddaddy well enough. And I liked my father fine. We were all in good company. But I could not relate to either one of them as men, so whatever relationship we would build out of this moment, however we would find a way to be with each other, it would start from a place of differences. We shared the same blood. We looked the same. We walked the same, talked the same. But we were not the same—could never be the same.

My grandfather lived in a modest house, in a militant way. He was seventy-three years old, lived by himself. He had his routines—ate the same foods every day, went to bed at the same time every day. Been that way for forty years. There wasn't a whole lot of furniture, but the place was nice, clean. He didn't have much, the way things looked, but he didn't seem to want for much, either. He took care of himself. There were no pictures of me and my sisters, but I could see a bunch of pictures of my father, my uncles, my great-uncles. Some of them had been great athletes, boxers, going all the way back to the time of slavery. There was a lot of family history in these walls, and as soon as I got used to where I was and who all I was with, I let myself take it in.

We had a good connection, me and Shadie Ray. It was a sweet thing, meeting him like this, a healthy thing. We talked and talked—and for the first time since we'd set out from my hotel, my daddy kept quiet. The time flew by, and then we fixed ourselves a little something to eat, and then we drove off. On the way back, there was less talking—probably because it was late and we were both tired. But there was also a lot to think about. It was still a little unreal to me that I was sitting in the front of this vehicle with my father—a man I'd never really met until this day. He said he thought about me every day, and I took that as a lie, but the truth was *I'd* thought of him every day, and not in a good way. *I'd* thought of the obstacles he'd placed in my life, in the lives of my mother, my sisters. *I'd* thought of the ways he failed us. *I'd* thought of the legacy he left behind—the one I'd worked so hard to erase all through high school. And now here he was, sitting right across from me, close enough to touch. The man looked like me, talked like me, but he was not like me in any way that mattered.

And in that moment I realized I no longer needed to think of him every day—at least, not in the same ways. No, I could think of the man I'd become, instead of the boy I'd been. I could think of my own children. I could pledge to love them even more, be there for them even more, fill up all those spaces in their lives where my daddy should have been in mine.

My own sisters, they wanted nothing to do with this man. They would have told you *I* was their father, not this man in the front seat with me. *I* was the one who'd raised them, looked after them, fought for them. Not him. *I* was the one they came to when there was something going on. But I had to let all of that go. Meeting my grandfather like this and seeing my father like this let me see it was time to let the bitterness slide. My whole life had been bitter. My whole career, I was bitter, angry. It's how I played the game. I had my *mad* on, and I laid it out all over that field. But I didn't need to hold on to that bitterness any longer, I realized. I was good. My mom and my sisters were good, too. No, this man who called himself my father didn't change a single diaper, didn't make it to a single one of my games, didn't lift a single finger for a single moment in the service of a single one of his children. And it wasn't just me and my twin sisters—he had ten children in all, scattered all over, and I could bet he was just as useless each time out. But I started to think that without this man's uselessness, I wouldn't have pushed myself so hard.

So out of that long day in North Carolina, we found a way to reconnect—and I must say, I liked being in my father's company. Hard as it was for me to believe, a relationship took shape. I didn't set out looking to keep this man in my life, but here it is. We get along. I look forward to our talks, our visits. It can be a one-sided relationship at times, he tends to call for money more than he calls just to talk, but that doesn't mean I don't enjoy hearing the sound of his voice, hearing the richness of his laughter, seeing myself in him. He is the father I am not—meaning, everything I am to my children, *for* my children, it's because of what this man was *not* for me and my sisters. I am the positive to his negative, and I count this as a great good thing.

Very quickly, music became our bond. My daddy loves to sing, and so do I, and every so often we'll fall into it together. He'll start in on a hymn or an old gospel song, and I'll join in. Or maybe it happens the other way around. The music lifts us up and helps the pain of all those absent years melt away. We are not the same, made from different stuff, but when we lift our voices, none of that matters.

Now, it just worked out that one of our favorite movies is *The Five Heartbeats*, which tells the story of an R&B singing group that folks say was modeled on the Temptations, the Four Tops, and the Dells. We'd each come to the movie on our own, long before that day in North Carolina, but once it came up that it meant something to each of us, separately, we made the time to watch it together. We both knew the story: the lead singer of the group was a character named Eddie Kane Jr., and the first time I saw that movie, long before my daddy and I reconnected, I saw his story as my father's story. In the movie, Eddie Kane had every gift, same as my daddy. He was good-looking, same as my daddy. He could sing, same as my daddy. He had a way with the ladies, same as my daddy, who went Eddie one better because he was also a great athlete. But they shared the same dark side, because the character in the movie also struggled with drugs and alcohol and all kinds of poor choices, and my daddy was cut this way, too.

In the movie, Eddie Kane's life is so out of control that the other members of the band kick him out. He'd been the main heartbeat of the Five Heartbeats, but he can't keep it together, so they continue on without him. That's how it goes in life, right? Either you can cut it or you can't. Eddie's girl, Baby Doll, leaves him when he's at his worst, but she comes back to him, stays with him, marries him, helps him get the Five Heartbeats back together, too. There's this rousing moment toward the end, when the group is singing this one song in church, "I Feel

Like Going On," and there was just something about that song, man—it got us going. It sang like an old spiritual, like folks had been singing these words for generations. Me and my daddy both, we responded to it.

> Though the storm may be raging,
> And the billows are tossing high,
> I feel like going on . . .

That song, it spoke to us. It *sang* to us, and for a while in there, every time we got on the phone with each other, I started in on this song. Why? Because it tells of the way this man persevered. Though the storms were raging, and he went through some tough, tough times, my daddy kept on keeping on, and I applaud him for staying in the fight. On his side, he feels the same way about me, so we trade off, and when he sings I know he's thinking of me, and all his other children, and the tough times he put us through. Those billows were tossing high for us—because of *him*, so he sings to celebrate *us*.

I feel like going on . . .

Yes, yes I do. Always.

What I learned from my father was the kind of father I would not be. It was my greatest motivation in life, to be a real father to my children, and I felt it rise in me the first time I held my son Junior in my arms. Ray Lewis III. It was a great day when Junior was born, the ultimate. I was still in school, his mom and I were still together, talking about everything to come. My dream, even then, was to have this big family—ten children, maybe more. I wanted kids running everywhere. I wanted to become the old man sitting on the rocker on the back porch, watching the kids out in the yard. I wanted to be that dude walking down to the creek with a fishing pole on his shoulder and a cigar in his mouth, grandkids tugging at his shirtsleeves, a call coming in telling him that *all* his children and grandchildren are coming home for the holidays.

And in this moment, first day I held Junior in my arms, all of that was possible. Right there in the hospital, I could see how our lives would go. I was headed to the league. There'd be money coming my way. I could take care of my mama, my sisters, my brother. The game would take care of me and my own little family for a while. I would set things right and break that long run of no-account fathers cutting at my family tree like a buzz saw.

Things didn't end up working out with Tatyana, Junior's mom. She wanted to stay in Florida. Oh, she came up to Baltimore from time to time, and for a while it was still looking like we'd find a way to be together as a family, but once Junior started school, that happened less and less. By this time, we had two more boys—Rayshad and Rahsaan—only, we weren't together in the same way as a family. This was a great sadness to me, but I swore that when I had kids I'd never be out of their lives—and I never have. Never treat them like my father did me—and I never have.

That picture I'd always carried, of me and my great big family? For the longest time, I could close my eyes and see it, but when I open them now the picture looks a little different. My dream of a big family is coming true in new ways—ways I hadn't figured. They're at that age where they don't need me shining a big light on how things are with us and how things aren't, but let me say that I love them all and can't imagine a world any different than the one I have with them. I wish I could have my children under my roof, but I've found a way to roll with it. Junior, Rayshad, and Rahsaan were down in Florida with their mom most of the time I was playing, but I always found a way to be present without *always* being present. Their mom knew how important that was to me. And while I was making my life in Baltimore, there came my daughter Diaymon. And then there was my son Ralin and my daughter Rayvyn. Later on, Ralin's mom had a daughter without me, Kaitlin, and I've embraced her as my own as well. So, no, it's not how I pictured it—seven kids, by four different women. Not even close. But it's the picture God has taken for me, and so that's the one I've put up on the mantel. That's the picture I choose to celebrate. I've started telling people I've got four kings and three queens—all living under different roofs—not my own, but we make it work, we do. One of the ways we make it work is to be present in each other's lives—*fully* present. The holidays, that's our time together. We've worked it out with my kids' moms over the years that we all get together at my house in Baltimore. Thanksgiving. Christmas. Summer vacation.

One thing, though: the game was a drag on those holidays. I loved having all seven kids under one roof for the holiday, together with all my siblings, my mom, my aunts and uncles and cousins, but the way it usually worked during my career was I always had one eye on the clock, one foot out the door. We'd have our celebration, we'd wake up the next morning, all my kids would be piled onto my bed, roughhousing, just being together as a family, and my bags would be all packed, sitting by the door. And then, too soon, I'd have to head out, and my kids would look at me like I was pulling some kind of plug. That's the great heartache in the life of a professional athlete. Middle of the season, you're someplace else. Even if you're around and it works out that your schedule sends you home, your *head* is someplace else.

Each year, it got harder and harder to walk out that door, and at some point I realized the game will get rid of me after a while. I realized that the life I was in was bigger than just me—

and for me, *bigger* meant my family. And so that first Thanks-giving away from the game in 2013 was a sweet, sweet moment for me and my family. There was no place else I needed to be, nothing else I needed to think about. It felt to me like I'd *arrived*. My whole life, I'd been working *toward* something, powering through. But now I was here, at home, my giant family spread all over the house. Wherever I was headed, all those years, I had finally arrived.

Now, I don't want anyone getting the wrong idea—this didn't mean I was in the kitchen, helping out. Afraid not. You see, in my family, we do it old school. The women, they take charge of the kitchen. The men, we head to the other room, kick back and relax. And let me tell you, it felt good to finally *relax*.

That first Thanksgiving, my nephews sitting on my lap, my nieces to either side, my kids running every which way, one of them came up to me after a while and said, "Dad, you're not mad anymore."

This was true. I'd always been on edge, wired tight. But once the game was gone, there was only this right here—there was only *family*.

Understand, I haven't given up on that dream of one big family, all up under one roof. Trouble is, I still haven't met *the one*—the woman who's meant to be my partner on this ride. Sometimes, you get with someone when you're young and you grow in different ways, on different paths. That's all. Now that I'm older, a little more set in my ways, I'm hoping to find some-one who's also a little older, a little more set in *her* ways—and that our ways might fit together. And when *that* happens, and it will, we'll start in on another bunch of kids, start filling up the house all over again.

The parenting part, I've got that down by now. I *know* how to be a father to my children. They know my rules. They might get away with this and that when they're at home with their mamas, but when they're in my house we go a certain way. We don't watch R-rated movies. We don't listen to music that degrades my daughters and pushes my sons toward a lifestyle that doesn't fit with who we are. We're clear on that.

We carve out our special times together—and in between those special times, I'm back and forth to wherever they are, taking in their games, driving them to school, getting something to eat—whatever I can do to stay in their faces, in their heads, in their hearts. In our own way, we live as if we're all up under the same roof, and when it works out that they're under *my* roof—well, then things go a certain way. My kids know that when they live with me, they live by my rules, and just so we're clear on what those rules are, I put them up on the fridge.

On the fridge, it says:

WE WILL ALWAYS PRAY TOGETHER BEFORE BED
WE WILL ALWAYS EAT TOGETHER AT THE TABLE
WE WILL FIND SOME TIME TO READ A BOOK EACH
   AND EVERY DAY
WE WILL ALWAYS DROP OUR PHONES ON DADDY'S
   DRESSER AT TEN O'CLOCK EACH NIGHT—UNLESS
   SOMEBODY ELSE IS PAYING FOR IT

If you stick to what's on the fridge, you're good. But there are also plenty of other rules in my house that are clear and easy to enforce: about homework and working out, and how much television they can watch when living in my house. When my children are back with their mamas, there's not a whole lot I can do, but I like to think I'm instilling a mind-set in them, a work ethic that lets them stick to most of these rules even when I'm not around to check up on them.

All in all, we're one big happy family, in our own way, and

it all flows from the patterns my father could not set for me. It comes from my own mother, who had to be both a mother *and* a father. It comes from the strength of family I felt with my brother and sisters. It comes from knowing the hurt that was visited on me and my family by these other men. It comes from the promise I made to myself in childhood that I would not live a day in my father's name and that I would not raise a child by his example. The fact that we've made repairs to our relationship and found a way to enjoy each other's company doesn't change the pain this man caused us all those years. It doesn't erase the past. But it does help me to set that past aside and look ahead—because, got to say, I feel like going on. Whatever it is I've been put on this earth to do, I'm not done yet.

I feel like going on.

I do.

I will.

I must.

TWELVE

"This Ain't Over"

Man deals with the possible . . .
God deals with the impossible . . .

Those were my words to our team doctor, Leigh Ann Curl, when she checked me out on the sidelines that day in Baltimore. October 14, 2012. The day I busted up my triceps in the sixth game of the 2012 season, a season I knew would be my last. When I said those words to the doc she looked at me like I was plain crazy. She could see what my arm looked like just then. She could see the injury was bad upon bad—said she didn't need an MRI to tell her what was plain as day. Said she knew from experience that people my age don't recover from that kind of injury.

People my age. She didn't mean it that way, but the words stung.

And here's a funny thing—only, *funny* is probably not the right word. It was more *curious* than *funny,* but I kept smiling. The more the doc looked me over, the more she flashed me this worried look, the more I could only smile. Finally, it got to where she said something—said, "Why are you smiling, Ray? This isn't good. Your triceps is torn."

I said, "I'm smiling because we're gonna win the Super Bowl. I'm smiling because this injury is nothing."

She said, "You're not hearing me, Ray."

I said, "Oh, I hear you, Doc. But you're not hearing me. I'm gonna be okay."

Right there on the sideline, the game still going on, my mind was off in a whole new direction. I was smiling because, throughout my career, whenever I had an injury, I used to call it my "cocoon time." I had this whole little science project worked up in my head. Don't ask me where it came from, this type of thinking, but I'd always been fascinated by butter-flies—at first, they were just something to wonder about. I'd watch them flying around on a nice summer day and I'd study them, wonder what they were up to, so I started reading up on them. I learned that the life-span of a butterfly was about ninety days—that's all, just ninety days. And that's at the long end. Some die after just a week or so, some make it about a month, but they get a whole lot done, whatever time they have. As caterpillars, they're able to make one of the purest silks found on this planet—something man can't make, but it comes out of the mouths of these little old caterpillars. Really, they're the most amazing creatures, capable of doing the most amazing things, and probably the most incredible thing about them is the way they're able to transform themselves. They spin themselves this little cocoon and shut themselves inside. They can't take their mamas with them. They can't take nobody with them. They're on their own, and they tuck in and wait. That's all they do, just wait. And in the waiting, that's where this strange magic happens.

These were the kinds of things I used to think about when it was time for me to heal. Told myself it was like a gift, an opportunity to block my mind off, to wrap myself in this nest of hope, possibility, whatever you want to tell yourself is going on inside that tight cocoon. You can't take anyone in there with you. It's just you, alone, facing that long slog back to recovery. People called it rehabilitation, but I called it rejuvenation—

the way I set it up in my mind, it wasn't a hard road, but a journey. I'd tuck in and be by myself and just deal with it. I'd *just wait*—for this strange magic to happen. So when I started going through my surgeries, recovering from various injuries, I took the time to turn inside myself and really heal. Kept telling myself it was *my* time. Kept telling myself there was nothing to worry about—in fact, the only folks with something to worry about was whoever had to deal with me once I got back to the field, because I'd had all that time to rejuvenate.

I'd come back refreshed, recharged, repurposed.

Don't know when I started smiling through my injuries, but I do remember one time, a game against Cincinnati, when I snapped my finger so bad it looked like it was hanging by the skin. But I kept on—said, "Tape it up, let's go!" Because my finger was just my finger. End of the game, no matter what, it would still be hanging like that, so might as well play through it. Might as well see it to the end and smile through. That's an old-school way of thinking I got from guys like Ronnie Lott. You tell yourself the pain don't matter—and, just like that, *it don't*. And once you buy into that, there's no going back. So this injury to my triceps, I would just find a way to deal with it.

Meanwhile, my boys had to deal with this game. The Cowboys were driving, down just one possession, time running out. Tony Romo kept dinging us with short passes, finally connected on a four-yard touchdown pass to Dez Bryant with about thirty seconds on the clock. The two-point conversion failed, would've tied the game at 31–31. But then they got the ball back on an onside kick, and we got called for pass interference on the very next play. It put the Cowboys in field-goal position, but they missed a fifty-one-yarder and we held on for one of those *sigh of relief*-type wins, 31–29. And let me tell you, there wasn't anybody in that stadium with a *sigh of relief* louder than mine, because I knew what that win could mean on the string of a long season. I knew what it cost us, me not being on the field for that last series. I knew I might be out for a while, knew I had some work to do. But I knew I'd be back, and that we were still in this fight together, and we were headed to the Super Bowl.

These things, I knew.

That night, I spent some time with my family, tried to make it a celebration. I had everyone together—they were all at the game—and it was meant to be a joyous time. They could see I was hurting, they took turns being down, but I kept trying to lift them back up. One by one, I told them we were good—told them it was *all good*. I didn't let on how serious the doc thought it was. I didn't let on that there was any cause for worry. There would be time for all that.

For now, we could only look ahead—all of us, together.

Next morning, I went to see Dr. Curl. We did an MRI, looked at pictures. She told me what we were looking at, but I was like the doc on this. I didn't need an X-ray to tell me what I already knew. Wasn't anything she didn't already tell me down there on that field, except here she could point to the film so I could see for myself what she was talking about. Here she started talking about surgery—there was no other choice, she said. Even if I never played another down of football, I'd need surgery. She talked about the long odds against me. She used that phrase again—*people your age*—set me off the first time I heard it, and here it set me off again. Still, I heard her out, and when she ran out of things to tell me I said, "You done?" Like I was impatient, itching to move on.

She said, "Ray, this is serious."

I said, "I know it's serious. I'm serious."

She said, "You got that look." Meaning, I was smiling, planning something.

I said, "Hell yeah, I got that look."

She said, "What are you going to do?"

I said, "I'm gonna do what I always do."

I got on the plane the next morning for Miami, went to see Dr. John Uribe—only orthopedic surgeon I trusted around me with a knife. He was our team orthopedist at Miami, and he'd done every one of my surgeries—actually, every surgery but one.

(The one he didn't do? I'd torn the labrum in my left shoulder, and I had that operated on in Vail, Colorado. But Dr. Uribe was at the knife for every other surgery: on my thumb, on my back, on my left shoulder, on my right shoulder, on my right ring finger, on my right hamstring, on my wrist—too many to count, almost.)

I flew down with my X-rays, with Dr. Curl's report, and as soon as I handed the material over to Dr. Uribe, he knew what I was facing, what I was planning.

He said, "Don't tell me, Ray."

I said, "Just look at the film, Doc. Tell me how soon you can fix it."

He popped the X-ray onto this little light box in his office and gave it a quick look—said, "Ray, it's gone." He showed me a picture to explain what he was seeing, and the way he described it to me was the same way Dr. Curl had described it—said it's like that muscle was a piece of meat. Once I'd snapped that ligament, the muscle just kind of rolled up, like a snap cord on a vacuum cleaner. There was no good way to roll it back and expect it to hold—not under the stress and strain of the game.

He said, "Forget football. Let's just worry about getting you the use of that arm."

I said, "Forget football? Doc, you serious?"

He said, "This is a major tear, Ray."

I said, "So let's get to work. When can you do the surgery?"

He said, "I can do it in the morning." He was resigned to it—couldn't tell me *no.*

I said, "Well, then I'll see you in the morning."

This was on a Tuesday, two days after the game against the Cowboys. Wednesday morning, I was in the operating room at Doctors Hospital in Miami. Dr. Uribe, he told me he could repair the shoulder, but he couldn't guarantee that I would play football again. It was a question in his mind—but it wasn't a question in mine.

He said, "Ray, if you re-tear this, you might not get back the use of that arm. It's a big risk."

This was him talking to me before the surgery, before he put me under, telling me how it would go.

I said, "Don't mind that. Just tell me how soon I can get back."

He said, "Best case?"

I said, "Best case."

He said, "Twelve weeks."

Twelve weeks would have put me into the postseason. When you're playing, you don't need to look at a calendar. You count the time by the games on your schedule. We'd just played our sixth game, had a bye week coming, so twelve weeks meant my season was gone. Twelve weeks meant my teammates had a job to do, had to hold up their end, find a way to take us to the post-season. If they could get us to the playoffs, I could come back and help the rest of the way. But it would be on them, for now.

The surgery went the way it was supposed to go. Dr. Uribe did what he was supposed to do. Now it was on me to do my job, and as I came to in that hospital bed, I set my mind to what lay ahead. A lot of folks, they change things up when life gets hard—but me, I'm cut a different way. I always tell people that if you show me your failures, I'll show you your future, and here I would not let myself fail. After all, it's your struggles that define you, and compared to what I'd been through this was nothing, so I started in on my cocoon time, turned my full focus on getting back to whole.

First couple days, I was in traction. They had my arm up in a fixed brace, rested on a pole pressed into my hip. I looked like a soldier returned from battle. I wouldn't take any of the pain medication they brought for me—my thing was to just deal with the pain, find a way to set it aside. As soon as I could travel, I arranged for a driver to take me to Orlando, and from Orlando the plan was for me to take a private jet to a clinic in Arizona, where I was putting together a full-throttle rehab program. I talked to everyone I knew, everyone I'd ever played with, everyone who'd gotten close to a similar injury. I was determined to work with the best of the best, so I got recommendations coming and going, up and down. But first, I arranged it so I could go to Junior's game—another reason to smile. That's why I flew through Orlando. During the season, I didn't get to sit in the stands and cheer on my boy, so I wasn't about to miss this chance. Even an injury like this one to my shoulder, it comes with a silver lining—you just have to know where to look for it. So I sat there in the stands, a stool up under my arm to support that pole, keep that traction going.

And Junior just tore it up down there on that field. It was something to see, so I took in this blessing. Counted myself lucky that this little piece of goodness was coming out of this injury. Here I was, spinning my little cocoon, but I was doing a better job than those caterpillars, because I'd found a way to take the people I love *inside*. My whole career, football season kept me away from my kids, this time of year. My son was making all this noise on his high school football team, and I couldn't even watch him play, so this was part of my healing. This would make me stronger.

I stuck around after the game, just to check in with Junior, have a little time together before I took off. And here's the thing: once I brought Junior into that cocoon with me, I wasn't about to let him go, so I kept shuttling back and forth from Arizona to Florida—didn't miss one of his games the whole rest of the season. The way I worked it was I'd put a pin in my rehab routines, get on a plane, do what I could while we were in the air, and sit myself down in the stands and let some of that *proud dad* medicine help with the healing.

It was a good trade all around. Whatever time I lost in therapy I made up for in restoring my spirit.

In Arizona, I probably averaged about three hours of sleep each night. All day long, I had therapy. If the doctors suggested two sessions each day, I pushed for four. As soon as they cut off my cast, I hopped on the bicycle and did what I could to keep up my fitness level. I wasn't just working to get my shoulder back in shape. I had to keep the rest of me in football shape so I could hit the ground running once I was cleared to play. A lot of folks, an injury like mine, they would have used a stationary bike—but, no disrespect, a stationary bike is for people who play tennis. Us football players, we have to *move*. We have to feel those miles in our legs, climb those hills, drop those gears and max out the resistance—otherwise, you're just spinning your wheels, man.

Let me tell you, I experienced more pain in those first weeks after my surgery than I'd ever known—and it was all because I was pushing myself *way* past what these doctors and therapists were telling me. That twelve-week timeline? It wasn't quick enough for me, so I had to double down and dial in. Somewhere in there, I even found time to fly to Switzerland for some cutting-edge plasma therapy, let the doctors over there take my blood and spin it around for a while in a centrifuge before injecting it back into my shoulder—it was supposed to speed the healing process, and I was determined to try anything.

Every waking moment was given over to my rehabilitation.

Back in Arizona, I'd be out of bed at six o'clock each morning, out the door by six thirty, in the gym by seven. I'd work out for two and a half hours, go to therapy, take a quick lunch, do a couple hours on the bike, therapy again, another workout, and on and on. In between, I'd find time to run through my deck of cards—sit-ups only, to start, until I was able to build up and start back in on those push-ups. End of the day, I'd have to ice for two hours, just to cool down from all that activity, and when I finally climbed into bed my mind would be racing a million miles a minute and I'd toss and turn for another few hours before I could fall off to sleep.

Next day, I'd get up and do it all over again.

The whole time, the Ravens left me alone to do my thing. My rehab schedule, my doctors, my therapists were all on me. I directed my care, the whole way—paid for everything myself, too. Only thing I asked of the Ravens was to keep me off the Injured Reserve list. The way it works, you go on IR, you're out for the whole year. That's it—you're done. So this was the one thing I told Ozzie Newsome I needed. I said, "You have to trust me on this."

And to Ozzie's great credit, he did. It cost him a roster spot to carry me the rest of the season, and I'm sure he caught some flak for it around the league, but he knew I wouldn't be asking if I didn't think I could make it back—and of course there was no reason for me to be busting tail like this if I wasn't eligible to come back and rejoin the team.

That whole time I was working to get myself back in shape, I kept thinking of that great Denzel Washington movie about Rubin "Hurricane" Carter. Carter was this middleweight boxer wrongfully convicted of murder and finally freed after twenty years in prison, and there's this powerful montage in the movie where Denzel was putting his body through all these insane paces, turning himself into a machine. That's the picture I kept in my head while I was working out, rehabbing. I was in the middle of my own movie, getting my body back to where I needed it to be, turning myself into a machine.

And as I pushed myself, as I rode that bicycle, as I powered through my routine, over and over and over, I kept hearing this voice inside my head—going, *They don't know.* Going, *Nobody knows.*

I was coming back, *willing* myself back. And I was coming back *pissed.* I was on a mission, because this was my last ride out of here.

And I had to make it count.

The whole time I was out, there was talk in the papers, talk on the radio about how I was done.

Ray Lewis will never play again—those words stung, too.

I'd try to tune all that out, but of course the negativity was bound to creep in—and when it did, it got me riled. I'd think, *These people don't know me.*

My teammates, they knew me.

The Ravens coaching staff, they knew me.

The front office staff, they knew me.

And they knew to steer clear. I'd given them all my word, told them I'd be back. And I would not be diminished. I might not be back at full strength—but even if I could only come back at 60 percent, 70 percent, it would be enough to get it done. Nobody would know I wasn't all the way healed, because I'd find a way to beat you, no matter what.

Underneath all that talk, I started to hear a buzz about how I'd come back—when, in what kind of shape, in what kind of role. We were looking ahead to the postseason. My teammates—to *their* great credit—they were doing their part on the field. Oh, the Ravens stumbled a bit right after I was hurt—losing big to Houston, 43–13, Week Seven of the season. But after that they went on a sweet little momentum run, with victories against Cleveland, Oakland, Pittsburgh, and San Diego—that last one in overtime. That put us at 9–2 on the season, so it was looking like a playoff spot was in reach.

I returned to practice that week—no plans yet on when I'd be ready to play, but it was good to be back with the team. It was good to be back in pads, getting my work in. And the guys, they were happy to have me back in the fold. That was *my* locker room, and I was a powerful force inside those walls. I most certainly was. Even if I wasn't contributing, I found a way to *contribute*—you know, to make myself heard. Every chance I got, I reminded folks of the promise I'd made to them after that loss to New England in the championship game the year before. The promise I made to the city of Baltimore. They didn't need reminding, but I reminded them anyway.

This ain't over . . .

No, it wasn't. Not by a long shot. And now that I was back in the mix, it was time to get down to it. To deliver on that promise. But then we went and lost back-to-back games, to Pittsburgh and Washington—that second one also in overtime—and I started to realize my team needed me in the mix more and more.

Still, at 9–4, we remained in control. A playoff spot was ours if we wanted it. Of course, it helped that year that there was a ton of parity in the AFC. At least, that's what the so-called experts and prognosticators called it. Me, I called it mediocrity. There were a lot of weak teams, up and down the league. If you look at the final standings, you'll see that there were only six teams in the conference to finish above .500, and all six of those teams went on to the playoffs.

At 9–4, only three games left to play, we were close to a lock, but we couldn't count on making the playoffs just yet. We had some work to do, had to win at least one more game to clinch, and it was right after that overtime loss to Washington that I started thinking about getting back into a game. I wasn't ready to play just yet, but I was ready to put a plan in place, and it worked out that Ravens owner Steve Bisciotti happened to call that week as I was doing my stretches. I had my daughter Diaymon with me, and we just happened to be talking through my return when my phone started vibrating.

Diaymon and Junior were the only two people I'd let in on my thinking about this being my last year. Even now, all this time later, they were the only ones who knew for sure what I was fixing to do. Now that there was all this talk, all this speculation, they'd become my sounding boards—don't know that they wanted that role, but I appreciated their advice, knew they had my best interests at heart. So here I was, telling my daughter that I thought I was ready to play, and she was trying to convince me to hold out a little bit longer, to get a little bit stronger. Me, my whole focus was on helping the team. I didn't care about my injury. I only wanted to lift these boys to the greatness that was ours—whatever it cost me. As long as I could lift my arm and get it to do what I needed it to do, I could play.

Diaymon saw it a different way. She said, "No, Daddy. You should come back in the playoffs." Like she knew what was best for me, best for the team—best for the fans, even.

She had my back, this one—an eye for a big spot, too. She knew what it cost me, what I'd put myself through, getting myself ready after my surgery. Last thing she wanted was for me to come back in a meaningless game and maybe get hurt, knock myself back out before there was anything on the line.

But better believe these last couple games mattered. Until we clinched, every game mattered—especially if we wanted to lock up home-field advantage. The reality, though, was we only needed to *qualify* for the playoffs. Everything else would flow from earning this spot—because I had a vision. Because *I knew*.

Steve Bisciotti was thinking the same way, it turned out. I told him where I was in my rehab, how close I was to being ready. He said, "You should pull a Willis Reed"—meaning, I should find some dramatic moment in the playoffs to step back onto the field and lift my teammates, just by showing up. But this was another something I didn't want. Nothing against Willis Reed, a great competitor, but the man was *hobbled*. Think back to that Game Seven of the 1970 NBA Championships. Willis Reed could barely move, but just by being on the court he was able to jump-start the New York Knicks and send them on to a championship. It was a great, great moment. *No doubt.* A storybook ending to a storybook season. *No doubt.* But I'm sorry, that wasn't my thing. I didn't want to *just* show up. I didn't want to play hobbled. It wasn't enough to just *inspire* my teammates. Hell no. I wanted to lift my team on my back and *carry* us to the Super Bowl.

(Michael Greene)

With current Ravens owner Steve Bisciotti, another great supporter.

I wanted to *contribute*—anything short of that, what was the point?

We decided I'd remain on the sidelines for our home game against the Denver Broncos that weekend. We'd take it one game at a time. I kept doing my thing in practice. I kept making my noise, rallying the troops. I came out to the stadium, went to the locker room, went out to the field—no big thing. And really, it wasn't. The guys were all happy to have me around, and I was happy to be back, but it felt to me like I was stepping inside someone else's office. They all had a job to do. Me, I was just showing my face.

We ended up losing that game to the Broncos—our third loss in a row, setting us back to 9–5. Truth was, if the rest of the schedule broke our way, we could have probably slipped in through the back door and qualified for one of the Wild Card spots even if we lost our final two games. But who wants to head into the postseason with five straight losses?

How it shook out was the Steelers ended up losing later that day, so it ended up we did qualify for the playoffs on the back of these three straight losses. Still, we had to win at least one more game to clinch the division, which would let us keep our first-round game at home. So our game the following week, at home against the New York Giants, was pretty damn big. And it was our last game of the season in front of the Baltimore fans and a chance to stop this ridiculous losing streak before it ran away from us. I wasn't ready to play just yet, but I made myself more of a presence in practice. I started to *hit*. I tried to get some things going.

My triceps, it wasn't *right*. I would not be at full strength, I was realizing. But full strength didn't matter to me just then, because I had a world of strength to go around.

THIRTEEN

The 40-Yard Line

I followed Diaymon's lead and waited out the final two regular-season games on the sidelines. She was right—there was no good reason to play just yet. My triceps, it could still do with some healing, strengthening. My team, they could fight to the postseason without me. There were some bumps in there, but we did manage to beat the Giants at home to put an end to that dreadful losing streak and set the stage for my return to the field in front of our home crowd. The way the standings were lining up, the final game of the season, against our division rivals from Cincinnati, didn't really mean anything. We were at 10–5, and they were at 9–6, but we owned the tiebreaker, so the division was ours even if the Bengals beat us.

Wasn't any reason for me to return just yet. Wasn't any reason for *any* of our key guys to play in that game, really—and John Harbaugh pulled his starters after just a couple plays and left the game to the second string. It didn't matter. The *postseason*, that's what mattered, and as we were getting ready for our first-round game against the Indianapolis Colts, it felt to me like the right time to tell my teammates what was up with me. All along, I didn't know if I would say anything about my decision to retire, or if I would just let the games play out and deal with it later. But there was buzz, speculation. Also, once it worked out that we were playing the Colts in that first round, it seemed to fit. I mean, the Colts had been Baltimore's team, way before the Ravens. There was still a big fan base that kept rooting for their beloved Colts, even after the team quit the city for Indianapolis in 1984. And here I was, the last remaining player from that original Baltimore Ravens team of 1996, a team that helped to chase the sting from the Colts leaving, about to put on the pads for my final home game. I just *had* to say something, right?

So I did.

I told John Harbaugh first—it was on a Wednesday, heading into our first playoff game. Didn't go into any details with him, but I gave him a heads up, asked him if I could speak to the team. I said, "Coach, this day had to come."

And right then, just off of these few words, he knew.

Coach called a team meeting and gave me the floor and I talked and talked. I had no idea what I was going to say, but the words, the emotions just flowed. For thirty minutes, I went off. Took a while for me to get to the headline, but I started out talking about what the game had meant to me, what my career had meant to me, what the relationships I'd built on this team and in this city had meant to me. All of that. I talked about Atlanta, too, and how I'd struggled to win back my good name. It started out like a pep talk. I reminded my team that this was our fifth straight trip to the playoffs and that the past four trips had ended in disappointment—only, they didn't need reminding. I talked about the job we had to do on the field, how I'd fought back from my triceps injury just to be here with them in this moment, to change the way our season would end. We would go out on top, I told them. There was no other option.

And then, finally, I got around to it—said, "This is my last ride."

There were some *oohs* and *ahhs*, some rustling. But I kept going—said, "Everything that starts has an end. It's just life."

To a man, I believe they knew—but, still, there were plenty of emotions. Wouldn't say it took anyone by surprise, the fact that I was retiring, but there were tears. Mine, too. I'd known this was it for me all along, but it took putting it out there for it to feel real to me, for me to think there was no turning back.

We stayed in that room for a while—time enough for everybody to come up and give me a hug, shake my hand, say something. I'd been with some of these dudes a long, long time, so this was a tough spot. For them, for me. And then it got a little tougher, because by the time we broke there were reporters waiting for me outside. Word travels fast in the world of professional sports—and, once the news was out, it spread like a firestorm. I was the top story.

Wasn't how I wanted to play it, because we had some work to do, but it was a big story. I *got* that.

And now there was a bigger story we were about to tell.

One more home game.

That's all we had left to us. Didn't matter if we won out, who else won out. This first-round game against the Colts, with their rookie quarterback, with their Baltimore history, with their big-time receivers—this was it for me, in this city, in front of these fans. And even though it was an emotional transition for me, I was at peace with it. I was—kept telling everyone, "I'm good, I'm good." Because I knew it was my time. Because I'd worked so hard to get back to this spot, to finish what we'd started the year before—to finish what *I'd* started, first time I ever touched a football.

A lot of folks, in the few days we had leading up to the game, they'd come up to me and say, "Suppose you lose?" It's like they were asking if maybe I'd change my mind, come back to fight another day.

But I'd just say, "I don't live on *supposes.*" I'd just say, "We're *not* losing." And I'd say it like a matter of fact, because I'd *seen* this. I'd *dreamt* this. I'd made a promise to my teammates that we would come back and finish this.

This ain't over.

I told my teammates how it would go: Indianapolis, first round. Denver, in the divisional round. New England, in the AFC Championship. After that, who knows? Just then, it was looking like San Francisco was the team to beat in the NFC, so in the back of my mind we were preparing to play them, too.

That final home game—man, it was something. I talked to John Harbaugh before the game, made sure he was good with me bringing one of those little cameras out there on the field. Didn't want him thinking it was a distraction, that I was disrespecting the game in any way. You're not *really* supposed to do that, you know, take a camera out there with you. But I wanted to capture everything, hold it close, because we weren't coming back to Baltimore. Whatever happened, here on in, this was my last dance in front of this home crowd—and that stadium was electric. It's like the whole city was crammed inside that building, everybody hopped up on Red Bull and coffee, jumping up and down. It was exciting. It was emotional. It was crazy. I kept my helmet on, because I didn't want the whole world to see me crying. It's like I had my own little suit of armor, my shield. I hid behind that helmet, hid behind that little camera, kept my crying to myself.

(Baltimore Ravens/Shawn Hubbard)

My pregame prayer. Wild Card game versus the Colts in 2012.

My last dance? It came from a place deep down. The moment was emotional enough, but I added to it. I found a little extra fuel, and it came from the movie I'd watched the night before this last home game—*Ali*, with Will Smith. And in this one scene, where Ali fought George Foreman, they played this one song—and that was the song I was playing on my headphones as I came out of that locker room, before I stepped onto that field to play the Colts. It was an Alicia Keys song called "Fight," and it had this one line in it that kept ringing in my head:

Didn't come all this way just to lose.

No, sir. I did not. And as I listened to that song and took in its message, I kept saying to myself, *Man, listen here. Your arm hurts like hell. You are seventy-percent healthy, and you can't really move your arm without pure pain. So what you gonna do?*

Well, there was only one thing to do, really. I told myself that if I was gonna go out, I would go out on that battlefield. Just like Ali. I was too far *in*. I'd already announced I was playing, so there was no backing out. So I walked out there, and I looked at that crowd, and you cannot tell me different, that I was not stepping out there for all black folks, for all underdogs, for all the people who were ever told *you can't* or *you will never* or *you can't have* or *you will never do*. Whatever it is, stand for something. That's the message that was driving me when I came out of that tunnel.

Whatever pain I was feeling, it didn't matter. But I didn't come all this way just to lose.

There was a game to be played, so we got down to it. And you have to realize, all that time rehabbing, all that time in the gym, I never really tested my arm to see what kind of pain I would feel at full impact. It's the kind of thing you don't really know until you *know*, and what I knew was this: My strength was okay. My range of motion was okay. My flexibility was okay, too. No better than that, but once that whistle blew, it was *on*. First quarter, I shot through the gap on a blitz and reached to make the tackle, landed on the ground hard. I felt the *crush*, and I popped back up and my arm was throbbing so bad I couldn't believe it. But then I looked up at the crowd, and I got this tidal wave of adrenaline, and I howled, "It don't matter!" And just then, the throbbing, the pain—it didn't matter. Not one bit.

So I played through the pain. Just set it aside. Made a bunch of tackles, a bunch of plays. Those Colts—Andrew Luck and them, Reggie Wayne and them, Vic Ballard and them—they kept coming, but we just set them aside, too. We didn't control the game the way I would have liked, wasn't the way Coach Harbaugh drew it up for us, but we kept the Colts out of the end zone. That was our goal, heading in to this game—to keep the Colts from *their* goal. All the Colts could manage were three field goals, so we had a solid victory on the scoreboard, 24–9, and at the end of the game someone came up to me and told me I had fifteen tackles. Fifteen! Honestly, I didn't know. At other times in my career, I would've kept a solid count, a running total in my head, but on this day each tackle, each hit, took so much out of me that I wanted to get past it. I thought if I counted it, it would stay with me, so I shook each one off and looked ahead to the next play.

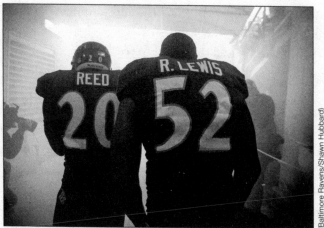

(Baltimore Ravens/Shawn Hubbard)

Walking out of the tunnel with Ed Reed during the 2012 playoffs.

At the end of the game, Coach Harbaugh did a wonderful thing. We'd just gotten the ball back on downs, time was running out. The game was in hand—we needed but one first down to run out the clock. He said, "Ray, you know the fans want to see you out there one last time."

I said, "What you mean?"

He said, "The city wants this."

He meant for me to take the field one final time, lined up in the backfield. It wasn't scripted. It wasn't planned or talked about—or, if it was, it wasn't planned or talked about *with me*. So I ran out there and took my spot on the field and listened to those fans sing down to me a final time. It was like a curtain call—right there on the 50-yard line, which I thought was appropriate. Better, like a salute. And as Joe Flacco took a knee on that last play, I caught myself wishing I had my little camera with me, so I could capture this moment and keep it close, but just as I caught myself wishing in this way I looked around and saw all these flashes popping around the stadium. Thousands and thousands of folks snapping their own little cameras, capturing *their* versions of this moment, so I realized I didn't need a camera of my own.

It was there for all the world to see.

Coming out of that first-round Wild Card weekend, I looked at the rosters of all the teams remaining in the playoffs. A lot of the players, I already knew, but I looked at the second units, the special teams—up and down the lineup. The coaching staffs, too. San Francisco. Green Bay. Denver. Seattle. Atlanta. Houston. New England. Over four hundred individuals, and I couldn't find one who would call God's name if he won the Super Bowl. Not one. This troubled me and inspired me, all at once, but I don't mention it here as a knock on any of these great players and coaches, because to get to this league, to get to the postseason, there was greatness running through these teams, most definitely. Go ahead and believe what you want to believe. Go ahead and celebrate how you want to celebrate. But for me, how *I* believe, this was a motivating thought, an *empowering* thought, because it told me I had an obligation that was bigger than football, an obligation that was bigger than the promise I'd made to my teammates, to the city of Baltimore—to myself, even. I had an obligation to Him—to sing His glory, to sing His praise.

As if I needed any more reason to play my heart out.

Next up was Denver in the divisional round, just like I'd seen it—only, this game wasn't easy, either. Wasn't how I'd pictured it. This game had some Baltimore history to it, too, because Peyton Manning was in his first year as the Broncos quarterback, and he'd been the face of the Indianapolis Colts for a long, long time—so all those old Colts fans in Baltimore had a soft spot in their hearts for him. Don't think those *soft spots* were enough to get them to pull for Peyton in this game, but it's tough to root against an athlete you've made a place for in your heart.

It's funny, how it all worked out, first two games of the postseason, the Ravens fans being pulled every which way—me retiring, the Colts returning, Peyton Manning going up against us with his new team. It reminded me that God doesn't make any mistakes. It played out this way for a reason, by design— me, carrying my city on my back. The postseason can be an emotional time, but it doesn't usually work out that it's *this* emotional.

The Denver fans, they didn't care at all about what was going on back in Baltimore—and rightly so. They did what they could to get under my skin. There were signs everywhere in that stadium:

RAY LEWIS WILL NEVER PLAY ANOTHER GAME!

BYE BYE, RAY.

THE CAREER STOPS HERE!

There was none of that blind hatred I'd seen back in Pittsburgh, first game after my trial. This was just good old-fashioned heckling, gamesmanship, but it got me going. It stoked the fire, picked me up, drove me forward. My arm wasn't right, coming out of that game against the Colts, so this was a worry—not a big deal, but a worry. If I had to measure it, I'd say I was at 50 percent, maybe 60 percent. But I was on a journey, and 50 percent would have to be enough. Worry or not, I could still get to the ball. Worry or not, I could still put a hurt on someone. Only thing I couldn't do, really, was reach for the ball with my bum arm. But the game was mostly about beating your man, and I could beat my man, no problem.

I told my coaches, "I'm good."

And I was—only, if I was being completely honest, I was just "good enough."

It was a battle, this game.

Denver scored first on a ninety-yard punt return.

We answered back with a fifty-six-yard touchdown pass from Joe Flacco to Torrey Smith.

Next, Corey Graham picked off a Peyton Manning pass and ran it back thirty-nine yards for the score, but then Manning threw a fifteen-yard touchdown pass to Brandon Stokely.

And that was just the first quarter.

I was getting my tackles. I was hurting, but I was beating my man, getting to the ball. I was *dictating*—only, each time I *dictated*, my arm barked back. The Broncos couldn't tell that I was hurting. My teammates, don't think they could tell, either, because I was playing like I was *burning*. But I couldn't extend my arm, so I was a wounded warrior. Every time we got the ball back, I'd gather myself on the sideline, braced against the pain I'd just endured, the pain still to come. A couple times in there, I caught myself wishing the clock would hurry up and move, so I could get to the end of this ordeal.

(Baltimore Ravens/Shawn Hubbard)

Even though I still wasn't at a hundred percent
coming into those games, I'd come to play.

At halftime, I called the team together and showed them this ring I'd started wearing around my neck. It was sent to me by this kid in Florida who'd heard me give a talk one day and quote from the book of Isaiah 54:17. He was inspired to make me this ring, with his own hard-earned money, and it carried the inscription: NO WEAPON FORMED AGAINST YOU SHALL PROSPER. So I gathered my teammates, asked them to join me in this prayer.

We stood as a group and recited that line three times:

No weapon formed against you shall prosper.

We traded touchdowns the rest of the way, ending with a seventy-yard touchdown pass from Flacco to Jacoby Jones— what a lot of folks started calling the "Mile High Miracle," because there was less than a minute to go in the game. That play, it kept us alive, but it also added a whole new dimension to our game, because Ravens football had always been hard-hitting, nose to the grindstone–type football. We were known for our defense. We'd never been known as a big-play team—wasn't our style—but here on this one play, Joe Flacco let the world know we would find a way to beat you on *his* side of the ball, too.

Anyway, that put the score at 35–35, and that's how it ended in regulation, and then we traded punches for a while—stop, stop, stop . . .

Finally, Corey Graham grabbed *another* interception—the dude was playing *out of his head*—and we ran off another few plays to gain some field position. Then, fourth and five, ball on the Denver twenty-nine, we sent in the field-goal unit.

I'd started having these strange dreams, around the time I told my teammates I was retiring. I couldn't understand these dreams at first, but they all had the number 40 in them. I wasn't sleeping well to begin with. That's how it goes when you're nursing this kind of injury—you only sleep on your good side, so when I tossed and turned I shot up in pain. Sometimes I'd wake up and just have this image in my head of a giant number 40. Or maybe the number 40 was a part of the story of the dream. Once in a while, there'd be a stadium, with a giant number 40 on the scoreboard, a giant 40 on the field, whatever. Some of the dreams had to do with football, some of them just with *life*, but always there'd be the number 40, over and over.

And here I took the time to notice that our field-goal kicker, Justin Tucker, was standing on the 40-yard line as he lined up to take the kick. Back of my mind I thought, *Hmmm . . . that's interesting.* And when that ball sailed through the up-rights and gave us the win, I went out onto the field and did my little dance in celebration, and halfway through I noticed I was standing on the 40-yard line, too. Again—*Hmmm . . . that's interesting.* Laid my head down on that field, right at the 40. Don't know why—didn't even think about it. And I don't know that I'd fully made the connection just yet, between these little "40" moments and the dreams I'd been having, but it registered, and I guess I filed it away.

It was something to think about.

Meanwhile, the Patriots were taking care of business in *their* divisional game against the Houston Texans, so that set us up for a rematch of last year's AFC Championship—and let me tell you, there was a whole lot of trash-talking heading up to that game. Some of it wasn't even trash, wasn't even coming from the Patriots camp. In fact, a company that owned a bunch of billboards started putting up these LED countdown clocks all over the Boston area, ticking down the time to "Ray's Retirement Party," setting it up to get everyone thinking the Patriots would knock us out of the playoffs and this would be my last game. It got a lot of attention, that move—it certainly got mine, but not in the way those folks probably meant. It got me irritated, infuriated—and that's not something you want to do when you're about to face me in a big game.

Like a lot of athletes, I played with competitive fire—been that way my whole life. And here I was already fired up to begin with. Here the pain in my arm was fire enough. The pain of last year's loss in this same game was fire enough. So my message to my teammates going into this game was to hit, to hurt. I said, "Every person touches the ball, punish him. We're in the *punishing* business." We *punished* that New England team. Wasn't even a match, but it took us a while to get our points. Biggest play of the game? We were down 13–7 at the half, but then we crawled back, put a couple nice drives together, made a couple key stops. Scored a touchdown to take the lead, midway through the third, another to start the fourth quarter, and this one put us up 21–13. It was still just a one-possession game, and with the ball back in Tom Brady's hands, we had to keep sharp. The Patriots had this power play they used to run, and I told my boys, next time it came round, I'd try to cut out the lineman's legs, cause a big pile. It was just like that

Eddie George play—I had it read. And the pile left the Patriots running back Stevan Ridley one-on-one with our strong safety, Bernard Pollard. And Bernard hit that boy and made him fumble . . . *on the 40-yard line*. Bernard just about put him to sleep—*night, night!*

On the 40-yard line.

So many great stories came out of Super Bowl XLVII. It was the first time in Super Bowl history that two brothers faced each other as head coaches—John Harbaugh on our side of the field, and Jim Harbaugh on the San Francisco side. And Beyoncé was set to play the halftime show, so that also got a lot of coverage. Heading into the game, I gave a ton of "last dance" interviews, but I didn't talk about the pain I was dealing with. It worried me, but I didn't let on—pain had never stopped me before, and I wasn't about to let it stop me now. It was just something to deal with, to get past—a gauntlet all its own. But *this* pain in my arm was like nothing I'd ever experienced. *This* pain was debilitating. Playing *through* pain, it was no big thing. But this wasn't about playing *through*. This was about powering past, rising above, getting my body to do things it wasn't designed to do. Every one of these playoff games, it set me back, sent me reeling. All those tackles, those hits, they sucked a little life out of me—and by the end of this postseason run, I'd be credited with fifty-one tackles, a playoff record I'm betting won't be broken anytime soon. Got to where I couldn't lift my arm without feeling like I'd be better off just ripping it from my shoulder. Got to where, the night before the Super Bowl, holed up in my hotel room in New Orleans, I had to rig a makeshift traction device just to get some relief. I tied some shoelaces together, made myself a sling, ran it over the little sprinkler head that came out of the wall over my bed. And I sat like that—half asleep, half not—trying to close my eyes, trying to will myself past the pain, waiting for the sun to come up so I could get ready, get to the stadium and get dressed. Distract myself from the pain by putting myself through these paces one final time.

For a beat or two, I didn't think I'd make it. It hurts me to admit it, but it was so. I couldn't even crawl into the bathroom to splash some water on my face, but then I found a way to scramble to the sink, and as I let that faucet run I looked at myself in the mirror. There was the story of my life, right there in my reflection. There was the pain of my father abandoning me. Abandoning *us*. There was the pain of these other men, beating on me, beating on my mother. There was the pain of going hungry, the pain of all that weight I had to carry as a child, taking care of my brother and sisters. There was the pain of losing my best friend to the butt end of a rifle, the pain of being falsely accused in Atlanta. The pain of being incarcerated, abused, violated. The pain of being judged for a terrible crime that had nothing to do with me. The pain of fighting back from a career's worth of injuries, surgeries.

And finally, there was the pain of this right here—only, I couldn't tell anybody about it. I couldn't tell our team doctor. I couldn't tell my coaches, my teammates. I could only stare myself down in that bathroom mirror and find a way to power through. To rise above. To ask my body to do the impossible. I thought about what it meant to be a leader—because, really, that's the spot I was in. I thought how I might *lead* if I couldn't really *play*. I thought, *How do you go into the greatest battle ever and not tell your soldiers what's really going on?* But to tell them would have been to take away one of our greatest weapons. Didn't matter just then that I couldn't *fire* with the same intensity I'd always brought to the game. Didn't matter that I couldn't *execute*. It only mattered that

I took the field and put it out there that I was a force to be reckoned with. The same force I'd always been. I could *lead* my teammates just by putting on my helmet and lining up on that field.

I ran the shower, thought I'd stand and soak for a while, maybe calm down the pain in my triceps. But finally I just had to suck it up and roll. I made my way to the stadium, to the locker room, the whole time trying not to let on the kind of pain I was in. I couldn't drop my arm—it wouldn't go. But I thought if someone saw me carrying my arm in this way, favoring it, we were done.

As I walked into the locker room, I locked eyes with Brendon Ayanbadejo, a special-teams player out of UCLA—a solid guy, played some linebacker for us, too. He could see I was suffering, struggling. There was no one else around, and I could see in Brendon's eyes that he didn't know what to do, what to say. And in my eyes, he could see that this wasn't something we needed to talk about. All he said as I walked past was, "I ain't gonna say nothing."

And I said, "Please. Not now."

There would be time for all of us to say something later. For me, now, it was time to lead. I couldn't *play*—not the way folks *expected* me to play—but I could *lead*.

And, so, I did—tried to, anyway. I knew that my job that day, on that field, was to set an example, to set a tone. To *lead*.

All week I had this kid quarterback in my head. We'd run through all these great quarterbacks just to get to this game: Andrew Luck, Peyton Manning, Tom Brady, and now we had Colin Kaepernick, who could do things with the football *none* of those other three could do. Man, that's a *gauntlet* right there. The young guns and the old guard. That's a big-time lineup—potentially, four future Hall of Fame quarterbacks—and we picked 'em off, one by one. But Kaepernick required a whole

Readying for battle before heading out to the Super Bowl.

different game plan than the other three. Those guys were classic pocket passers—they didn't move around a whole lot, so you could contain them with a decent pass rush. But this kid out of Nevada? Oh man, he could run. He could take a broken play and turn it into something special, so he was in my head when I took the field. A good distraction from the pain.

We came out strong to start the game—just took it to them that first half. Headed into the locker room with a score of 21–6. The 49ers could only manage two field goals, so we were rolling.

Second half, coming out of that locker room a second time, I was hurting. For the longest time, I was hurting. In the Super Bowl, the halftime runs longer. There are all those commercials, all those commentators need time to do their thing. Beyoncé, she needed time to do her thing. They had to set up that big stage and break it down. And all that time, me cooling down, fighting through that pain, it just made my arm worse. Whatever adrenaline I'd had to get me through that first half, it had leaked away, and now I didn't know how much longer I could play through this intense pain, and as we walked back out to the field, I dropped to my knees in prayer. I made like I was tying my shoes, didn't want anyone to step in on this private moment, this personal moment, but I needed some guidance, man. I needed to know how He wanted me to play it.

And just then, inside this personal moment, me kneeling in prayer by the side of the field, pretending to tie my shoes, He spoke to me. He did. I could hear Him, clear as day, through the din of that Superdome crowd.

It was me who spoke first. I said, "We're up by a lot of points, but I don't know if I can hold my arm up any longer. I don't know what you want me to do."

He said, "Trust Jacoby."

Like I said, clear as day—like the voice that spoke to Kevin Costner in *Field of Dreams*. *If you build it, they will come . . .*

Trust Jacoby . . .

And then: "Give him your strength."

I thought, *What? Trust Jacoby? Give him your strength? What does that mean?* But then it came to me. Then I knew. I ran over to Jacoby Jones, who was getting ready to run out to receive the second-half kickoff. I grabbed him, spun him around. I said, "I'm just doing what God is telling me to do."

Jacoby, he looked at me like I had a couple screws loose, but he didn't do anything, say anything. He just stood there, waited. So I put my hands on his chest and ran them down the front of his jersey. That's all. And as he ran out to receive the kick, I looked down and saw where we were standing: *on the 40-yard line.*

Where else?

Next, I heard God speak to me again. He said, "Watch this."

So I watched Jacoby Jones, deep in our end zone, catching that drive off the foot of the San Francisco kicker, David Akers, tucking it, breaking tackles, and dancing the length of the field. One hundred and eight yards! The longest kickoff return in

Super Bowl history. At a time in the game when a *leader* looks to put the hammer down on his opponent.

Oh my goodness. *Oh my goodness.* I was bursting with what I was seeing. I was dancing up and down that sideline myself, telling my coaches, "I just touched him! I just touched him!"

It was the craziest thing, the most beautiful thing. The purest thing.

In that moment, the game was ours. There was nothing that could stop us. And then there was that "lights out" moment when the Superdome went dark. Folks started calling it the "Blackout Bowl" after that, treating it like a joke, but it was no joke. It took us out of our game. We'd been up 28–6, been keeping the 49ers out of our end zone, but then there was this power outage nobody could explain, the game was delayed more than a half hour, and we got out of our rhythm. Whatever momentum we'd had—and it was *huge* after that 108-yard kickoff to start the second half—it was gone. Don't know how it happened, but we let San Francisco back in the game.

Just like that, we were scrambling. Just like that, it was a whole new ballgame. Colin Kaepernick was a different dude coming out of that delay. It's like he'd been playing tentative, the big moment maybe just a little too big for him, but then he had this little pocket of extra time to catch his breath and take in the scene without any of the glitz and noise of the Super Bowl, and he calmed down, started to *play*. First, it had taken him a while to adjust to us, to adjust to this giant stage, and now it took us our own while to adjust to *him*.

The 49ers came out of that blackout and scored seventeen unanswered points—touchdown, touchdown, field goal—which cut our lead to 28–23 at the end of the third quarter.

We hit back with a field goal to go back up by eight. And

then Kaepernick did some *leading* of his own, racing his team across the field for another touchdown. Then Jim Harbaugh looked to tie the game with a two-point play, but Kaepernick failed to connect with Randy Moss and we were holding on to a tiny two-point lead, midway through the fourth quarter.

Joe Flacco led us on a nice little drive, ate up some clock, ended with a field goal to put us up by five, 34–29, and here is where I had to suck it up one more time. I went out there determined to make one last stand—only, these 49ers, they kept coming. They connected on a pass, pushed the ball on the ground, kept moving those chains. And then, Frank Gore busted a thirty-three-yard run around the left end, took the ball all the way down inside our 10-yard line. There was about two and a half minutes left on the clock, and this was where we doubled down, dialed in. This was where, whatever hurt I was hurting, I had to set it aside. This was where, whatever prayers I was praying, I had to turn up the volume. I knew that if I rushed this one lineman, hard, I would free up a lane for Dannell Ellerbe. I knew it would hurt, but I knew we'd have that clear path to Kaepernick and we could pressure the quarterback, so I counted it a good trade—and as soon as I made that hit, my arm went numb. But the pass fell incomplete, so it was all good. And as I walked back to the huddle, I brought my good hand up to that necklace and ran my fingers across that inscription:

No weapon formed against me shall prosper.

I kept saying these words, over and over, mumbling to myself beneath my helmet, and when we huddled up I let those words spill out—along with a couple more. I said, "Nobody got to be heroes." I said, "Just give me one more play." I said, "One stop at a time, we walk out of here champions." And we held them. We did. Two short passes to Michael Crabtree, incomplete, and we had the ball back on our 5-yard line, 1:46 left in the game.

All we had to do was run out the clock, and it ended up, third and eight, we had our punter, Sam Koch, line up in the end zone and run off a little more time, take the safety. The scoreboard worked out in our favor, made sense to push San Francisco deep into their own territory and let time run out on the free kick.

And I'm telling you, as soon as that clock switched to all zeroes, you could hear "Purple Rain" blasting through those Superdome speakers. Confetti flying everywhere. People going crazy. And in this huge, beautiful moment I took the time to speak the truth to the man who brought me here. I said, "God, I will never go against you."

Bringing the Super Bowl trophy to the Baltimore fans.

POSTGAME

My City Is Burning

Before I finish, I want to go back to what happened in Atlanta, the tragic deaths of those two young men, the way I was falsely accused, the way I was treated. I know I said that it was time to set the incident aside and that I didn't want it to *define* me, but those low moments have come back to me recently with what's going on in some of our cities—in my *own* city, even. In fact, when I was working on this book the city of Baltimore was being torn apart. What set it off was a twenty-five-year-old African American man named Freddie Gray being arrested by Baltimore police officers for no good reason on April 12, 2015. The police roughed him up so bad that he fell into a coma and died a week later, igniting a firestorm of protest across my city, across the country. A week after *that*, as Freddie Gray was being buried, the storm turned violent. Police officers were pelted with rocks, protesters were clubbed and sprayed, cars were turned over, fires set, windows smashed.

There were ugly, terrifying images of Baltimore flashed all over the news, all over the world, and in this one flashpoint my city was added to the list of hot spots where incidents of police brutality showed a simmering racism that continues to terrorize, marginalize, and antagonize our young people. It wasn't *just* Freddie Gray in Baltimore. It was Michael Brown in Ferguson, Tamir Rice in Cleveland, Walter Scott in South Carolina, Eric Garner in New

York, and on and on. And those are just the folks we've come to know by name—can't even put a number on those who've been beaten down away from the public eye. And think back just a little ways, and there are more names we can add to the list: Rodney King in Los Angeles, Abner Louima in New York, and on and on.

Things got so bad in Baltimore, the mayor declared a city-wide curfew. President Obama took the time to calm people down. There were hundreds of arrests, hundreds of people hospitalized. Our city had come to a bad boil. Store owners were afraid to close up shop at night, there was so much looting and vandalism going on. I had a lot of emotions over that week, but one of the strangest moves for me was the Baltimore Orioles playing a game against the Chicago White Sox in an empty stadium because city officials didn't trust that police officers, the National Guard, and whoever else they were bringing in could keep control. I can't imagine what that was like for the ballplayers to play for no one but the cameras. For a professional athlete used to playing in a big-time arena, the crowd can be everything. Even when the crowd is against you, it can impact the game—and so those pictures that came out of this one "silent" baseball game were chilling.

The whole sad episode tore me apart. I couldn't just stay at home and watch it on television. I had to do something, so I went downtown to work with the Baltimore police officers to keep the peace—to do what we could to get the rioters and protestors to dial down their rage and frustration.

I said, "What are we doing? This is not how we solve our problems."

For whatever reason, folks responded to me on this, so I helped to lead some peaceful protests, helped to quiet some of the noise, to still some of the violence, and as I did I kept thinking back to those low moments in Atlanta. It felt to me like there was some kind of connection, so I wondered at where I'd been, alongside where we now were, and I started to realize that race relations had gotten *worse* in the fifteen years since those stabbings. This was just my take, I know, but this was how I'd come to see it, and it saddened me to think how things were for our young African American men. It troubled me—not *just* because of what I had to live through myself, although that's a part of it. But the world has changed. Back then, I was *blamed* for a crime I didn't commit, while today these police officers are lashing out at these kids before a crime is even committed. I suffered the prejudice of judgment. Freddie Gray suffered the prejudice of prejudgment. Might not seem like a big shift—but to me, it's everything. To me, it's the world we've made for our children, and it scares me to think of these black kids in the hood—what are they supposed to do? Where are they supposed to go? We've written them off— same way *I* was written off all those years ago. Same way Freddie Gray was written off by these six police officers who arrested him and put a beating on him—*just* because of the color of his skin.

You have to realize, I've been listening to this noise for fifteen years, and I'll probably hear it for the rest of my life, but I've learned to tune it out. Oh, I heard it all before Atlanta, but it took on a different tone after my name had been dragged through the papers. And yet what people say about me, it doesn't affect me. It can't touch me. I found a way to deal with all that hatred that found me in Pittsburgh my first game back, where I was called a murderer, a nigger, a child killer. How do you deal with that? Man, I don't wish that kind of hatefulness on anyone—especially the young black males in America who seem to have to face it most of all.

I can't help but worry for my sons. I worry about how the world sees them, what the world expects of them. I worry about how they'd respond if they found themselves in the wrong place at the wrong time, up against a wrong-minded individual or group of individuals inclined to write them off—like they did me. Like they did Freddie Gray, Michael Brown, Tamir Rice, Walter Scott, Eric Garner . . .

I don't know what to do with that worry, but I do know this: rioting is not the answer. No, the way forward is for *all* our brothers, for *all* black men to stand and be counted. If you've been done wrong, do right. If you've been done bad, do good. Be your own man. Live in your own skin. Serve your own God. Know your own mind.

That day at Three Rivers Stadium, the word *nigger* raining down on me as I sat on the bench, waiting to go back into the game, I turned to one of my teammates and smiled—said, "This ain't about me." And, really, it wasn't. It was about the folks doing the name-calling—it was a place to put their prejudices. That's all. So I came up with a line I'd end up repeating for the rest of my career, whenever somebody confronted me on this.

I said, "I'm gonna let my smile represent my past, and I'm gonna let my heart represent my future."

And in those words, there was tremendous power. In those words, there was freedom. Because if I smiled, my enemies would never know what I was thinking. If I smiled, the haters would never know what was in my heart. So even when somebody cursed me, even when somebody wronged me, I would smile anyway, pray anyway. I was good. As long as you didn't touch me or my kids, I was good.

Look, I know what it's like to be in pain. I've played in pain, trained in pain, lived in pain. Those two and a half weeks in an Atlanta jail cell, it felt to me like I might *die* in pain. But the greatest pain of all was living every day of my life knowing I didn't have a father. Knowing I was too small to protect my mother—to *see* her being hurt. To *feel* that hurt for her. The pain of other people's words? The pain of other people not *liking* me? Come on—that's *nothing*. That time after Super Bowl XXXV, against the Giants, when those Walt Disney folks turned away from me *right on the field* because they didn't want to associate with me after I'd been named MVP, didn't want me saying "I'm going to Disney World!" It bothered me in the moment, can't lie, but it only bothered me enough to notice. It didn't bother me enough to *get* to me—I wouldn't let it. In fact, a dozen years later, when I stepped away from the game, who came calling to give me a job as a football analyst? ESPN, which of course is part of the Disney company—not exactly the circle of life, but it was the *circle of justice*, at least. And I was only too happy to smile and go to work for these people and let my heart represent my future.

Four days before my thirty-fifth birthday on May 12, 2010, I was honored by the city of Baltimore with the naming of a section of North Avenue as "Ray Lewis Way #52." It was an incredible day that I got to share with my children.

I know that I played the game the way God told me to play it, lived my life the way God told me to live it. And now that I've left the game, I'm still cut the same way. When I sweat, I sweat for me. I sweat for my kids. I sweat for my legacy. I sweat for these young men grappling to find a way out of these tough neighborhoods.

A great name is rather chosen than all the riches on this Earth . . .

That's a line from Proverbs and I find myself thinking on this a lot these days. But what is a great name? If you wake up in the morning trying to please people, you've lost the battle. If you spend your time thinking on what folks say about you, you've lost the battle. A great name is not *that*. In Proverbs it goes on to say that it is better to be respected than to be liked. Think on that for a moment. Our current culture is all about being liked. How many *likes* we have—that's how we take our measure. There's no *respect* button on Facebook—the word itself, it doesn't even come up. Think about the two words that are everywhere online—*like* and *follow*. They're our currency. But if you're a child of God, your world should be built on *respect* and *leadership*. Real people don't *follow*—they *lead*. Real people don't need to be *liked*—they earn our *respect*.

My mama did one helluva job on me, she did. I'm telling you, *she* is the reason I am who I am. I respect her. I do. More than anyone else. She was with me all through my career— every down, every game. I could feel her strength, hear her voice. She was *with* me in the way I mean to be for my children.

And in her presence, I find a great lesson: Be an example. Be a force for good. And know that everyone with a great name has been through *something*. A great deal of something. It's not about doing what everybody else is doing. It's just about being true to yourself. Whatever the majority of people are doing, go ahead and do the opposite—if you know what you're doing to be right and good and true. Live your legacy. Do your thing.

Walk in a certain light.

I've put Atlanta behind me—I've let that anger go. And someday—soon, I hope—the folks in Baltimore will let this fresh anger go as well. It doesn't mean they'll *forget* how Freddie Gray was treated. It doesn't mean they'll *forgive* those police officers. But they'll find a way to let their smiles represent their past, for their hearts to represent their futures.

ACKNOWLEDGMENTS

Of course, I have to start out by thanking my children, who are the driving force in my life. Everything I do, I do for them. Really, from when my oldest was born, there's not been one moment of my life that has not been for my kids. I might have dedicated this book to their grandmother, but I've dedicated my life to my children. So thank you from the bottom of my heart for being my four kings and my three queens.

My brother and sisters, I want to thank all four of them for walking through life together with me, through the ups and downs—I have no better friends in this world than my brother and sisters. To my extended family—my aunts, my uncles, my grandmothers, my grandfathers . . . every bloodline that's connected to me—there is no me without you. Every story that's never been told, it flows through you, so I want to thank you as well for being in my heart and keeping me in yours.

To every coach who's ever coached me, I am in your debt. I never gave up, never even thought about giving up, because these good men rolled into my life. You guys shaped me into becoming the man I am today.

To my hometown of Lakeland, Florida; to the entire community at Kathleen High School; to the University of Miami and all supporters of the U and Hurricane football . . . thank you for lifting me up, raising me, cheering me on.

254 | ACKNOWLEDGMENTS |

To the city of Baltimore, we were supposed to be connected. When God connected us, He knew that I would never stop loving this city, and I want to thank the people of Baltimore for loving me and embracing me as one of their own. To the Ravens organization, I've been through a lot of things in life, but I want to thank you for your dedication, your friendship, your support, and for your willingness to stand as a first-class organization in everything you do. Steve Bisciotti, Art Modell, Ozzie Newsome, Dick Cass . . . over seventeen years and four contracts, we never had one dispute. Thank you for letting my legacy start and end in Baltimore.

To every teammate I ever played with—from high school all the way to the NFL—I not only want to say thank you but I want to honor you. I don't care if it was one day of practice or many years of practice, you made an impact on me. You pushed me forward. Like it says in Proverbs 27:17—iron sharpens iron. Thank you, my brothers.

And finally, this book you now hold in your hands didn't up and happen on its own. I'm grateful to my assistant, Ashley Knight, for helping to organize my life and my thoughts so I could focus on this right here. I'm grateful to Jay Mandel at William Morris Endeavor, and his assistant Lauren Shonkoff, for setting this project in motion. Also to Josh Pyatt at WME, who makes everything possible. And I'm grateful to their WME colleague Mel Berger for introducing us to Dan Paisner, who worked with me to capture my voice and my spirit. Thanks also to Matthew Benjamin and the entire Touchstone team— including David Falk, Brian Belfiglio, Shida Carr, Meredith Vilarello, Elaine Wilson, Martha Schwartz, and Kyle Kabel— for believing in my story and putting it out into the world in such a compelling way. Behind the scenes, I'm especially grateful to my brother Rohan Marley for providing a home-away-from-home in New York—a place where Dan and I could do our work in a relaxed environment. Also, thanks to Rich Berman for taking the time to read the early drafts of this book and weighing in with notes and comments.

My heart is full—and my life is filled with rich friendships, too many to count. I'm grateful for all of them—for all of you. You are all a blessing to me, and you have my blessings in return.

INDEX

ABOUT THE AUTHOR

Ray Lewis is widely considered to be one of the most dominant defensive players in the history of the National Football League. Lewis led the Baltimore Ravens to victory in Super Bowl XXXV (where he was named Super Bowl MVP) and again in Super Bowl XLVII, in what would be the final game of his career. The Ravens' all-time career leader in tackles and fumble recoveries, Lewis was selected for the Pro Bowl thirteen times (a record for linebackers) and named AFC Defensive Player of the Year three times before retiring in 2013. Today Lewis devotes his time to being a father as well as an analyst for the NFL on ESPN.